Planning with Neighborhoods

Urban and Regional Policy

and Development Studies

Michael A. Stegman, Series Editor

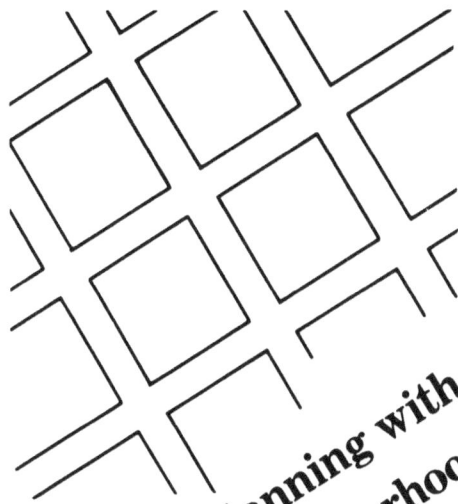

Planning with Neighborhoods

William M. Rohe and

Lauren B. Gates

The University of North Carolina Press

Chapel Hill and London

Library of Congress Cataloging in Publication Data

Rohe, William M.

  Planning with neighborhoods.

  (Urban and regional policy and development studies)

  Bibliography: p.

  Includes index.

  1. Community development, Urban—United States. 2. Neighborhood—
United States—Planning. I. Gates, Lauren B. II. Title. III. Series.

HN90.C6R64   1985   307′.12   84-17221

ISBN 978-0-8078-1638-7

ISBN 978-0-8078-4133-4 (pbk)

To our parents for
their love and support

Contents

List of Tables
and Figures

Figure

Preface

Upon reviewing the literature on neighborhood planning in preparation for teaching a course in this area, we discovered that very little had been written on the effectiveness of contemporary neighborhood planning programs. The available works consisted of either "how-to" guides or simple descriptions of programs with little or no evaluation. Their authors typically justified neighborhood planning programs on philosophical or theoretical grounds, not on measurements of performance. Our desire was to go beyond the existing literature to provide students, practitioners, and scholars interested in neighborhood planning with concrete examples of accomplishments and with prescriptions for developing successful programs. Hence, we began conducting case studies of operating programs seeking to uncover both their strengths and weaknesses. We also decided to survey all neighborhood planning programs in the country to obtain a sense of the diversity of program styles and more data on the accomplishments and problems associated with these programs.

The data reported herein were collected over a two-year period between 1979 and 1981. Since that time, some of the programs have been revised in response to internal evaluations or simply shifts in political currents. This does not diminish the relevance of these findings, however, since we are interested in evaluating a general class of programs and developing general recommendations, rather than evaluating specific programs.

In addition to any usefulness this study may have as a description and evaluation of the state of neighborhood planning in the United States, we hope it will aid in the development of neighborhood planning programs in cities where they do not exist and contribute to the improvement of currently operating programs.

Ultimately, we seek to improve the effectiveness of American city planning in achieving an improved quality of life for urban residents. The development and improvement of neighborhood planning programs, we believe, is a major step in this direction.

We wish to thank Jon Howes of the Center for Urban and Regional Studies at the University of North Carolina at Chapel Hill, who helped arrange initial funding for this project. Other funding came from a Junior Faculty Development Award provided by the University of North Carolina.

Our faculty and student colleagues at the University of North Carolina at Chapel Hill also deserve thanks for their support, encouragement, and insight. They have helped create a supportive intellectual environment that makes scholarly activity both more productive and more enjoyable. Finally, we owe a special debt of gratitude to the citizens and planners who took time out of their busy schedules to talk with us about their work. The enthusiasm and genuine concern demonstrated by these individuals made this project both exciting and personally meaningful.

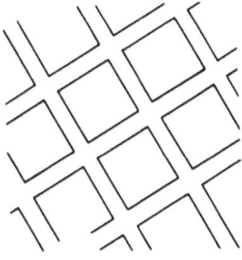

Planning with Neighborhoods

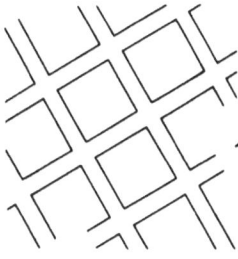

1 Introduction

If we are to speak realistically of pre-conditions for effective change, it must be recognized that the neighborhood—not the sprawling, anonymous metropolis—is the key.
—The National Commission on Neighborhoods, *People Building Neighborhoods*

The city is far from simply a collection of people and buildings. Rather it is a mosaic of distinct neighborhoods, each with its own character and reputation created by the characteristics of residents, housing types, ages and styles, and economic activities. Moreover, these distinct neighborhoods have different needs, issues, and problems which necessitate different kinds and styles of public programs.

Throughout this century, the neighborhood has been a major focus of attention among those concerned with urban affairs. This focus on neighborhoods stems from the belief that they represent the building blocks of the city. The health of a city is largely dependent on the vitality of its individual neighborhoods, and the physical and social conditions in neighborhoods to a large extent define the quality of life for urban residents. They affect individual decisions to stay or to seek more desirable living conditions in suburban or rural locations. Those decisions, in turn, affect the local tax base and the overall viability of urban areas.

Contemporary neighborhood planning programs represent attempts to address the quality of life in neighborhoods. They seek to identify problems, as defined by residents, and to prevent future problems from developing. They are designed to improve or stabilize neighborhood characteristics important to citizen perceptions of quality of life. Neighborhood planning programs address the "smaller" issues of concern to local residents and crucial to the continued viability of neighborhoods and ultimately the city as a whole. Their method is based on a respect for the unique perspectives of local residents and involves substantial citizen participation in both the development of plans and their implementation.

Currently three forms of neighborhood planning are being practiced in the United States. The first involves independently organized efforts sponsored by indigenous neighborhood organizations. Although these organizations may receive grants from public agencies or private foundations, they are not sanctioned or controlled by them. These efforts typically aim to address a perceived problem or set of problems in the neighborhood through self-help or advocacy efforts.

The second form of contemporary neighborhood planning consists of federally sponsored community development programs. Planners employed by local municipalities are charged with identifying problem areas, called neighborhood strategy areas (NSAs), developing a comprehensive rehabilitation program, and administering the implementation of that program. Although citizens have opportunities to comment at several public hearings required by federal regulations, their involvement in designing and implementing improvements is often limited. Furthermore, program activities are typically limited to a relatively small number of neighborhoods compared to the total number in any city.

The third form comprises locally sponsored, city-wide neighborhood planning programs. These programs seek to involve all neighborhoods in public planning and municipal affairs. They are sponsored by municipal government, although federal funds are often used to subsidize their operation. Participating neighborhood groups become involved in a wide variety of issues, including zoning changes, evaluation of local service delivery, comprehensive planning, and local problem solving.

This book is particularly concerned with the third form of neighborhood planning. Our purpose is to provide a description of these programs and a preliminary evaluation of their effectiveness. Neighborhood planning, as defined for the purposes of this study, refers to municipally sponsored programs that seek to involve neighborhood groups throughout the city in one or more of the following activities.

First, neighborhood groups may be involved in the review of plans or proposals developed by municipal agencies which may have an influence on neighborhood life. Groups are responsible for reviewing plans before they are presented to the city council or mayor and either negotiating changes directly with the sponsoring agency or attaching their comments to the plan or proposal as it goes forward for consideration. Neighborhood planners are typically provided by the city to help keep neighborhood groups abreast of relevant city-initiated proposals and to help analyze the potential effects of specific proposals on their neighborhoods.

Second, the city may give neighborhood organizations the responsibility for producing their own plans for the development of their neighborhoods. Typically, neighborhood planners provide technical assistance in developing these plans. In some instances neighborhood plans become a part of the official comprehensive plan for the city. In others the plan is a means of communicating the needs and desires of individual neighborhoods to developers, planners, and city officials.

Third, participating neighborhood groups are encouraged by the city to become involved in self-help activities. Technical assistance or partial funding is often provided to groups that want to sponsor a neighborhood improvement activity. Neighborhood planners are typically involved in helping groups organize activities and write grant proposals to public and private funding agencies. Activities range from neighborhood clean-up campaigns to major housing rehabilitation projects.

Over fifty locally sponsored neighborhood planning programs have been adopted in the United States in the last two decades. Several societal forces have encouraged this growth in neighborhood planning. First, many citizens and citizen groups have been demanding a greater role in the process of public planning, as well as in other spheres of government. This, to a large extent, is a reaction to the many unpopular planning projects undertaken in the 1950s and 1960s, such as Urban Renewal and federal highway programs.

Second, requirements for citizen participation in many federal programs have established a norm, or at least an expectation, of citizen involvement in the planning of physical and social services. The Community Development Block Grant Program, for example, requires that applicants must "provide residents of the community with adequate opportunity to participate in the planning, implementation and assessment of the program." Many neighborhood planning programs were originally established to satisfy this requirement, but have been broadened to encourage participation in all spheres of local planning.

Third, public officials have wanted a better means of communicating with citizens. As cities have grown larger and more diverse, public officials have found it difficult both to assess citizen views and to explain their own views to citizens. Neighborhood planning programs provide a mechanism for accomplishing these goals.

Finally, many public planners have recognized certain limitations in traditional comprehensive planning. Critics suggest that comprehensive planning has ignored the needs of local neighborhoods in favor of business districts, excluded citizens from meaningful participation, and failed to achieve an equitable distribution of public goods (Chapin, 1965; Friedmann, 1971; Perin, 1967). Neighborhood planning, as a decentralized, participatory, action-oriented planning process, has been seen as a means of addressing the limitations of comprehensive planning.

As a means of organizing citizen participation, neighborhood planning programs differ from other mechanisms of involving citizens in several important ways. Unlike most other forms of citizen participation, citizen involvement in neighborhood planning programs is organized by territorial units with particular significance for citizens: the neighborhoods. Citizens are particularly concerned about their neighborhoods since they often have considerable economic and social investments there. As Naparstek and Cincotta write: "In real terms, people live in neighborhoods, not cities. In real terms, their investments, emotional as well as economic, are in neighborhoods, not cities" (National Commission on Neighborhoods, p. 1). People are also more familiar with the conditions and problems in their local neighborhoods, making them better able to contribute to planning initiatives.

Moreover, neighborhood planning programs encourage continuous involvement as citizens meet on a regular basis to discuss issues and proposals. This might be expected to lead to more informed citizen input as citizens become more familiar with the issues, techniques, and constraints of city planning.

Finally, neighborhood planning allows local neighborhood organizations to set their own agendas rather than simply respond to the agendas set by local planners or public officials. Neighborhood organizations are free to bring up any issue of concern, making this an active, rather than solely reactive, form of involvement. The neighborhood groups meet on a regular basis or when they feel there is a problem, not just when called upon by public officials.

Particularly important given the fiscal crisis facing many American cities, neighborhood planning programs often give rise to self-help approaches to solving local problems. Citizens not only become involved in advising public officials but also undertake their own projects to improve or maintain conditions in the local area. These often include physical improvements, such as beautification and housing rehabilitation, and service improvements, such as community crime prevention and recreation programs.

To date there has been no systematic evaluation of the performance of neighborhood planning programs. In undertaking to provide that evaluation we seek to answer a host of questions, including: What are the various mechanisms being used to involve neighborhood groups in planning? What responsibilities and opportunities are provided to neighborhood groups through these programs? How do citizens, planners, and planning directors evaluate the effectiveness of these programs? What concrete accomplishments can be credited to these programs? What factors have limited these programs from achieving their full potential? and, Which program structures are working better than others? A main objective is to develop a set of recommendations for improving the performance of these programs.

Approach to the Evaluation

Program evaluations typically take one of two forms: an in-depth study of the effects of a specific program or an overview of the activities of a class of programs. The former has the advantage of providing detailed information but does not allow one to generalize from the results. Looking at only one program, it is difficult to isolate the specific causes of success or failure and to know if the same program would be successful in a different context. The overview approach, on the other hand, can provide information on the importance of program characteristics and context, but often lacks an in-depth analysis of program operation.

Taking advantage of the strengths of both approaches, the present evaluation relies on a survey of fifty-one neighborhood planning programs across the country and six in-depth case studies of operating programs. The survey was designed to provide an overview of the characteristics, accomplishments, and problems of these programs, and the case studies were designed to provide detail and insight.

The Mail Questionnaire

A mail questionnaire provided data used to describe the characteristics of programs in the United States and assess their success in achieving specific program objectives. Further, the questionnaire provided data for an analysis of factors associated with program success.

The questionnaire consisted of thirty-four items divided into three sections (see appendix A). The first included questions on program staffing, program budget, sanction, initial proponents and opponents of the program, method of defining neighborhood boundaries, and methods of organizing neighborhood groups. The second section contained questions on the roles of the neighborhood planners and the neighborhood groups in the program and on the activities of the neighborhood groups. The last section included questions on the specific accomplishments and problems of the program, the level of support given to the program by individuals and groups in the city (for example, mayor, city council, other city departments), and the characteristics of the city that affected program performance.

Questionnaires were sent to the directors of city departments that administered neighborhood planning programs. These departments were identified from lists available in published sources (Center for Governmental Studies, 1976; Hallman, 1977; Rafter, 1980), from a letter-writing campaign to major cities, and from interviews with researchers and others interested in neighborhood planning programs. The initial list included seventy-one city departments thought to have programs that fit the definition of neighborhood planning presented earlier in this chapter. Although, undoubtedly, some programs have been missed, the list represents a fairly complete roster of neighborhood planning programs operating in the United States. (See appendix B for the complete list of programs.)

In a cover letter directors were asked to complete the survey or, where appropriate, to pass it on to the director of the
neighborhood planning program in their city. In many cities a
deputy or assistant director is in charge of the program.

After three follow-up letters and a phone call to nonre-
spondents, sixty-six of the seventy-one program directors responded, a response rate of 93 percent. Fifteen responses
were from cities with programs that did not fit the definition of
neighborhood planning presented above; these were excluded
from the sample. Thus the total sample consists' of fifty-one
programs.

Literature describing the programs and their accomplishments—such as annual reports, brochures, administrative and
procedural manuals, neighborhood plans, and other descrip-
tive documentation—was also collected from sponsoring departments.

The Case Studies

The case studies were designed to provide an in-depth assessment of neighborhood planning programs. Six cities were selected for study based on two important program dimensions:
(1) whether they worked with officially sanctioned neighborhood groups, with independent groups, or with both types of
neighborhood groups, and (2) whether the cities had a one-,
two-, or three-tiered program. Past research has suggested
that these dimensions have important implications for all aspects of program operation, including citizen influence on political decisions, the development of plans and projects, and
citizen-government relations (Hallman, 1977; Rafter, 1980).

Secondary criteria for selection included geographic cover-
age and city age. The intent was to include cities varying in
age and located in different parts of the country. Based on
these criteria six cities were selected: Atlanta, Georgia; Cincinnati, Ohio; Houston, Texas; Raleigh, North Carolina; St.
Paul, Minnesota, and Wilmington, North Carolina. Interviews
were conducted with the planning directors, neighborhood
planners, and citizen representatives working with these programs. A total of forty-eight interviews were conducted in the
six cities.

All interviews were conducted during two-day site visits in
the spring and fall of 1981. Interviews typically lasted from

one to one and one-half hours and were guided by interview schedules developed for each of the three participant groups (see appendix A). Interview items consisted of both open-ended and closed-ended questions. Probes such as "Can you give me some examples?" or "Can you explain a little?" were used with both question types when necessary. Participants were interviewed privately, and they were assured that all information they provided would not be attributable to them by name. The purpose of the study as described to participants was to identify accomplishments and problems with the program. Agency documents pertaining to the program were also collected during the site visits.

The Evaluation in Perspective

Because of the lack of previous research on the effectiveness of neighborhood planning programs, we decided to take a broad look at the accomplishments and problems of these programs rather than a narrow look at one specific issue. Our larger purpose in this study is to evaluate neighborhood planning programs within the set of broad propositions to be presented in chapter 3 and to develop a set of recommendations for developing effective programs.

Given the nature of the propositions and the large number of programs involved, we chose a qualitative rather than a quantitative methodology. This methodology relies on program documentation and surveys and interviews with those involved with the programs. Qualitative research methods, such as case studies, are generally accepted by the social science profession as appropriate for program evaluation (Weiss, 1972). As stated by Glaser and Strauss, "There is no fundamental clash between the purposes and capacities of qualitative and quantitative methods or data. . . . Each form of data is useful for both verification and generation of theory" (1967, pp. 17–18). Even Campbell, originally a staunch advocate of quantitative methodologies, has come to accept the legitimacy of case studies, which primarily involve interviews with those involved with the program, as an acceptable evaluation methodology (Campbell, 1979).

The question of the objectivity of the respondents in both

the case study interviews and the survey must still be considered; in the end, each reader must make his or her own assessment of the strength of the evidence. Several points should be
kept in mind, however.

First, much of the data used to describe programs and their
accomplishments comes from annual reports, administrative
and procedural manuals, and other documentation on the programs. Although one could argue these data sources are not
totally objective, they do seem to provide a reasonably accu-
rate description of the programs, their operations, and the
more specific projects undertaken by program participants.
Moreover, to cross-validate these descriptions and accomplishments, descriptions of program operations and projects were
elicited from citizens, neighborhood planners, and directors of
these programs.

Second, although much of the data comes from interviews or
surveys of individuals working with the programs, indicators
of accomplishments, problems, and factors leading to successful programs were developed by summing across all programs. Individual bias, then, would tend to average out. If
most respondents within a program and across programs cite a
particular accomplishment or problem, this is strong evidence
that the accomplishment or problem is not the result of individual bias. The inclusion of citizen interviews in the case studies also provides a check against the validity of the statements
made by program directors and neighborhood planners. Having been careful to corroborate our evidence with information
from a range of different sources and individuals, we feel con-
fident in the validity of the results and the conclusions drawn.

Finally, it is clear from our interviews and from the number
of problems identified that respondents were willing to criti-
cize programs and were not simply trying to make the programs look good. Directors, neighborhood planners, and citizen representatives all had a lot to say about the shortcomings
of these programs.

This study is not intended to offer the final word on neighborhood planning programs. Rather, it is intended to provide
preliminary evidence on a wide range of propositions. We hope
to encourage more narrowly defined studies of the propositions presented, as well as of propositions not considered in
this evaluation.

Organization of the Book

Chapter 2 begins with a history of neighborhood planning in the United States, which is designed to place contemporary neighborhood planning in a historical context. Three historical approaches are reviewed and their major accomplishments and limitations are identified. Chapter 3 presents a review of social, political, and planning theories that justify a neighborhood approach to planning and delineates eight propositions concerning the benefits of neighborhood planning. These propositions are used to guide the study. Chapter 4 explores the diversity of neighborhood planning programs in the United States by presenting a description of the characteristics of programs surveyed and of the six programs evaluated in the case studies here. The major accomplishments of these programs are discussed in chapter 5, and factors associated with the accomplishments are presented in chapter 6. Chapter 7 presents a discussion of the major problems or obstacles encountered by these programs. Finally, in the conclusion the propositions presented in chapter 3 are considered in light of the study findings, contemporary programs are placed in historical context, and recommendations for improving neighborhood planning programs are presented.

In most of the data chapters we have integrated the data from both sources, rather than present the survey data followed by six case studies. This was done for several reasons. First, in reviewing both data sources we found considerable similarity in program accomplishments and problems. Differences were more in degree than in category. Thus presenting the survey data followed by six discrete case studies would have resulted in considerable redundancy. Furthermore, our major objective is to assess the accomplishments of and problems endemic to neighborhood planning programs, not to evaluate specific programs. This objective is better served by organizing the data by topic (for example, accomplishments, factors associated with accomplishments, problems) rather than by program. What we lose in not giving an integrated presentation of the case studies we more than make up for in the clearer focus we are able to provide on the accomplishments of and problems experienced by these programs. The survey data provide an indication of the pervasiveness of the accomplishments and problems, while the case studies provide specific examples.

Contemporary neighborhood planning programs are progeny of a rich ancestry of neighborhood-oriented programs. They are the result of a century of experimentation with programs for improving the quality of life in urban neighborhoods, and their development has been influenced by the successes and failures of these earlier programs.

A review of these programs is important in developing a full understanding of contemporary programs. Accordingly, this chapter will trace the modern evolution of neighborhood planning, emphasizing the successes and failures of earlier approaches, and illustrate how contemporary neighborhood planning has been influenced by a long history of public and private involvement at the neighborhood level.

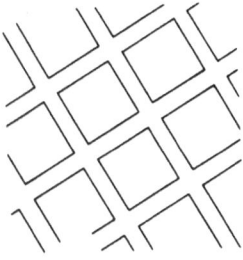

Three eras of neighborhood planning are discussed, each characterized by a different approach to the improvement of the quality of life in urban neighborhoods: the settlement house approach, the neighborhood unit approach, and the community action approach. As we shall see, each approach emphasizes different aspects of neighborhoods and adopts a different tack in solving neighborhood problems. Each of the three approaches will be described and analyzed in five areas: (1) its definition of the problem; (2) its method of defining neighborhoods; (3) its philosophical underpinnings; (4) the relationship between citizens and the program sponsor; and (5) the major accomplishments of and problems with the approach.

The Settlement House Approach: Emphasis on the Social Neighborhood

The social settlement movement grew out of the reform-minded spirit of the late nineteenth century. Preceded by the establishment of charity organizations, improvements in the conditions of penal and mental institutions, and housing reform, the settlement movement was a bold new attempt to address the problems of urban poverty, illiteracy, ill health, and criminal behavior.

During this period the Industrial Revolution was in full swing. New production processes required a concentrated labor force, which in turn created increased congestion, overcrowding, and unsanitary conditions in working-class areas of cities. The result was high rates of morbidity, disease, and crime.

Yet the Industrial Revolution also brought a new reverence for the power of science and a new breed of reformers who believed that science, blended with fellowship, could be used to solve the problems associated with rapid industrialization. Reformers associated with the settlement house movement did not limit their mission to one specific problem, such as delinquency or health, but were willing to tackle a wide range of problems as identified by scientific analysis of existing conditions. Moreover, the settlement house perspective focused on the local community as a means of addressing urban problems. The local community or neighborhood was seen as an important social unit that could be used to help solve the problems of poverty, illiteracy, criminal behavior, and ill health. It is this emphasis on the analysis of existing conditions and on the local community as an important social unit that qualifies this movement as an early form of neighborhood planning.

The formal beginning of the settlement house movement dates back to the opening of Toynbee Hall in the Whitechapel area of East London in 1884. Attempting to generate interest in helping the poor of his parish, Samuel Barnett, vicar of the Whitechapel church, initiated contacts with professors and students at Oxford and Cambridge universities. This led to the formation of a committee of university professors and others who solicited funding from philanthropists for the first settlement house. The house was to be a place "where twenty university men live in order to work for, to teach and to learn of the poor" (Barnett, 1909, p. 18).

The settlement house concept quickly spread from England to the United States. The first settlement in this country was established in New York in 1886 by Steven Coit, and soon after, houses were opened in Boston, Pittsburgh, Philadelphia,

Chicago, and other cities. The National Federation of Settlements was established in 1911, and the first international conference on settlements was held in London in 1922. By 1930
there were 160 settlements in the United States.

The activities undertaken by settlement houses broadened over time. In the beginning, they placed great emphasis on education and the appreciation of "the finer things in life," including art, literature, dance, and music. Settlements typically sponsored social activities, clubs, athletic programs, and classes in subjects ranging from civics to handicrafts. Activities were programmed for all age groups.

Very quickly, however, settlements broadened their activities to address some of the immediate problems facing local residents. Hull House in Chicago, for example, became involved in labor organizing and political organizing to address working conditions and the lack of public services in the local area. Jane Addams wrote: "The settlement, then, urges first, the organization of working people in order that as much leisure and orderly life as possible may be secured to them in which to carry out the higher aims of living" (1895, p. 40). Settlement workers also lobbied and demonstrated for better sanitary inspection, schools, sewage disposal, streets, parks, and other public services. Settlement staff were also urged to run for political office and to adopt an advocacy role in dealing with city government (MacMahon, 1914, p. 108).

Definition of the Problem

Settlement house activists defined the problem as a failure of low-income and immigrant groups to integrate into modern middle-class, industrial society. These groups had not adopted the values that were thought necessary to be a part of mainstream society. Important values included a work ethic, stable family life, frequent physical recreation, and the appreciation of art and cultural activities. They placed the majority of the blame for this not on the individuals themselves but on a society that did not provide the opportunity of self-advancement. In the words of Woods:

> The great city—the typical product of civilization—
> shows by multiple effects the danger of having people
> cut off from the better life of society, and breeding with

phenomenal rapidity all the evils with which society is cursed. The task is to make provision so that every part of society shall not only have a full supply for its fundamental human wants, but shall be constantly refreshed from the higher sources of happier and noble life (1923, pp. 2–3).

In particular, they held class segregation responsible for the failure to assimilate the poor into mainstream society. This segregation further inhibited the development of compassion among the upper class for the plight of the poor. In the United States, since many of the poor were recent immigrants, class differences were accentuated by ethnic differences. A major focus of many settlements was to facilitate the assimilation of these groups into traditional American society.

Settlement leaders also blamed modern capitalism for stimulating mobility, which broke up families and destroyed important community ties. Coit commented: "The more urgent is the influence of the Neighborhood Guild [another name for a settlement] in preserving the family life because modern industry in its demand for perfect mobility of labor, strikes a blow directly at the home life of working men" (1892, p. 28). Unlike the socialists of the time, however, the settlement house advocates did not see the capitalist system as fundamentally opposed to their objectives. Instead, they placed much of the blame at the individual level. Capitalism could work, they argued, if individuals were aware of the consequences of selfishness and took an interest in the well-being of the poor. Whereas the socialists believed that revolution was necessary to change social conditions and government control of capital was necessary to control selfish interests, advocates of settlements felt that knowledge of the consequences of material selfishness (the private accumulation of capital) would awaken reform. The fundamental problem was not with the capitalist system but with the individuals in the system.

Settlement leaders also criticized modern social organizations for breaking down the family and creating divisions between social groups. Typical social organizations—including political clubs, Christian men's groups, and labor unions—only involved one member of the family (typically male) and often established adversary relations with other social groups. This, they said, led to a splintering of families and communities. In

commenting on a wide range of traditional social institutions,
Coit stated: "All of these [traditional social institutions] by
separating their social life, young and old, boys and girls, men
and women, Tories and Liberals, or men of different trades
and women of different trades, maim and cripple the many-
sided humanity of the persons they would benefit" (1892, p.
26). They also saw the increase in the number and influence of
vocational organizations and other special-interest groups as a
threat to the interests of both the general public and the local
community (Woods, 1923).

Finally, settlement activists charged politicians and administrators with contributing to the problem by ignoring health
and safety problems in poor areas. They found the provision of
public services to poor areas to be inadequate, particularly in
the areas of sanitation and housing and health inspection.

Definition and Use of the Neighborhood Concept

To those involved in the settlement house movement, the
neighborhood was primarily defined as a social entity. It was
an area in which individuals of the same social class and ethnicity lived. No clear neighborhood boundaries were established; rather, the neighborhood was operationally defined as
the poor or ethnic area around the settlement house.

Beyond this, though, they saw the neighborhood as a system of social relations. They judged the health of the neighborhood by the degree to which residents participated in both
formal and informal social and political activities. Woods comments: "Disorganized neighborhoods must be reconstructed
by encouraging the active participation of its citizens in these
areas of concern: health, vocation and recreation" (1923, p.
154). Thus, the major goal of this movement was to create
strong social neighborhoods by facilitating social relationships
and mutual concern among residents. Only through developing neighborhoods, they thought, could the ills of the city and
nation could be solved.

Philosophy

The settlement house movement was driven by a blend of ide-
ologies, including the Christian ideal, the democratic ideal,
and the scientific ideal. The exact proportions of the blend var-

ied over time and from settlement to settlement; yet their influence is evident at all times.

The settlement house movement was a means of putting into practice the Christian principles of compassion and universal fellowship. It was, to some extent, domestic missionary work. Settlement workers were to teach local residents, by setting positive examples, to develop fellowship with their neighbors and faith in God.

> Only through fellowship (which for us Christians is the work of the spirit) can the kingdom of God be possible. And fellowship means bringing together men of every class and group in the interest of life worth living. . . . The settlement group, no matter how variously constituted, through its common life is working toward a common faith and in so far is adding to the religious experiences of the world. (Simkhovitch, 1938, pp. 140–41)

However, no standard religious dogma was taught, and typically settlements were independent of any specific religious denomination. Yet many of the early settlement house directors were either church affiliated or had seminary training, and this greatly influenced the nature of settlements.

This religious ideal was intertwined with a democratic ideal. Democracy itself was seen as an expression of Christian principles. "A belief in a progressive realization of democracy is a religious belief. Only when the followers of Jesus really adopt His method and live His spirit will Christian unity come true and democracy be a fact" (Simkhovitch, 1938, pp. 141–42). According to the settlement house philosophy the benefits of democracy could be expanded to include the poor. To do this, however, a mechanism was needed to educate the poor and to develop strong families and strong communities. The settlement house was to be that mechanism and thus further the development of democracy.

Whereas Christian and democratic ideals framed the goals of the settlement house movement, the scientific ideal formulated the method of achieving those goals. Strong connections between settlement houses and universities led to an emphasis on documenting and analyzing the conditions and ways of life in slum areas. The purposes of these studies were to inform society of the terrible living conditions in slum areas and to better understand both the types and extent of problems faced by the residents of these areas. Through these studies, settlement activists sought to identify problems and to develop a better understanding of the causes of those problems. This information was also used to develop settlement programs. Woods comments: "Corresponding to such lines of investigation and indeed as a result of the study of the particular needs of the immediate neighborhood, several settlements are introducing practical economic experiments toward the improvement of the economic conditions of the working people" (1923, p. 44). Thus, the settlement approach to neighborhood development involved empirical analysis, using both participant observation and statistical techniques, and applied this information to program development.

These philosophical positions led to four specific principles that guided settlement house activities. The first was that settlement workers should have close personal contact with those they wished to help. This meant that settlement workers should not only live in poor neighborhoods but should have frequent informal contacts with their neighbors and "learn to sup sorrow with the poor" (Holden, 1922, p. 12). They were expected to live simple lives to understand the experience of their neighbors. In the words of Jane Addams: "A settlement accepts the ethics of its contemporaries that the sharing of the life of the poor is essential to the understanding and betterment of that life" (1895, pp. 29–30). This informal contact was also seen as an effective means of transmitting knowledge and appropriate social values to the poor.

The second principle of settlement work was the development of strong family and neighborhood units. Settlement activities were designed to involve all members of the family and to foster association among neighbors. They thought that by involving the whole family, the prospect of individual change was greater. "Since the guild consists of a group of clubs for all ages and both sexes, each club in it exercises a wholly different moral influence upon its members from what it would if isolated" (Coit, 1892, p. 26).

Similarly, settlement activists sought to involve neighbors in settlement programs to provide support for individual change and the development of local norms for socially desirable behavior. The settlement also provided the organizational framework for bringing the community together to work for social and political change. Coit comments: "All people, men, women and children, in any one street, or any small number of streets, in every working class district, shall be organized into a set of clubs, which are by themselves, or in alliance with those of other neighborhoods to carry out, or induce others to carry out, all the reforms—domestic, industrial, educational, provident or recreative—which the social ideal demands" (1892, p. 21).

The third principle involved the maintenance of a flexible organizational structure. Settlement activists recognized that each area had a unique combination of people and problems and that no one program or set of activities was appropriate for all areas. Moreover, they knew neighborhoods changed over time and that both populations and problems would come and go. They also wanted to avoid being seen as bureaucratic organizations, wanting instead to be seen as houses where "helpful people lived." MacMahon comments: "The thing to be most dreaded in the settlement is that it loses flexibility. It must not be too closely organized lest we lose just those delicate kinds of influence which cannot be carved through too rigid an organization" (1914, p. 109).

This concern for flexibility led those in the settlement movement to reject the idea of seeking public funding for their work. They felt that public funding would restrict the activities that could be pursued, impose a set of rules, and stifle new initiatives (Holden, 1922, p. 96).

The fourth principle of the settlement movement was self-help. Their goal was to provide local residents with the necessary skills and motivation to better their lives and enter mainstream society. In the words of Elliot: "There is an old saying: 'Help men to help themselves.' And this has been the standard by which we have judged what people to help and how" (1915, p. 117). In practice, the self-help principle meant teaching reading, writing, and social graces and encouraging participants to put those skills to work in bettering their lives.

Relationship between Program Sponsors and Citizens

Settlement houses were established by the upper class to aid the lower class. In this sense, the relationship between program sponsors and those served can only be described as paternalistic. Altruistic members of the upper class wanted

to teach the lower class to appreciate what they had come to
value: art, music, literature, and other subjects thought necessary to lead a productive life. Coit comments: "The way to
save and prevent is often by educating the intellect and cul-
tivating the taste of the person in danger or already fallen"
(1892, p. 23). Settlements in areas with many immigrants were
concerned with Americanizing the population, although they
did recognize the importance of their retaining some ethnic
identity.

Settlements relied on philanthropists to provide the necessary funding and on university students and volunteers to provide the manpower. This reinforced the paternalistic image of
these efforts. This reliance on philanthropy was, in fact, recognized as a problem by those involved with the movement, and
some called for a greater emphasis on generating funds from
the neighborhood residents themselves. Pacey writes: "The
stigma of philanthropy which plagued the early neighborhood
workers grows constantly less as neighborhood people unite
with them, contributing whatever of time and financial aid they
can afford" (1950, p. 6). Nonetheless, settlements still involved
the imposition of the values of one social class on another.

Accomplishments and Limitations

The settlement house movement can be credited with a number of accomplishments. Clearly, the movement resulted in the
betterment of living conditions for a number of individuals, as
many local residents took advantage of the informal and formal services offered by settlements. Settlements also brought
pressure on local governments to improve services in settlement areas. Their success in bringing about actual change,
however, varied from settlement to settlement. The more active settlements, such as Hull House, appear to have had a significant influence, yet most appear to have had minimal impact
in influencing public service delivery. Settlements were small-
scale organizations in areas where voting rates were low;
hence, they often lacked political clout.

Possibly the greatest accomplishment of the settlement
movement was in educating the general public about living
conditions in low-income areas. The many studies conducted
by settlement workers were instrumental in generating public
sentiment for a greater public role in efforts to improve living

conditions in poverty areas. Settlement programs often became prototypes for later public initiatives. Furthermore, the settlement house movement was successful in introducing the use of scientific analysis in the identification and analysis of urban problems and in focusing attention on the importance of the social neighborhood in solving these problems.

There were, however, a number of limitations with the settlement approach to solving neighborhood problems. First, the faith of the settlement leaders in the existing political system and their emphasis on individual change limited their influence in bringing about structural changes in political systems to better represent the interests of the poor. They placed their emphasis on individual improvement rather than political organizing and sought no new avenues of political access and influence. Rather, they focused their efforts on securing minor concessions in specific areas of public responsibility and in specific subareas of the city. Settlement leaders were concerned with helping individuals move out of the lower class rather than eliminating the lower class. Second, the self-help principle was poorly operationalized. Settlements often relied on staff who were typically from outside the area to speak for the area and its problems. Furthermore, citizens relied on the settlement house for their organizational life. They were not encouraged to develop local organizations independent of the settlement houses. The reliance on philanthropists to fund programs also goes against the principle of self-help, at least in its purest form. Third, settlements were limited in number; hence, they were limited in effect. They only served a small proportion of the needy in any one city. Only those in the immediate area of a settlement house benefited from its services.

The Neighborhood Unit Approach: Emphasis on the Physical Neighborhood

As we have seen, the settlement house movement was primarily concerned with improving the social conditions in low-income areas and relied on philanthropy, rather than public funds, for its support. During the period when settlement houses began to open in American cities, other reformers were focusing on urban physical conditions thought to be related to poor health and inefficiency. These reformers believed that it was the responsibility of local government to rectify existing physical problems and to assure that new development did not lead to similar problems. Areas of major concern included the lack of recreation areas, excessively high residential densities (which limited the amount of natural light and fresh air inside housing units), congestion, and poor sanitation facilities (Rohe, 1982).

Throughout the early 1900s reformers pressured cities to adopt regulations controlling new development. While zoning and subdivision regulations proliferated during this period, there was no widely accepted normative template to guide new development. Howard had proposed the garden city concept, but this was not particularly applicable to small developments on the periphery of existing cities. Perry provided a template applicable to small-scale development which offered the promise of safe, healthy, and socially satisfying urban development (1929).

In 1929, Clarence Perry's now classic paper describing the neighborhood unit concept was published in *The Plan of New York and Its Environs*. In this paper Perry advocated neighborhood-scale development projects and presented six basic principles of good neighborhood design. This paper officially began a new era of neighborhood planning that focused on the physical design of new residential areas.

Perry's formulation was the synthesis of a number of diverse ideas and experiences. In the early 1900s the community center movement grew out of the settlement house movement. It was, in essence, the application of the settlement idea of providing a facility for community activities to middle-class areas. The community center movement sought to open up public schools for neighborhood cultural, recreational, and social activities and thus create a greater sense of community (Perry, 1939). According to Mumford, "Adherents to this movement sought to animate civic life by providing a common local meeting place to provide a forum for discussion and to serve as a basis for community activities that otherwise had no local habitation" (p. 260).

In 1909, Perry was hired by the Russell Sage Foundation to study this developing movement and identify problems in achieving its goals. He investigated many programs and publicized their activities. His eventual focus on the elementary school as the focal point of the neighborhood unit was undoubtedly influenced by this experience.

Perry was also influenced by planned communities of his

day. His own experience as a resident of Forest Hills Gardens in Queens, New York, promoted by the Russell Sage Foundation and designed after successful British developments, contributed to the development of the neighborhood unit concept (Perry, 1939). Perry admits analyzing Forest Hills Gardens and deriving many of the neighborhood unit principles from what he considered to be successful design features. For example, Forest Hills Gardens contained approximately five thousand persons, which was large enough to support an elementary school and seemed to be an ideal size. Other principles, however, were derived from what he considered to be shortcomings of this design. The area designed for civic functions, for example, was located on the periphery of the neighborhood and served commercial functions as well. Perry observed that a neighborhood required special communal facilities, in a central location to develop a strong sense of community. A business district, he suggested, did not properly serve this function.

Many of Perry's contemporaries were also experimenting with designs similar to the neighborhood unit. In England, Ebenezer Howard proposed that his ideal Garden Cities be subdivided into wards containing five thousand people, each with its own elementary school, local government, and radial road boundaries. These same principles were also employed in the design of such London suburbs as Bedford Park and Hempstead Gardens. In the United States, the Chicago City Club held a competition which focused attention on the process of integrating public and private facilities into local areas (Mumford, 1954). Stein and Wright also used the neighborhood as a basic unit of design in planned communities of Sunnyside Gardens, Long Island, and Radburn, New Jersey. Perry was responsible, however, for pulling these ideas together and presenting them as a series of design principles.

Once introduced, the neighborhood unit concept was widely accepted by city planners, real estate developers, social reformers, and others concerned with urban problems.

Definition of the Problem

Perry and other supporters saw the neighborhood unit formula as the solution to a number of physical, social, and political problems. Perry was particularly concerned with two shortcomings in the urban residential environments of his day: the

lack of play space and the lack of conditions that create neigh-
borliness (Perry, 1939). Existing high-density development resulting from the necessities of the machine age, he suggested,
did not provide for play space for preschool children or play
areas for older children where they would be supervised. He
wrote: "Students of crime have often speculated on why it is
that large cities, with elaborate parks and playground systems, still show a high delinquency rate. Some of it may be due
to the wide unprotected gulf which lies between the apartment
home and the play field. When the youngster tells his mother
he is going to the public playground, how can she be certain
that he actually reaches it?" (p. 119). A lack of nearby recreation areas was seen as contributing to larger social problems,
such as poor health. Thus, a main goal of the neighborhood
unit formula was to allow people to live near their daily oc-
cupations, yet still have access to recreation opportunities in
their neighborhoods.

Perry was also critical of residential environments for promoting urban isolation (1939). He blamed congestion, a lack of
a distinctive and personal atmosphere, and a lack of facilities
conducive to communal activities for individual alienation
and low rates of political and social participation. "The multifamily way of life has reduced the opportunities for vigorous
games, for wholesome companionship, for securing neighborly
help and advice. . . . Does this fact help to explain the cities'
insanity and suicides? When the need of people is for warm
personal sympathy, just how much consolation can they find in
a rich supply of books and education?" (p. 23).

The neighborhood unit was designed to rectify this problem
by providing common recreational and commercial facilities.
These, he thought, would encourage neighboring, friendship
formation, and participation in community affairs.

The culprit in the development of these problems was un-
planned and piecemeal development. Perry felt that good residential design was impossible unless individual land parcels
were big enough to be planned as entire neighborhoods. Yet
subdivision practices resulted in multiple ownership, which inhibited coordinated development and made the provision of
residential amenities financially unfeasible. Uncoordinated development was also responsible for a decline in urban property
values and for urban blight. The low levels of residential satisfaction that resulted from the lack of amenities and mixed land

use led to rapid residential mobility and declining property
values.

Definition and Use of the Neighborhood Concept

For Perry and others concerned with the design of new residential areas, the neighborhood was a physical entity that produced certain social consequences. The ideal neighborhood
would "embrace all the public facilities and conditions required
by the average family for its comfort and proper development
within the vicinity of its dwelling" (Perry, 1929, p. 50). This
definition was further specified by Perry as six principles of
neighborhood design. These are:

1. *Size.* A residential unit development should provide
   housing for that population for which one elementary
   school is ordinarily required, its actual area depending upon its population density.
2. *Boundaries.* The unit should be bounded on all sides
   by arterial streets, sufficiently wide to facilitate its
   bypassing, instead of penetration, by through traffic.
3. *Open Spaces.* A system of small parks and recreation
   spaces, planned to meet the needs of the particular
   neighborhood, should be provided.
4. *Institution Sites.* Sites for the school and other institutions having service spheres coinciding with the
   limits of the unit should be suitably grouped about a
   central point, or common.
5. *Local Shops.* One or more shopping districts, adequate for the population to be served, should be laid
   out in the circumference of the unit, preferably at
   traffic junctions and adjacent to similar districts of
   adjoining neighborhoods.
6. *Internal Street System.* The unit should be provided
   with a special street system, each highway being pro-
   portioned to its probable traffic load, and the street
   net as a whole being designed to facilitate circulation
   within the unit and to discourage its use by through
   traffic. (Perry, 1929)

These principles define the physical form of Perry's ideal neighborhood.

Perry also gave thought to how neighborhood units could be

constructed. In his original presentation of the neighborhood unit concept, Perry advocated the use of public condemnation to assemble land parcels large enough to construct well-planned neighborhoods. These parcels would then be sold to development corporations who, in return for this benefit, would develop according to the neighborhood unit formula. He felt that the neighborhood unit formula assured sufficient public benefit to warrant public condemnation. In his subsequent book *Housing for the Machine Age*, however, he backed off from this idea and emphasized cooperation between individual landowners instead.

Under this new scheme, a city planning commission would decide on a location for a new neighborhood and identify the various landowners and their shares in its total present value. The city planning staff would then prepare a tentative layout for the area based on the neighborhood unit formula and lots would be laid out for subdivision. The original owners would be offered a proportion of lots equal to their original contribution and a share of the school site, with the expectation that this would later be bought by the municipality for the construction of a school. The potential benefits to landowners included higher property values from the added amenities, free subdivision service, prompt installation of services, protection of property values, and easier access to mortgage money (Perry, 1939).

Although not all planners accepted the details of the neighborhood unit formula, they generally accepted the desirability of basic principles and they began to think of the neighborhood as primarily a physical entity. The neighborhood became a basic building block of many new communities. Radburn, New Jersey; Greenbelt, Maryland; Greenhills, Ohio; Greenbrook, New Jersey; Levittown, New Jersey; and Columbia, Maryland, to name a few, have all relied on the neighborhood as a basic unit of development. Many of the neighborhood unit principles have also been incorporated into subdivision regulations. It is now commonplace, for example, for these regulations to require the setting aside of land for recreation purposes and a street design that discourages through traffic.

The neighborhood unit movement was based on two major be-
liefs. First, its supporters viewed close social contacts between members of a local area to be important for individual
and social health. Second, they felt that the proper design of
residential areas would help to bring about these contacts. In
essence, they believed in physical determinism.

Early advocates of the neighborhood unit viewed it as a
means of reversing what they saw as a breakdown in local
social interaction and political participation caused by rapid
large-scale urbanization and technological advances, such as
the improvement of transportation technology. Influenced by
sociologists such as Charles H. Cooley, they sought to recreate
villagelike social relations—the natural form of social organization—in urbanized areas. Dahir comments that although
some are attracted to an urban way of life based upon anonymity and namelessness, these people are not truly happy.
The alternative is to be integrated into a neighborhood and
"have a new and personal part to play, a new healthy ambi-
tion" (1950, p. 233). Similarly, Mumford writes: "In the neighborhood, if anywhere, it is necessary to recover the sense
of intimacy and innerness that has been disrupted by the increased scale of the city and the speed of transportation" (1954,
p. 269).

These advocates saw the development of local associations
as the solution to many urban problems, including crime and
mental illness, and also thought that neighborhood units would
increase political participation. In commenting on the importance of a central square, Perry wrote: "The square itself will
be an appropriate location for a flagpole, a memorial monu-
ment, a bandstand or an ornamental fountain. In the common
life of the neighborhood it will function as a place of local cele-
brations. Here, on Independence Day the flag will be raised,
the Declaration of Independence be recited and the citizenry
urged to patriotic deeds by eloquent orators" (1929, p. 65).

The neighborhood unit was to bring about social contacts
and political participation in several ways. First, the provision
of recreation areas and other community facilities would provide the impetus for people to associate, become friendly, and
develop a sense of community. Perry, for example, wrote: "Vast
numbers of urban dwellers are not acquainted with people

next door. When, however, residents are brought together through the use of common recreational facilities, they come to know one another and friendly relations ensue" (1939, p. 215). Second, the homogeneous housing styles advocated by most neighborhood unit advocates would provide a sense of community and "feeling of kinship" to residents (Kostka, 1954). Moreover, homogeneity of housing styles assured a certain degree of social homogeneity, at least with respect to income. This was thought necessary for the development of positive social relations and voluntary action. Third, clear neighborhood boundaries and a curvilinear street pattern would result in community cohesion. The curvilinear street pattern was to discourage through traffic and facilitate internal interaction.

It is clear from the writings of early advocates of the neighborhood unit that they believed in physical determinism. Physical arrangements, they believed, produced certain social behaviors. Perry, for example, in commenting on Forest Hills Gardens wrote: "When reduced to general terms the basis of the Garden's community life was simple. It grew directly out of the physical plan of the development. The plan, in most of its aspects, either compelled association or made it easy and enjoyable" (1939, p. 213). As reviewed below, however, subsequent empirical research has not substantiated these claims.

Relationship between Program Sponsor and Citizens

Like the settlement house movement, the neighborhood unit movement was paternalistic. The responsibility for planning residential areas was invested in the professional city planners, and there was no attempt to elicit citizen input. The planner was the expert who, armed with the neighborhood unit formula, knew what would promote the greatest satisfaction among future residents. Keller comments: "Many planners advocate planned neighborhoods not because they have reliable evidence that this is what urban residents desire or need, but because this conforms to certain cherished values that they hope to preserve" (1968, p. 127). They assumed that future residents would hold the same values and preferences for residential environments that they held.

The sponsor-client relationship in the neighborhood unit movement, however, was different from that of the settlement house movement in one major way. In the settlement house movement sponsors and clients came from different social classes, whereas in the neighborhood unit movement they were essentially from the same social class. Typically, both the clients and sponsors in the neighborhood unit movement were middle and upper middle class and, as such, were likely to share social values and preferences.

Accomplishments and Problems

The neighborhood unit movement focused attention on the design of residential areas and provided clear guidelines for orderly growth. Before its introduction, planners were more concerned with beautification and transportation projects (Scott, 1969), and gave little attention to planning new residential areas. Thus, the neighborhood unit movement helped create more desirable residential environments by focusing attention on the residential sector of the city. Moreover, as mentioned earlier, many of the neighborhood unit principles have become incorporated into modern-day subdivision regulations. They have provided basic standards for residential development. In particular, the emphasis on the provision of appropriately located recreation, commercial, and public facilities throughout residential areas was a contribution to the practice of planning. It has also helped to preserve open space in urban areas.

Furthermore, the movement emphasized the comprehensive planning of new residential areas. Transportation, recreation, housing, and public and private facilities were considered as a system rather than as discrete elements of urban development. This movement also introduced the idea that physical planning could and should support social behavior, particularly face-to-face human contacts. Most planning before this time was based on aesthetic or functional criteria, not social.

Finally, the movement must be credited for its longevity and persistence. Since its inception, the neighborhood unit has remained a popular approach to residential development. A study by Solow, Ham, and Donnelly (1969) indicates that 80 percent of practicing planners actually use the neighborhood unit concept in practice.

Not everyone accepted the desirability of the neighborhood unit, however. One of the most vocal critics has been Reginald Isaacs. In a series of articles written in the late 1940s, Isaacs was critical of what he considered to be the discriminatory nature of the neighborhood unit concept. He speculated that

the concept—with its emphasis on homogeneous areas—became popular because it coincided with the first major black migration since the Civil War to northern cities and the first expression of concern by real estate interests over the "invasion" of white residential areas. He viewed the neighborhood concept as a means of enforcing social segregation and maintaining ghetto areas. Planners, he believed, should be working to provide increased housing opportunities for the poor by encouraging the integration of all social classes and racial groups. The neighborhood unit concept, he believed, was working against this purpose (Isaacs, 1948a). Isaacs and others also criticized the neighborhood unit for promoting segregation among those in different life-cycle groups. The neighborhood unit, he argued, is designed to serve the needs of those in the early childrearing stage of the life cycle and provides limited support for such groups as the elderly or single adults. Keller notes that "neighborhood units which are supposed to be a microcosm of urban life fail because of segregation by income and family composition" (1968, p. 132).

The neighborhood unit concept has also been criticized as a romantic notion that does not recognize the reality of modern urban life. Urban lifeways, according to this argument, include transience in both place of residence and interests. It is unrealistic, then, to expect to achieve stable villagelike residential neighborhoods. Isaacs cautions that "in planning urban development it is well to realize that change is characteristic of modern urban life. . . . This involves a shift from a static conception of the city to that of the city as a dynamic, changing organism" (1948b, p. 180). The neighborhood unit concept promotes a static approach to urban development. Furthermore, critics argue that, regardless of urban form, people will work, shop, and socialize in areas away from their local neighborhoods. Both the ease of transportation and the proliferation of special-interest groups work against extensive participation in local groups and activities. Hence, the neighborhood unit is idealistic and not practical for modern urban life-styles.

Even if neighborhood units could change these patterns of behavior, many argue that local isolationism breeds conflict and deprives residents of many of the advantages of urban life. Dahir (1950), for example, argues that many people want the anonymity of the city and enjoy the city's high level of stimulation. The neighborhood unit concept assumes people desire intimate face-to-face relations with their neighbors. Yet, critics argue, this is not true of many people.

Whereas the above criticisms focus on the goals of the neighborhood unit concept, others focus on the means of realizing those goals. The physical determinism implicit in the neighborhood unit concept has received particular criticism. Pahl (1970), for example, asserts that Mumford and other planners who sought to create social relations between citizens by using physical planning principles have made unsubstantiated statements. In fact, studies of the relation between physical design and neighborhood social interaction have typically shown weak or nonsignificant relationships between these variables (Kuper, 1970; Gans, 1961; Solow, Ham, and Donnelly, 1969). The influence of resident social characteristics, social values, norms, attitudes, and other variables has been found to mediate, if not overshadow, any influence of physical design.

Other more specific assumptions of the neighborhood unit concept have also been criticized. A population size of five thousand people, for example, is said to be too large for neighborly relations to develop (Keller, 1968). Moreover, Isaacs suggests that the local facilities called for in the unit concept are inadequate and are often too far from some residents. He also criticizes the school as a focal point of the community as impractical and overly child centered (Isaacs, 1948b). Furthermore, critics also question the utility of a common meeting area, given the diversity of individuals usually found in urban areas.

Finally, the economic efficiency of the neighborhood unit concept has been challenged. Critics argue that the neighborhood unit is too small to act as a service district for urban services. The idea of providing each neighborhood with its own elementary school has received particular criticism. Neighborhood schools would be too small to undertake the specialized activities that become economically feasible in large schools. The proliferation of small parks and other public open spaces would also necessitate expensive maintenance service.

The Community Action Approach: Emphasis on the Political Neighborhood

Although the neighborhood unit concept had a major influence on the development of new residential areas, it had little affect on the problems of inner-city neighborhoods. As development

expanded outward, the central cities were largely ignored.
During the 1930s and 1940s, however, two events had a significant influence on our view of the role of government in addressing urban problems. Although the seeds of the welfare
state had been sown many years earlier, the Great Depression
and World War II were responsible for an expansion and consolidation of the view that the public sector should have the
ultimate responsibility for the well-being of every individual in
society (Janowitz, 1976). During the Great Depression welfare
programs were expanded to meet the needs of the large numbers of unemployed and to stimulate the economy. Keynesian
economic principles were put to the test and were given pass-
ing grades. The mobilization for World War II helped to emphasize universalism and create procedures and institutions
conducive to the welfare state. As Janowitz notes: "A society
that could mobilize for total war was defined as one that could
also mobilize for social welfare. Thus, it was the actual performance of the central government during the war that was
crucial in the thrust toward a welfare state. . . . The achievements of wartime mobilization created cadres of administrators and administrative structures that could be adapted to
large scale societal 'intervention'" (1976, pp. 37–38). Thus the
stage was set for large-scale government involvement in the
problems of urban areas.

For its part, the planning profession during the 1940s and
1950s was preoccupied with the notions of comprehensive and
regional planning. Many believed that a wider and more encompassing approach was needed to solve the problems of urban areas. The rapid growth in metropolitan development
after World War II reinforced this emphasis, as new residential construction expanded well beyond municipal boundaries
and metropolises grew into megalopolises. The rapid growth
on the outskirts of urban areas, however, did little for the long-
standing urban problems of poverty, unemployment, and
crime. In fact, it exacerbated these problems by enticing the
middle class to flee traditional urban locations, resulting in
falling municipal revenues and a concentration of the poor.

To address these problems of slum living and falling municipal revenues, the federal government, in the Housing Act of
1949, offered cities the power and resources to engage in acquisition and redevelopment programs. The program allowed
municipalities to acquire properties in areas defined as slum
neighborhoods through eminent domain and sell them to pri-

vate entrepreneurs at reduced prices. Land acquired through the act could be used for a variety of purposes, including luxury housing, low-rent private housing, commercial or industrial activities, and public facilities. Many cities took advantage of the provisions of this act and began clearing slum housing. As Frieden and Kaplan note, however: "Urban renewal, begun in 1949 as a slum clearance program with the avowed purpose of improving living conditions for slum residents, was converted during the 1950s into a program for strengthening the central cities against suburban competition" (1975, p. 23).

In the Housing Act of 1954, several important changes were introduced, but they did not significantly change the basic structure of redevelopment activity. There was a new emphasis on the rehabilitation of housing and the conservation of neighborhoods, and cities had to develop a "workable program" including a plan for relocating those displaced by program activities, a program for citizen participation, and a housing code setting minimum standards. Unfortunately, however, these new provisions did not seem substantially to change the manner in which renewal programs were implemented. The federal government was lax in enforcing the requirements for citizen participation and relocation, and many participating cities ignored the emphasis on conservation (Gans, 1965; Weaver, 1965).

The failures and abuses of the urban renewal program set the stage for the community action approach to neighborhood planning. It became clear that razing physically deteriorated areas was not going to solve the broader range of urban problems which included crime, poverty, illiteracy, and unemployment. New initiatives were necessary to address these problems, and they began to emerge in the early 1960s.

The roots of the community action approach can be traced back to the Ford Foundation's Gray Areas Projects and the President's Committee on Juvenile Delinquency. The purpose of the Gray Areas Projects was to stimulate broader and more coherent approaches to solving the physical and human problems of the deteriorating sections of urban areas (the gray areas). According to Marris and Rein: "They sought to challenge the conservatism of an impoverished school system; open worthwhile careers to young people disillusioned by neglect; return public and private agencies to a relevant and coherent purpose; and encourage a respect for the rights and dignity of the poor" (1982, p. 15).

Although concerned with adopting a comprehensive approach to the problems associated with poverty, the first grants awarded in 1960 went to seven school districts to support what were considered innovative demonstration programs, such as home-school coordinators, adult classes, preschool programs, and after-school programs. Yet these grants did not facilitate the coordinated and comprehensive approach that was being sought. During the following four years, six more grants were awarded, but this time the recipients were associations comprising a number of city agencies—including private voluntary agencies and, occasionally, county agencies—which were to coordinate the efforts.

Shortly after the first round of Gray Areas project grants, newly elected President Kennedy established the President's Committee on Juvenile Delinquency and Youth Crime. The committee's purposes were to promote coordination between federal agencies with delinquency prevention programs, stimulate experimentation and innovation, and encourage cooperation between federal, state, and private organizations (Executive Order 10940). The committee defined its task broadly to encompass the relationships between delinquency and educational problems, unemployment, and the limited opportunities available to inner-city youth. The committee also promoted the Juvenile Delinquency and Youth Offense Control Act of 1961, which provided funds for demonstration projects and required the secretary of the Department of Health, Education, and Welfare, who controlled the funds, to consult with and consider the recommendations of the committee. During the next three years, major demonstration projects were funded in six cities, as well as a number of smaller projects.

These two programs are important in the evolution of federally initiated community action in that they emphasized demonstrations and innovations that sought to address urban problems in a comprehensive and coordinated manner. Through collaboration between public and private agencies, they hoped to address a wide range of interrelated problems. Furthermore, the programs promoted systematic planning and evaluation as a means of assuring more effective programs. Finally, these programs encouraged applicants to involve citizens in the planning for demonstration projects. The method and

extent of citizen involvement, however, was not clearly specified. These themes were to be carried over into the broader
and more ambitious federal community action programs to
follow.

In 1964, with the backing of President Johnson, Congress
passed the Economic Opportunity Act, which provided funds
for the Community Action Program and led to the creation of
the Office of Economic Opportunity (OEO). The purpose of the
Community Action Program was "to help urban and rural communities to mobilize their resources to combat poverty" (Community Action Program Guide, 1965). Approved Community
Action Agencies received considerable latitude in developing projects to combat poverty. Remedial reading, literacy
courses, job training and employment counseling, health services, neighborhood multiservice centers, and related programs were all eligible for funding. In the early years of the
program, the federal government funded 90 percent of the
costs of community action programs and, after 20 August 1966,
50 percent of the costs. By September 1965 more than five
hundred community action agencies had been funded. In 1965,
$237 million was provided in support, and in 1966 this amount
rose to $628 million.

The local Community Action Program (CAP) agencies were
designed to be independent of city hall. Their governing bodies
or advisory committees were composed of (1) representatives
from the chief elected official or governing body of the city,
the board of education, the public welfare agency, and major
private social service agencies; (2) representatives from important community organizations such as labor, business, religious, or minority groups; and (3) representatives from residents of the areas and members of the groups to be served,
including at least one representative from each of the neighborhoods or areas in which the CAP would be concentrated
(Community Action Program Guide, 1965).

Most of the objectives and strategies of the earlier programs
were continued within the Community Action Program, although the relative emphasis changed. In particular, much
more emphasis was placed on citizen participation. The original legislation called for "maximum feasible participation of
members of groups and areas served." Although the exact intent of the phrase was at first unclear, subsequent regulations
specified that participation should include hiring the poor to

work with the poor and involving citizens in both planning and
policymaking. The representatives of the poor were to be selected by "traditional democratic approaches and techniques." In practice, this often included elections to select representatives or appointments that were made by neighborhood groups. In any case, this represented a major change from earlier programs in which representatives of the client group were selected by public officials.

A second, less-noted phrase in the original legislation also had a major influence on the eventual nature of this program. A long-range objective of the act was "to effect a permanent increase in the capacity of individuals, groups and communities afflicted by poverty to deal effectively with their own problems so that they need no further assistance." This phrase provided the justification for local CAPs to engage in community organizing designed to strengthen the indigenous political power of low-income neighborhoods. Newly created organizations and coalitions often directed their activities at city hall, which resulted in the alienation of city mayors and other officials. When local political power turned against the programs, Congress passed an amendment granting cities the right to take over the private nonprofit community action agencies. Furthermore, as the program evolved, increasing amounts of funding were earmarked for national programs, such as Head Start and the Jobs Corps, allowing for less local discretion in program selection. In 1971, President Nixon abolished OEO, and many programs administered under the Community Action Program were transferred to other federal departments. Existing CAPs, stripped of many of their functions, were transferred to the Community Services Administration. Although this action did not abolish the Community Action Program, it marked a clear change. Nixon's abolition of OEO was motivated by a desire to move away from many of the basic tenets of the original program, including the necessity for coordination, institutional reform, citizen participation, and community organizing. As stated by Marris and Rein, "The poor were to receive money as needy individuals, not power as deprived communities devoid of a voice in their destiny" (1982, p. 256).

The next major federal initiative to address the problems of urban areas was the Model Cities Program. In 1965, President Johnson created a task force to recommend new initiatives to address the problem of poverty in the midst of plenty. The task force's recommendations were endorsed by the president and were written into law in the Demonstration Cities and Metropolitan Development Act of 1966. This act authorized the newly created Department of Housing and Urban Development to "provide grants and technical assistance to help communities of all sizes to plan, develop and carry out comprehensive city demonstration programs. These are locally prepared programs for rebuilding or restoring entire sections and neighborhoods of slum and blighted areas by concentrated and coordinated use of all available federal aids together with local, private and government resources" (Congressional Digest, February 1967, p. 40). The program sought to combine physical and social planning and development in selected low-income areas to produce a dramatic social, physical, and environmental reformation.

Operationally, the program awarded grants to Model Cities agencies in two stages. Initial grants were provided to cover up to four-fifths of the costs of developing a Model City plan. Subsequent grants were to carry out approved plans. Allocations included $12 million for planning in 1967 and 1968 and $500 million for implementation in 1969. The Model Cities agencies were placed under the jurisdiction of city halls and given the responsibility for planning and administering the programs. They were also expected to oversee the coordination and application of a wide range of federal programs in the neighborhoods and to exercise discretion in decisions regarding program funding.

Although many of the goals and principles of the Model Cities Program were similar to those of the Community Action Program and its predecessors, there were several important differences. First, the Model Cities Program was specifically targeted to individual neighborhoods. Concentration of program activities was intended to produce clear-cut and observable changes in target neighborhoods and thus act as a model for rehabilitation efforts. Second, Model Cities was concerned with physical rehabilitation as well as social rehabilitation. Earlier programs were primarily concerned with coordinating programs addressing social and institutional problems. Third, Model Cities was designed to avoid local political conflict and resistance by placing the control of the program clearly in the hands of city hall rather than with an independent agency. The mayor or city council had the final say on program activities. Fourth, the requirements for citizen participation were reduced. The legislation stopped short of calling for "maximum feasible participation," instead calling for "widespread citizen participation." Finally, the Model Cities Program not only was to plan for the expenditure of funds specifically allocated to the program but was to control funds that other federal agencies spent in Model Cities neighborhoods. By 1965 there were over forty separate federal programs for urban development involving thirteen departments and agencies (Frieden and Kaplan, 1975). One of the main concerns of the program was to coordinate the rapidly-growing number of federal aid programs for cities. Model Cities was to see that, at least in selected neighborhoods, these programs would be coordinated in a rational and efficient manner. As will be discussed later, problems arose with the application of many of these principles.

By 1974, when the Model Cities Program was largely replaced by the Community Development Block Grant Program, a total of 145 Model Cities projects had been funded in cities across the country. Many Model Cities agencies and programs received funding through the Community Development Block Grant Program and continued their activities.

Definition of the Problem

In the broadest terms, all the programs reviewed above were concerned with reducing poverty in the midst of plenty. More specifically, they shared common notions of why poverty persisted in spite of a healthy economy and earlier public and private antipoverty programs.

The designers of these programs viewed poverty as a consequence of a lack of opportunity for the poor to better their plight. The social and physical environments in poor areas inhibited local residents from assuming productive roles in society. Moreover, they indicted existing institutions serving those areas for their rigidity and inability to meet the special needs of the poor. Since they conceived of poverty as having multiple causes, they felt that no narrow single-focus program could break the "cycle of poverty." Increased opportunities for improved education, job training, employment, housing, and other social services were seen as necessary for success. Besides being overly narrow in their focus, these institutions, as they existed, were thought to have middle-class prejudices that inhibited them from effectively addressing the needs of the poor (Marris and Rein, 1982).

A lack of creative approaches to solving the problems of poverty was also seen as a problem. Traditional institutions were not experimenting with new approaches. Rather, they were adhering to standard ineffective programs. Advocates criticized this reluctance to coordinate efforts and to develop a comprehensive approach to the problem of poverty. All of the community action programs attempted to address this problem by requiring that local administering agencies be composed of representatives from a wide variety of institutions and by requiring that plans be developed which emphasized a comprehensive and coordinated attack.

The lack of client involvement was also defined as a problem with traditional programs, and with urban governance in general. In fact, Marris and Rein suggest that "community action was less an answer to poverty than to a sense of breakdown in the open, democratic structure of society. Each of its successive formulations—in the Gray Area Projects, the delinquency programs, the Economic Opportunity and Model Cities legislation—implied a need to reform the process of government itself" (1982, p. 273).

Supporters of the community action approach saw municipal governance structures as unresponsive to the real needs of the poor. Mandating involvement of the poor in the development and operation of programs was designed to correct this problem.

Definition and Use of the Neighborhood Concept

Throughout successive community action programs, the neighborhood concept played an increasingly strong role. The earlier Gray Areas projects and delinquency program made little specific reference to the neighborhood concept. Instead they were oriented toward larger sections of cities which were inhabited by the poor. The neighborhood was not used as a means of geographic targeting, nor was it seen as a potentially important political entity or social system that could be used to achieve program goals.

Within the Community Action Program, however, the neighborhood concept began to take hold. Several factors contributed to the acceptance of the neighborhood concept. First, the poor tended to be located in discrete neighborhoods bounded by physical obstructions—such as major roads, railways, and industrial or commercial areas—and identified with a particular ethnic or racial group or life-style. These residents also lacked mobility, which reinforced the need for decentralized services. Thus, in many instances, neighborhood multiservice centers were established. Second, one program objective was to organize residents of poor areas, and community organizing has traditionally been practiced at the neighborhood level. Third, in some areas neighborhood organizations already existed, and they lobbied for an active role in the program.

Thus the neighborhood began to be viewed as an important political entity. Spiegel comments that "it was that activity which recognized the organizational needs of the neighborhood as something distinct and separate from the larger community, even the Community Action Agency itself, which lent distinctive coloration to the Community Action Program" (1968, p. 59). Neighborhood organizations selected representatives to sit on the boards of directors and in many instances played significant roles in determining the nature of the local programs (Frieden and Kaplan, 1975).

The neighborhood concept continued to play an important role in Model Cities. The initial legislation emphasized the importance of developing a program "of sufficient magnitude to make a substantial impact on the physical and social problems and to remove or arrest blight and decay in entire sections or neighborhoods" (U.S. Congress, 1966). In effect, the emphasis on generating a substantial impact required programs to concentrate their activities in relatively small areas. The neighborhood concept was employed to define program areas, but no specific definition or criteria for selecting target area neighborhoods were provided. Thus, as Spiegel notes,

> Model Cities has made of it [the neighborhood] a geographic abstraction, an area whose boundaries have been delineated by the city in order to meet certain programmatic criteria promulgated by HUD. Conceptualized on this basis, neighborhoods may consist of a single neighborhood unit, or a group of units, or even parts of units. These constituent units may be defined according to a more sociological meaning of neigh-

borhood, namely in terms of their physical features and
natural geographic boundaries, as well as in accordance
with their social expectations, institutional loyalties,
group associations, values and aesthetics, educational
aspirations, or any combination of these and other factors" (1968, pp. 20–21).

The neighborhood as a political entity also played a role in the
Model Cities Program, despite attempts to discourage it. Local neighborhood groups, politicized by earlier programs, de-
manded to be involved in the program. Although there was no
specific provision in the legislation for involving neighborhood
groups, there was a provision for "widespread citizen participation." Neighborhood groups often used that clause to
demand inclusion in program planning and implementation
(Frieden and Kaplan, 1975). As noted by Spiegel: "In most instances, Model Cities decision-making systems evolved out of
a tough bargaining process between city hall and the neighborhood. . . . Neighborhood power and a measure of control
envisioned neither by HUD nor the cities, gradually began to
slip in under a number of negotiating tables" (1968, p. 62).

Philosophical Underpinnings

Like the earlier eras of neighborhood planning presented
above, the community action approach was based on a democratic ideal. Its sponsors were concerned with including the
poor in the benefits of democracy. If the cycle of poverty could
be broken, the promises of democracy—prosperity and freedom for all—could be kept. Particularly at a time of growing
Communist influence in the world, the United States was
acutely conscious of the image that poverty and slum areas
presented to foreign countries. America, the flagship of democracy, had large, visible signs of failure, at least for some
elements of the society. The contrast between poverty and op-
ulence in a generally healthy economy made it all the more
disturbing.

Cloward and Ohlin presented a more specific guiding philosophy (1963). Their influential book *Delinquency and Opportunity* is accepted as the basis upon which the original community action programs were designed (Marris and Rein, 1982).
In explaining the conditions that lead to the rise of delinquent

groups, they focused on "marked discrepancies between cul-
turally induced aspirations among lower class youth and the
possibilities of achieving them by legitimate means" (p. 78).
They argued that democratic industrial societies emphasize
competition between workers for skilled jobs. To motivate
competition, societies define success goals as potentially accessible to all, regardless of race, creed, or socioeconomic position. Yet, in reality there is often a wide gulf between aspirations engendered by the society and legitimate opportunities
for fulfilling those aspirations.

They recognized two types of barriers faced by lower-class
youth. One is a cultural barrier arising from subcultures within
society, while the other is a structural barrier, such as discrimination, lack of income, or the necessity to concentrate on
immediate concerns such as food, clothing, and shelter. Delinquent gangs provide alternative means of fulfilling success aspirations. Accordingly, the community action programs sought
to open up the societally sanctioned opportunity structure to
the poor and divert them from seeking alternative means of
achieving success. This accounts for the emphasis on education
and job-training programs within community action programs.

The work and writings of Saul Alinsky must also be credited
with influencing the nature of the community action approach
to neighborhood planning. Throughout the 1940s and 1950s he
and his associates at the Industrial Areas Foundation were responsible for organizing a number of communities across the
country and for training a large number of community organizers. Alinsky's philosophy, first put forth in *Reveille for
Radicals* in 1946, was based on a blend of Jeffersonian democracy, labor movement ideology, and the populist movement
(Lancourt, 1979). In the introduction to *Rules for Radicals*
(1971), Alinsky writes, "We are concerned with how to create
mass organizations to seize power and give it to the people; to
realize the democratic dream of equality, justice, peace, cooperation, equal and full opportunities for education, full and
useful employment, health and the creation of those circumstances in which man can have the chance to live by values
that give meaning to life" (p. 3).

Alinsky's philosophy included a number of principles which
were to influence the community action approach to neighborhood planning. First and foremost, Alinsky emphasized the
importance of developing local organizations. He believed that

"the foundation of a people's organization is the communal life of the local people" (p. 76). Local organization was more desirable and effective than mass organization, since individuals at the local level shared common cultural and social characteristics as well as common problems. The community action approach embraced this emphasis on local organization.

Second, Alinsky (1971) emphasized the importance of people doing things for themselves. The process, he believed, was as important as the product. "It is the most common human reaction that successful attainment of objectives is much more meaningful to those who have achieved the objective through their own efforts. The objective is never an end in itself. The efforts that are expended in the actual earning of the objective are part and parcel of the achievement itself" (pp. 174–75). This principle is evident in the community action approach in having residents on the boards of directors and acting as program staff.

Third, he believed in developing indigenous leadership to direct the effort for improving local conditions. The community action approach attempted to do this by providing residents with positions in local organizations, which facilitated access to the press and other means of influence.

Finally, Alinsky relied on confrontational, yet nonviolent, tactics, such as sit-ins, marches, and other forms of demonstration. His prescriptions on developing tactics include going outside the experience of "the enemy," staying within the experience of your people, and picking a target, freezing it, personalizing it, and polarizing it. These and other prescriptions for choosing tactics were employed by many organizers working within the community action approach to neighborhood planning.

Relation of Program Sponsor and Client

The relationship between program sponsor and clients in the various programs discussed in this section cannot be easily summarized, since it changed as the programs evolved and varied from locality to locality. In general, the commitment to involving citizens in program planning and implementation germinated in the earlier Gray Areas program, bloomed in the early years of Community Action, and withered slightly under Model Cities. The earlier programs required citizen involvement, but this was typically satisfied by a government-appointed citizen advisory council, which played only a minor role in program development and implementation. Under the Community Action Program, however, citizens from the area to be served made up at least one-third of the boards of directors of CAP agencies. There is some question, however, whether resident members of the CAP boards were effective in swaying policy, since they did not have the technical knowledge, information, or experience to develop forceful positions. Critics argue that although citizens were involved, this involvement did not constitute true citizen participation because no real power was distributed (Arnstein, 1969).

The intention of the Model Cities Program was to reduce citizen involvement in program operation and bring it more firmly under the control of local government (Marris and Rein, 1982). HUD program staff, however, lobbied for stronger participation requirements once the program was enacted (Frieden and Kaplan, 1975). The department issued a letter on participation requirements which required cities to provide organizational structures that involved neighborhood residents in planning, decision making, and implementation.

The actual degree of citizen involvement, however, differed considerably from city to city. Kaplan (1973) distinguished five classifications of local programs: staff dominant, staff influence, parity, resident influence, and resident dominant. The system adopted in individual communities was determined by (1) the degree of preprogram turbulence among neighborhood groups and between neighborhood groups and city hall; (2) the degree of involvement by the chief executive; and (3) the degree to which neighborhood groups were integrated and cohesive. Although Kaplan does not provide an overall assessment of the number of programs falling into each category, he does conclude that "most cities established an organizational structure that seemed to offer neighborhood groups opportunities for real influence in the program" (p. 76). Others were still unsatisfied with the degree of influence citizens had in the program. It is clear, however, that these programs provided substantially more opportunities for citizen involvement than any previous neighborhood planning program.

Accomplishments and Problems

Although the Community Action and Model Cities programs were short-lived, they can be credited with a number of accomplishments. In particular, both programs had significant effects on the political dynamics of local communities. They led to the creation of strong neighborhood organizations in many cities by providing a reason to organize: the promise of serious involvement in major initiatives. They also provided an opportunity for the development of indigenous leaders. As Marris and Rein suggest,

> Community action did provide a structure through which Black leaders could emerge and learn to argue with the political establishment. It gave them jobs, access to professional advice, a platform; it created a carrier for brokers between the ghetto and the society which enclosed it, drawing them into a network of political contacts which ramified from neighborhood to city hall and the Washington bureaucracy. It offered a way into conventional political careers (1982, p. 269).

Moreover, these programs created a new expectation in the area of citizen participation. As a result of these programs, citizen participation in community development programs has become standard procedure. Public officials now feel required to involve citizens in these programs, and neighborhood groups reinforce this by pressing for involvement. The Equal Opportunity Act and the Model Cities legislation also provided a basis for taking legal action against cities. Any group that felt excluded from participation had legal recourse. This often resulted in injunctions to delay political decisions until the outcome of the deliberations. This practice has been credited with starting the movement to protect the rights of the poor and to assure that all politically disadvantaged minorities are heard (Marris and Rein, 1982).

Both programs also initiated some degree of innovation and institutional change. The Community Action Program focused welfare agencies on job training and job opportunities, early education programs such as Head Start and Upward Bound, and the provision of legal services to the poor. Model Cities instituted model schools, created nonprofit neighborhood organizations and neighborhood multiservice centers, encouraged decision making by the poor, increased employment of minorities in local government, improved city management techniques, initiated improvements in intergovernmental cooperation, and increased involvement of elected officials in the problems of the poor (U.S. Congress, House, Committee on Banking and Currency, 1973). Not all of these innovations were successful, but they did represent new approaches to the problem of poverty.

Finally, both programs demonstrated the utility of social planning and systematic evaluation, required local agencies to develop coordinated plans for addressing poverty, and practiced systematic evaluation, which led to changes in program operation.

The accomplishments of both the Community Action and Model Cities programs, however, were limited by a number of problems, the most fundamental of which was the disparity between the goals of these programs and the resources committed to their achievement. Both programs established the ambitious aims of eradicating poverty and slum conditions, but the funds allocated were far too small to approach achieving those objectives. Each program provided approximately $500 million, but these monies were distributed among more than one thousand Community Action Agencies and one hundred and fifty Model Cities agencies (Marris and Rein, 1982). Thus, the funds available to local agencies were insufficient to produce the dramatic effects hoped for; often they were used simply to expand traditional services rather than to develop creative initiatives. Model Cities also suffered from an ambiguity in its mission: Was it a demonstration program or simply another program to funnel money to the poorest urban areas? Combined with the lack of funds, this lack of clarity in program goals precluded dramatic improvements and the emergence of a clear model for solving the poverty problem.

Disparity also existed between the program philosophy of local control and the realities of actual administration. Particularly in Model Cities, HUD often rejected initial proposals and plans for model neighborhoods, and as the program evolved, the department increasingly adopted stricter regulations. As noted in the Report of the President's Task Force on Model Cities,

> Instead of letting the cities proceed in their own way, the Model Cities administration persistently has substituted its judgment for theirs, thereby causing delay and uncertainty and eventually waste, confusion and frustration. The cities have been required, for example,

to follow very elaborate and stringent federal regulations in preparing their plans—regulations that took very little account of the realities of local government processes (1970, pp. 7–8).

Similarly, as the Community Action Program evolved, an increasingly greater proportion of funds was designated for specific programs and removed from local discretion. Thus, although greater flexibility was allowed under these programs, they did not fully live up to their promises.

Authority for implementing certain aspects of the program was also vague, particularly within the Model Cities Program. The requirement that other federal agencies contribute discretionary funds to Model Cities agencies, for example, was ill-defined. No amount of funding was specified, and there was no enforcement mechanism to assure compliance. Thus, agencies tended to spend their funds in ways that enhanced their own programs, rather than contribute them to a program for which HUD would get credit. Moreover, most of the agencies did not have large amounts of discretionary funds. Most funds were committed under statutory formulas.

Unclear guidelines concerning the nature of citizen participation also led to conflict between community groups and city hall, which in many instances resulted in the delay of program implementation and inflated project costs. Phrases such as "maximum feasible participation" were interpreted differently from program to program. Only after considerable conflict arose were more specific program guidelines offered, and by that time battle lines had been drawn. Given the desire of program planners to permit as much local discretion as possible, however, these conflicts may have been unavoidable. In fact, it may be argued that the ambiguities associated with the nature of citizen participation in these programs were instrumental in the development of strong neighborhood organizations. It provided an issue around which they could rally supporters and learn how to negotiate with city hall.

The tenuous nature of the political support for these programs represented another problem. The initiatives for both programs came primarily from the White House, which lobbied hard for their passage. They did not emerge out of conventional interest-group politics, and congressional commitment to the programs was tenuous (Frieden and Kaplan, 1975).

Moreover, in the case of Model Cities, agencies that were to contribute to the program were not even represented on the task force that proposed the program. Consequently, commitment to the program was minimal, and when critics attacked the program, few were willing to come to its defense.

Conclusion

A historical review of neighborhood planning illustrates that the neighborhood concept has played a major role in efforts to address urban problems. Successive programs, however, have emphasized different aspects of the neighborhood. The settlement house approach focused on social dimension of the neighborhood, stressing the importance of positive neighborly relations in a solution to problems of poverty. The neighborhood unit approach primarily focused on the physical dimension of the neighborhood, in the hope that changes there would bring about positive social relations. Finally, the community action approach focused on the political dimension of the neighborhood as a means of increasing citizen involvement in efforts to address poverty and related problems.

As this overview shows, the trend has been toward greater public sector involvement in neighborhood improvement programs. Sponsorship has changed from private philanthropic groups to local government to the federal government. These changes have been accompanied by greater citizen participation in program design and operation. Whereas in the earlier programs residents were the object of neighborhood-oriented programs, in the later ones they became more active participants.

Yet, these programs have had only limited success in meeting their goals. There are a number of reasons for this. First, there has been a lack of societal commitment to the goals of these programs. Given the magnitude of the problems addressed, the resources committed have been insufficient. Funding levels typically allowed only limited activities in limited geographic areas. Second, many of the problems that have been addressed by these programs are the result of larger structural problems and are not easily addressed by local action. The unemployment problem, for example, has not proved to be particularly amenable to neighborhood-oriented approaches.

Structural changes in the larger society would seem necessary adequately to address this problem. Finally, the emphasis in each approach on one dimension of the neighborhood rather than on a coordinated approach including social, political, and physical dimensions may have limited program effects. A comprehensive approach to neighborhood development may meet with greater success.

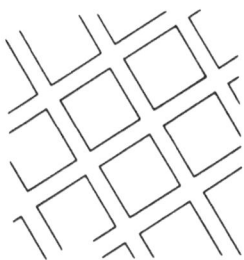

Three fields have contributed to the theory supporting the practice of neighborhood planning. First, the literature on planning is replete with critiques of traditional comprehensive planning and arguments for a more decentralized, participatory planning process. Comprehensive planning, it has been argued, has inherent limitations that restrict its ability to address the full range of urban problems facing American cities and this, in turn, has led to a general attitude among the public that planning is ineffectual. More specifically, these critics fault comprehensive planning for ignoring or misrepresenting the needs of local neighborhoods, excluding citizens from meaningful participation, achieving few tangible results, and overemphasizing physical development at the expense of service delivery and social and political development (Altschuler, 1965; Branch, 1972; Chapin, 1965; Friedmann, 1971). A decentralized, neighborhood-based approach to planning involving neighborhood groups has been put forth as a means of overcoming these limitations.

Second, social theory has emphasized several important social functions served by the local community or neighborhood which should be strengthened by neighborhood planning programs. The social functions of neighborhoods include the development of significant primary social relationships; the socialization of children and the development of informal social control; the provision of personal support networks; and the facilitation of social integration into the larger society (Fischer, 1982; Greer, 1956; Janowitz, 1975; Keller, 1968; Suttles, 1968; Warren, 1963; Warren and Warren, 1977). Neighborhood planning may be one means of supporting and strengthening these important social functions.

Finally, political theory has addressed the advantages of de-

centralized decision-making processes, including neighborhood planning programs. Three major claims made for decentralized government may apply to neighborhood planning
programs. These are increased citizen trust in government,
improved municipal service delivery, and increased social equity (Hallman, 1977; Schmandt, 1973; Yates, 1973; Zimmerman, 1972).

Drawing on these three bodies of theory, this chapter will
present eight propositions on the benefits of neighborhood
planning, which will provide the foundation for the evaluation
of neighborhood planning programs presented in subsequent
chapters. In the conclusion the legitimacy of these propositions will be assessed in light of the data presented.

*Proposition 1: Compared to traditional planning
approaches, neighborhood planning programs are more
responsive to local characteristics, desires, and problems.*

Traditionally, planners have relied on the comprehensive planning model to guide their activities. Among other attributes,
this model emphasizes the development of a general plan cov-
ering the entire municipality. As such, it is necessarily general
in nature and it emphasizes the larger projects of potential
concern to the entire community. These often include major
transportation, public facility, and recreation projects. Under
this model, planners are charged with developing proposals
for guiding physical development that serve the general public
interest. The assumptions are that an overall public interest
can be defined, that planners understand the overall public interest, at least with respect to the subject matter of their plans,
and that they possess the knowledge to gauge the approximate net effect of proposed actions on the public interest (Altschuler, 1965).

Many have argued, however, that there is no one public interest, but rather a number of public interests (Davidoff, 1965;
Meyerson and Banfield, 1955). The diversity of social groups
within urban areas produces a range of distinct interests, which
must be considered separately. Rather than ignore this diversity in favor of a unified view of the public interest, the planning process should recognize it and provide a mechanism for
its expression. Critics have also charged that the unified view
of the public interest is either politically naive or consciously

regressive because it ignores the distributive consequences of
planning decisions; in many instances, it has been used to promote the interests of the economically advantaged over the
disadvantaged (Davidoff, 1965).

The issue of how the public interest is defined is also important here. In the comprehensive planning model the planner is
responsible for defining the public interest through rational
analysis (Klosterman, 1980). Yet many question their ability to
do this given the limited knowledge planners have of the values of the various social groups and their tendency to view the
world from the perspective of their own social class (Gans,
1967). Although traditional citizen participation programs are
designed to provide a clearer sense of public concerns, these
have failed to involve a substantial proportion of the populace.

The work of urban sociologists has documented the existence of urban subgroups and shown that this diversity takes
on a distinctly geographic pattern. In particular, the work of
human ecologists has focused on identifying and describing
various social subareas within larger urban areas. Their work
has documented the existence of urban social subareas that
vary in ethnicity, economic rank, family structure, and occupational status (Duncan and Duncan, 1955; Greer, 1972; Shevsky
and Bell, 1955). More detailed analyses of these geographically
based social groups indicate considerable variation in their
life-styles, needs, and perceived problems (Fried and Gleicher,
1961; Gans, 1962; Michelson, 1976; Suttles, 1968). Rainwater
(1966), for example, reports differences among the poor, working class, and middle class in their concerns about housing.
Moreover, Michelson (1976) has shown that certain physical design elements are more or less conducive to various life-style
groups. Traditional comprehensive planning, which adopts a
city-wide perspective, is not well suited to accommodating
these differences.

Among its advocates, neighborhood planning is seen as a
means of accounting for the diversity in urban populations by
providing a mechanism for local residents to come together
and develop their own conceptions of their interests, rather
than rely on the planner to define those interests. Each local
community has the opportunity to express its unique values
and life-styles in the forming of recommendations for the future development of the area. In the neighborhood planning
model, local communities are also encouraged to develop self-

help projects to augment the services and capital improvements provided by the public sector. Finally, neighborhood planning programs provide a formal mechanism for communicating these unique values and desires to planners and, in many instances, directly to the local governing body.

The argument here is not that neighborhood planning should replace traditional comprehensive planning but that it is a necessary supplement to it. City-wide concerns need to be addressed, but the relative weights assigned to neighborhood and city-wide concerns have been overwhelmingly in favor of the latter. Neighborhood planning programs are an attempt to restore this balance by providing a mechanism for neighborhoods to participate in planning and development decisions.

Proposition 2: Compared to conventional approaches to planning, neighborhood planning programs result in an increase in the number of citizens participating in planning.

Traditional comprehensive planning has been criticized for its failure to involve a substantial proportion of citizens in the process of plan development. Although most comprehensive planning efforts involve some opportunity for citizen input, both planners and citizens are often disappointed by the amount of real input that results. There are several reasons for this.

First, citizen involvement in comprehensive planning typically comes at a very late stage in the planning process. Citizens are often asked to react to a plan in which a considerable investment of staff time and energy has been made. Thus, rather than respond to citizen concerns, planners often end up defending the plan. Moreover, since citizens have not been involved in the development of the plan, they are in a poor position truly to understand the constraints within which the planners worked or the trade-offs and choices they had to make. As a result, citizens often spend most of their time developing an understanding of the logic and intent of the plan and are in a poor position to provide insightful comments. Planners often leave with a feeling that citizens have little to offer, and citizens leave with a feeling that their participation was not genuinely desired.

Second, most citizens do not have a city-wide, long-term perspective. They have little idea of the current or future needs and problems of the city as a whole. Rather, they know and are concerned about the immediate problems in the areas

they experience on a daily basis—primarily their neighbor-
They come to planning meetings hoping to talk about solutions
to specific problems and end up discussing very general goals
and policies. In commenting on planning in St. Paul, for example, Altschuler writes: "St. Paul's planners hoped that vigorous discussion would follow publication of their Land Use
Plan. No one showed any interest in discussing it, however.
The reason seemed to be that the plan's stated goals were too
general. No one knew how the application of these goals would
affect him in practice" (1965, p. 80). Given the general nature
and future orientation of comprehensive planning and the
more specific and present-oriented concerns of citizens, low
rates of participation seem inevitable.

The consequences of public planning without substantial
citizen involvement have been addressed by several theorists
and researchers. Sennett (1970), for one, argues that conflict is
essential to human personality development. Traditional public planning, he suggests, has insulated individuals from the
conflict involved in planning issues and thus acts to inhibit the
full development of the personality in the individuals affected.
Roszak (1973) suggests that a reliance on expert knowledge
leads to the disintegration of the urban community because it
robs citizens of an important reason to come together and
work to solve problems in the cooperative spirit that forms
community solidarity. Moreover, traditional public planning
which relies on experts cannot incorporate the values and spirit
of the community. Comprehensive planning, Roszak believes,
results in manipulation and exploitation of the individual by
forcing reliance on the expert and robbing the individual of the
capacity for moral choice. Gans (1962), Friedmann (1973), and
others suggest that the lack of citizen participation results
in plans that are expressions of middle- or upper-class values
rather than of the full range of social values. Thus, the plans
often do not meet the needs of the working class and the poor.
Finally, because the business community does have city-wide
interests and is usually organized, it often participates to a
much greater extent. According to Altschuler:

> Downtown businesses . . . are accustomed to watch-
> ing the civic scene and searching for issues likely to af-
> fect their interests. They enter the discussion of any

proposal at a very early stage and understand its potential impact on their interests relatively early. Other
members of the public, however, tend to become aware
that something is afoot and then to conceptualize their
interests more slowly. After the perceptions begin to
dawn, most take quite some time to organize. (1965,
p. 82.)

Thus, comprehensive planning has tended to favor commercial
interests over residential interests.

Neighborhood planning programs are expected to be more
conducive to citizen participation for several reasons. First,
they put greater emphasis on local issues and problems more
familiar and personally relevant to local residents. This is not
to say that neighborhood residents or groups cannot address
city-wide issues through these programs; neighborhood planning, though, offers opportunities to address the more local issues often overlooked by comprehensive planning.

Second, neighborhood planning programs are designed to
involve citizens at an earlier stage in the planning process.
Neighborhood planning programs are designed to keep neighborhood groups informed of new initiatives and proposals and
to elicit their comments and suggestions before plans are for-
malized. This should provide greater incentive for involvement and a more satisfying experience for those who become
involved.

Third, neighborhood planning programs encourage continuous rather than sporadic involvement. This means that persons participate on a regular basis, become more knowledgeable about the issues, and learn how to work through the
political process to accomplish their goals. This is approaching
what Friedmann (1973) refers to as "transactional planning,"
defined as "planning in which processes of mutual learning are
closely integrated with an organized capacity and willingness
to act" (p. 247). Thus, continuous involvement should act to reinforce participation.

Fourth, neighborhood planning programs allow citizens to
establish their own agendas, rather than simply react to the
agendas established by professional planners. Thus it involves
community groups in what has been termed "the second face
of power" (Bachrach and Baratz, 1962 and 1970). Controlling
the agenda is an important source of power that has traditionally been denied neighborhood groups in their dealings

with public officials on planning issues. Within the context of neighborhood planning, citizens have opportunities to develop and recommend their own projects and raise their own concerns rather than simply respond to those identified by planners. This control over agenda setting should also reinforce participation.

Finally, participation in neighborhood planning programs takes place within familiar local neighborhoods, close to home and with familiar people. Residents are less likely to be discouraged from participation by unfamiliar and possibly intimidating people and places. Thus, higher rates of participation are expected in neighborhood planning programs.

Proposition 3: Neighborhood planning programs are more project rather than policy oriented and result in more local physical improvements and an increase in the political constituency for planning.

Traditional comprehensive planning has also been criticized for overemphasizing policy development at the expense of project development. Typically, comprehensive planning involves the development of a broad set of goals, objectives, and policies to guide the development and redevelopment of urban areas. The objectives of comprehensive planning stress the development of long-range, general plans. As defined by Black, a comprehensive plan is "an official public document adopted by a local government as a policy guide to decisions about the physical development of the community. It indicates in a general way how the leaders of government want the community to develop in the next 20 to 30 years" (1968, p. 350).

The development of these plans is a time-consuming process, and once developed, they are often updated every five years. The problem is that the comprehensive planning process itself does not result in more specific project plans needed to address the immediate problems facing the community, nor does it result in any immediate observable improvements. Moreover, once developed and adopted, these plans are often ignored by decision makers, bringing into question their overall relevance.

The long-range and general nature of the comprehensive planning process seems at least partially responsible for public apathy toward planning and a lack of a political constituency supporting planning efforts. Citizens often find it difficult to rally around general long-range plans. Developed by professional planners, such plans may not represent the perceived concerns of citizens. Thus, citizens are generally unconcerned with their implementation and politicians are free to ignore them without arousing citizen protest. For planning to be effective it must develop a stronger political constituency among the public.

Neighborhood planning programs have the potential to avoid these problems by focusing on short-term project planning. They provide citizen groups the opportunity to identify needed improvements in their neighborhoods and provide technical and sometimes financial support for those improvements. In this sense, neighborhood planning is more action oriented and should result in more immediate and observable changes in the local communty.

A more project-oriented planning process should also lead to the development of a stronger political constituency for planning. Citizens should have greater incentive for advocating and supporting local planning efforts. This should be particularly true in programs that involve citizen groups in the development of neighborhood plans. Citizens should feel a greater commitment to a plan that they developed and that represents their perceived interests.

Proposition 4: Neighborhood planning will result in a wider range of problems being addressed by the planning process and an improvement in public services.

A final criticism of traditional comprehensive planning is its emphasis on physical development. Rarely are social, political, or economic problems considered. This is particularly troublesome given the interdependence of these problems. High crime, for example, can precipitate the physical decline of an area as people move to safer locations and vandalism and other property crimes lead to physical decay. Similarly, lack of political organization or power in an area can lead to a relative lack of public services and improvements. Rarely are these relationships addressed in the comprehensive planning process.

This narrow focus on physical elements of the community contributes to the frustrations experienced by citizens involved in the comprehensive planning process. Their concerns are often much broader than physical planning, yet they are asked to focus solely on physical problems. For planning to solve urban problems, the relationship between physical, social, political, and economic problems must be addressed in both general plans and more specific action plans.

One area often excluded from consideration, but important to citizens, is public service delivery. Over the last several decades, the provision of these services has typically been consolidated in larger administrative units to achieve economies of scale and to assure greater control over the character of services and the activities of service providers. Advocates of decentralized government structures, however, see this trend as misguided. Based on studies that demonstrate the continuation of pluralism in American society, they argue that centralized service provision cannot hope to account for the variation in needs and desires of the various social subgroups. Centralized services, they argue, are rigid, insensitive, and ultimately dehumanizing (Schmandt, 1973). Public services have also been "professionalized," and citizens have much less opportunity to influence their nature.

Underlying these criticisms is the belief that economic efficiency, narrowly defined, is not a sufficient criterion for evaluating service delivery. As Altschuler points out, "It is possible for a remarkably 'efficient' government to produce disastrous results. Its objectives may be irrelevant, perverse or self defeating. Or it may be so overwhelming in its consequence that it destroys the capacity of its clients to help themselves" (1970, p. 207). Efficiency defined in terms of dollars per citizen or some similar criterion is not as important as assuring that the services provided meet the needs and desires of the populace. Any extra expense incurred in decentralizing services, it is argued, is well worth the improved quality of those services.

Neighborhood planning programs should broaden the purview of city planning and provide a mechanism for citizens to influence the nature of the services provided to their local area. These programs are often designed to encourage the consideration of social and public service delivery problems as well as physical problems. They provide a mechanism by which local communities can evaluate local services and communicate their concerns to city officials. Moreover, neighborhood planning programs can encourage the development of self-help projects designed to supplement the services provided by the city. Neighborhood clean-up, beautification, community crime prevention, and recreation programs are all examples of ways local residents can supplement city services.

Proposition 5: Neighborhood planning programs will result in more social interaction and a stronger sense of community in local areas.

Early sociologists, including Durkheim, Tonnies, and Simmel, bemoaned the loss of community in urban areas. These theorists felt that the persistent, personal, and satisfying relationships found in villages had given way to transient, instrumental, and nonsatisfying relationships in urban areas. Generally, they saw urban dwellers as lacking a sufficient number of primary relationships and as suffering from a sense of isolation and detachment from the society at large. The proponents of this perspective, however, present very little convincing empirical evidence to support their position. Typically, they cited the higher rates of crime and pathology in urban areas as evidence; yet these could have been caused by many factors.

More recent social theorists see the local neighborhood as a facilitator of feelings of community and belonging. Some, in fact, see the urban neighborhood "as the antidote to the alleged impersonality, specialization of interaction, and loss of comprehensible scale of the modern metropolis" (Wellman, 1977, p. 218). This is particularly true of those with limited mobility, including children, housewives, the elderly, and the poor. These groups, which make up a substantial proportion of the total population, are relatively placebound and are likely to develop their primary social relationships locally or not at all.

Janowitz (1952) coined the phrase "community of limited liability" to describe modern involvement with the local community. Individuals, he suggests, vary greatly in their involvement in their local neighborhood. In modern local communities people choose to become involved. Because of increased mobility there is no compelling necessity for their social involvement, as there was in earlier times. Moreover, their involvement is tenuous. If their needs or aspirations are not being met by involvement in the local community, they will withdraw from this involvement. Although this perspective is applicable to a large portion of the society, the substantial number of people who are relatively immobile do not have other choices.

The continued importance of the local neighborhood has been supported by a number of survey studies which show that a significant proportion of friendships occur in the local area and that attachment to the local area is often strong (Athanasiou and Yoshioka, 1973; Caplow and Forman, 1950; Fischer, 1982). One study comparing the number of primary social relationships in urban and rural areas found that they are more extensive in urban areas (Kasarda and Janowitz, 1974). Moreover, based on a large sample survey, Fischer (1982) found that, on the average, respondents named 4.8 local associates when asked about recent social encounters. This represented 41 percent of all associates. Comparing the locus and number of social contacts between urban and nonurban residents, he concludes that urbanism does "not reduce the absolute number of neighbors people deal with, but it does reduce the proportional role of neighbors. Put another way, urbanism adds social ties outside the neighborhood" (p. 101). A number of ethnographic studies have demonstrated that extensive social interaction still occurs in local urban and suburban areas and that this interaction plays a significant role in controlling individual behavior (Gans, 1962; 1967; Kornblum, 1975; Suttles, 1968; Whyte, 1955).

The importance of local social contacts has been underscored by research on the influence of social support systems on mental and physical health. Recent evidence indicates that personal support networks protect individuals from the ill effects of stressful life situations (Hamburg and Killilea, 1979; House, 1980). Fischer (1982) has identified three important types of social support: counseling, which includes discussing personal matters and seeking advice; companionship, which includes spending leisure time together; and practical support, which involves several kinds of material assistance, including assistance in and around the house, looking after the house while away and lending money. Furthermore, based on a large sample survey, Fischer reports that compared to relatives, co-workers, and friends, neighbors were the most often called upon for certain types of material support and were the second most frequently relied upon for spending social holidays and discussing hobbies.

Local interaction and a sense of community are also the

61
Theoretical
Underpinnings

basis for the development of informal social control. Warren and Warren comment, "It is on the local level that individuals encounter the culture and social systems of the larger society and are introduced into these systems and acquire appropriate attitudes and behavior patterns" (1977, p. 174). Beyond the family, the neighborhood is typically the first social system children are exposed to. Their behavior is influenced by their interaction with adult neighbors and other children. Moreover, adult behavior is constrained by the possibility of gossip, ridicule, and threats of social ostracism (Eames and Goode, 1977; Gans, 1962; Warren, 1962). According to Roland Warren: "These informal pressures, along with custom and local norms, operate directly on the decision-making of individuals as family or neighborhood members, along with the more formal controls operating through the law" (1962, p. 218).

Neighborhood planning programs are expected to increase local interaction and sense of community in neighborhoods and thus bolster the social support and social control functions of the urban neighborhood in two ways.

First, the designation of areas as distinct neighborhoods with distinct responsibilities is expected to strengthen the sense of common identity and common plight. As Altschuler comments: "There is a great deal of precedent for believing that a group's sense of unity can be cultivated by treating it as a group—i.e., by assigning it tasks which require collective decision-making and intense interaction among members, by distributing benefits through group channels and in accord with group policies, by refusing to negotiate except with official group spokesmen, and so on" (1962, p. 92).

The collective activities required of neighborhood planning programs provide a reason for people to come together, interact, and identify common perspectives and experiences. Futhermore, they provide a mechanism for the expression of these perspectives and experiences. Hallman, for example, concludes: "Looking at all phases of neighborhood decentralization, I find one of its greatest benefits is enhancing the sense of community. Where people have an organizational vehicle close at hand, they have a better opportunity to work together, and common action is a great booster of community spirit" (1977, p. 125). Treating an area as if it were a group by giving it certain responsibilities can lead to a sense of unity and common purpose. This, in turn, can lead to a cohesive social group.

Theoretical Underpinnings

Second, neighborhood planning programs should strengthen the social functions of the neighborhood by increasing local interaction. These programs provide the opportunity for residents to meet at neighborhood meetings and other social functions sponsored by the neighborhood planning program and develop personal relationships that transcend the performance of duties associated with neighborhood planning. Friendships and acquaintances with local residents are the likely result. The local groups started or supported by neighborhood planning programs can provide the basis for establishing and enforcing local social norms for property upkeep and the like. The sponsorship of community clean-up days, for example, may establish a norm for property maintenance, and those taking part might apply social pressure on others to maintain the cleanliness of the community. There is a considerable body of research indicating that those who participate in local voluntary organizations are more involved in informal social interaction in the local neighborhood. Studies by Ahlbrandt and Cunningham (1979), Bell and Boat (1957), Kasarda and Janowitz (1974), and Hunter (1974) all confirm this association. Although the causal ordering of these variables is uncertain, they are likely to have a mutually reinforcing effect. Those with more local associations are more likely to know of and join local groups. Those who join local groups are likely to develop informal associations with other members and affective attachment to the community as a whole. Neighborhood planning programs that establish local neighborhood groups or councils should lead to an increase in local social interaction and in sense of community.

Proposition 6: Neighborhood planning will result in a greater integration of participants into the larger society and increase the vertical ties between the community and larger social organizations.

Social theorists have emphasized the role of the neighborhood in providing an intermediate structure between the state or larger society and the individual. Durkheim, for example, wrote:

Where the state is the only environment in which we can live communal lives, they inevitably lose contact, become detached, and thus society disintegrates. A nation can be maintained only if, between the state and the individual, there is intercalated a whole series of secondary groups near enough to the individuals to attract them strongly in their spheres of action and drag them in this way into the general torrent of social life. (1964, p. 28)

Many contemporary social theorists feel that neighborhood organizations provide this necessary link between the individual and the state (Nesbit, 1966; Rubin, 1969; Warren, 1963). These organizations draw individuals into local public involvement and lead to more extensive participation in state and national affairs. They provide a local frame of reference and a base from which to relate to the larger society. This is particularly true of newcomers to urban life. Neighborhood networks and more formal neighborhood organizations are important instruments in the assimilation of migrants into a new way of life (Warren and Warren, 1977).

The vertical linkages between individuals and organizations in the local community and extra-community systems are also essential for maximizing the resources and power acquired by a community. Warren (1963) suggests that the strength of these linkages has an important influence on local conditions. Warren and Warren (1977) and Schoenberg and Rosenbaum (1980) go on to suggest that strong vertical linkages are essential for a healthy, viable community. Based on an analysis of five neighborhoods in St. Louis, Schoenberg and Rosenbaum conclude, "The viable neighborhood has linkages to public and private resource-givers through branch institutions in the neighborhood or through leaders who make linkages to outside institutions" (1980, p. 34). They see these linkages as essential for acquiring both the funding and political influence necessary to maintain or improve local conditions.

Neighborhood planning programs should provide a mechanism for integrating participants into the larger society by involving them in activities that require interaction with representatives of municipal government and other organizations outside the neighborhood. This patterned interaction should lead to the development of new vertical linkages, both increasing the integration of individuals into the larger society and improving the ability of the community to acquire resources from outside the community. Neighborhood planning programs that are responsible for creating new neighborhood groups should provide a new intermediate structure between the individual and the larger society and a mechanism through which local citizens can better understand and influence larger social institutions. Neighborhood planning programs should also provide new communication channels between citizens and municipal government. These should act to give citizens a better understanding of the activities of public officials and give public officials a better understanding of the concerns of citizens.

Proposition 7: Neighborhood planning programs will result in an increase in citizen access to and trust in local government.

During the last century, many writers argue, it has become increasingly difficult for citizens and neighborhood groups to influence the policies and programs of local government. Two actions are responsible for this trend: the consolidation of smaller jurisdictions into larger ones and the demise of the ward system of government.

Annexation of smaller jurisdictions by larger ones has severely weakened the influence that individuals and local groups have on government and strengthened the influence of business and financial interests. Kotler, for example, writes: "Through annexation, the strongest political unit in the region deprived other villages, towns and cities of their autonomous government and controlled their territory through political party organization, which was the instrument for domination for 'free' downtown. The strength of the party emanated from the power of that original city, which never lost its liberty" (1969, p. 6). Kotler views these annexations as imperial domination. Once autonomous neighborhoods are controlled for the sake of the economic and political interests of the central business district, tax expenditure and other important municipal decisions disproportionately favor the central business district. Regardless of whether one subscribes to Kotler's perspective, it is clear that during the last century annexations have increased the size and population of municipal jurisdictions and decreased the influence that any individual or local group can have.

The demise of the ward system, the second action that contributed to the decline of responsive municipal government, was a by-product of the municipal reform movement. In discussing this movement, the National Commission on Neighborhoods wrote, "While these reformers reduced parochialism, patronage and corruption, they also created structures that often made government more remote and less accountable" (1979, p. 277). In particular, at-large elections and professional nonpartisan management have been blamed for this lack of responsiveness and accountability. At-large elections decrease the influence of minority groups, while professional management tends to be rigid and ignore the needs and desires of citizens in favor of professional standards and operating procedures. Zimmerman comments: "The growth of a ponderous bureaucracy has slowed down the administrative decision making process and traditional municipal institutions have been unable to cope with the varying problems found in different neighborhoods. As a result, many citizens have become alienated from their local government" (1972, p. 11).

Some think that the reformers were simply unaware of these negative consequences, while others believe that at least some in the movement were trying to keep minorities out of government. Whatever the motivations, however, the result was to deprive local residential interests of a mechanism to define and redress local issues and problems. The demise of the ward system favored business and majority-group interests. Furthermore, it removed the mechanism for local participation and, according to some, led to a sense of political helplessness and apathy among residents (Hallman, 1977; Zimmerman, 1972). The average person was left powerless to influence the policy-making process in any significant way.

Neighborhood planning programs should increase access and trust in local government by allowing more citizen participation in municipal decisions affecting local neighborhoods. Providing greater opportunities for involvement should strengthen the representative structure and trust in municipal government. The communication channels established by many neighborhood planning programs should also help to inform citizens at an early date of projects affecting their neighborhoods. Thus citizens should be less likely to find out about a decision after it was too late to become involved in the political

process. Improved communication should also help citizens understand the necessity and logic behind municipal decisions,
thus increasing trust in municipal governance.

*Proposition 8: Neighborhood planning programs should
result in a more equitable distribution of public goods.*

Many have criticized municipal governments for failing to dis-
tribute public resources equally among all areas of the city.
The more well-to-do areas have traditionally had greater political power than poorer areas, and this power differential has
resulted in an imbalance in the expenditure of public funds
that favors the more well-to-do areas. As Hallman states,
"Municipal housekeeping departments have a double standard
of service, with quality correlated to neighborhood income" (as
quoted in Lineberry, 1977, p. 16). Harvey (1973) presents a
convincing argument that the mechanisms of income redistri-
bution in a complex city system typically increase inequalities.
   As Lineberry (1977) points out, however, there are many
definitional and operational problems with the concept of equity. Do equal inputs as measured by dollar expenditure, for
example, constitute an equitable distribution? Or are equal
outputs as measured by a standard level of service for all residents, for example, necessary? Equal outputs usually necessitate unequal inputs. In crime prevention, for example, equal
inputs would mean the same level of patrols regardless of the
crime rates, and equal outputs would mean deploying patrols
in a manner that would equalize crime rates across the city.
The use of subjective and objective measures of equity is also
at issue. Should we be more concerned with objective measures based on dollars spent or distance to facilities or with the
perceptions of individuals? Both measures would seem to provide useful information.
   Lineberry's analysis of public service equity in San Antonio
indicates inequities in the distribution of parks and libraries,
but finds that they were not related to socioeconomic status,
race, or political power. Instead, ecological variables such as
the age and density of the neighborhood were the most highly
associated with service levels. He concludes that in larger cities "pockets of discrimination can be found but probably not
patterns of discrimination" (p. 196).

Yet a number of documented instances of inequity related to race are to be found in court cases and other independent evaluations. In *Hadnott* v. *City of Prattville*, it was shown that while the white-to-black population distribution was one to five, the ratio of white-to-black park acreage was fifteen to one. Similarly, in *Hawkins* v. *Shaw* testimony showed that 97 percent of the housing units without sanitary sewers were occupied by blacks and 98 percent of the housing units not fronting on paved streets were black occupied. Finally, a study of library services in Chicago concluded that "over the years the Chicago public library has been putting an undue share of its resources into outlying sections of the city and not enough in disadvantaged areas" (as quoted in Lineberry, 1977). Thus it is clear that inequities exist in the provision of public services and that in some instances they are related to race and income.

Neighborhood planning programs should help diminish these inequities, whether they be related to race, income, or ecological characteristics, by providing opportunities for those who have traditionally been underrepresented to analyze the level of services provided and engage in the necessary political action to rectify the situation. These programs aid in the establishment or maintenance of neighborhood organizations, assist those organizations in assessing local problems, and provide opportunities for those organizations to become involved in local political activity designed to remedy their problems. This should lead to a more equal distribution of public goods.

Conclusion

Drawing on social, political, and planning theory, this chapter has presented eight propositions on the benefits of neighborhood planning programs. These programs are expected to be more responsive to local problems, increase citizen participation, improve local physical conditions and public services, increase local interaction and sense of community, foster social integration, increase trust in local government, and bring about a more equitable distribution of public goods.

It is interesting to note that many of these propositions are similar to the stated goals of neighborhood planning programs. A content analysis of the official descriptions of the fifty-one programs we surveyed indicates that almost half of the programs have increased citizen participation as an explicit goal.

Similarly, improving local physical conditions, solving local
problems, and improving communication were also frequently
mentioned goals. In evaluating the propositions developed in
this chapter, then, we are also evaluating these programs in
terms of many of their own goals.

The question we must now ask is, To what extent can these
propositions be supported based on the actual experience with
neighborhood planning programs? The data presented in the
next four chapters will provide a basis upon which to answer
this question. After presenting a description of the programs
and of their major accomplishments and problems, we will re-
assess the validity of these propositions.

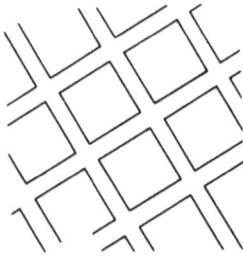

4 A Description of Contemporary Neighborhood Planning Programs

Although the goals of contemporary neighborhood planning programs are similar, the means of achieving them differ widely. Each program is the result of a local political process involving politicians, administrative personnel, and citizens. Variations in the balance of power between these elements and in local conditions result in programs that differ both in structure and operation. Each program is to some extent unique.

This chapter explores the diversity of neighborhood planning programs by presenting a description of the universe of programs operating in the United States. The description will focus on the organization of local neighborhood groups, overall program structure, program operation, interorganizational relationships, and community context.

Figure 4.1 illustrates the relationship between these five elements (after Gilbert and Specht, 1977). Local neighborhood groups are at the core of neighborhood planning programs. They provide the vehicle through which citizen concerns are defined and communicated to city officials. The questions of how these groups were organized, how they operate, and what role they play in the program will be of particular concern.

Elements of overall program structure are also important, as they provide the framework for interaction between citizens, planners, and decision makers. Variations in structural characteristics, such as the type of support offered to neighborhood groups and the official status of neighborhood organizations, should have a major impact on the focus of the program and on its effectiveness. How the programs are sanctioned, whether neighborhood groups have to go through a formal recognition process, the number of program tiers, and other important structural elements will be described.

Operational elements refer to important nonstructural aspects of the program, including indicators of the level of effort and the roles adopted by the various groups involved. More specifically, we will be concerned with the roles of the neighborhood planners and of the citizen groups, the training provided to planners, the number of staff positions, and funding levels. Interorganizational relations, or the larger political context in which the programs must function, will also be considered. Neighborhood planning programs are part of a larger political environment and must maintain political support to be effective. The support provided the program by the mayor, council, city manager, and other individuals and agencies will be discussed here.

Finally, the community context refers to the characteristics of the cities that have adopted neighborhood planning programs. The physical, social, and political characteristics of cities may have an important impact on the nature and effectiveness of programs. Here we will consider population, form of government, percentage of owner-occupied dwelling units, and percentage of residents below the poverty line.

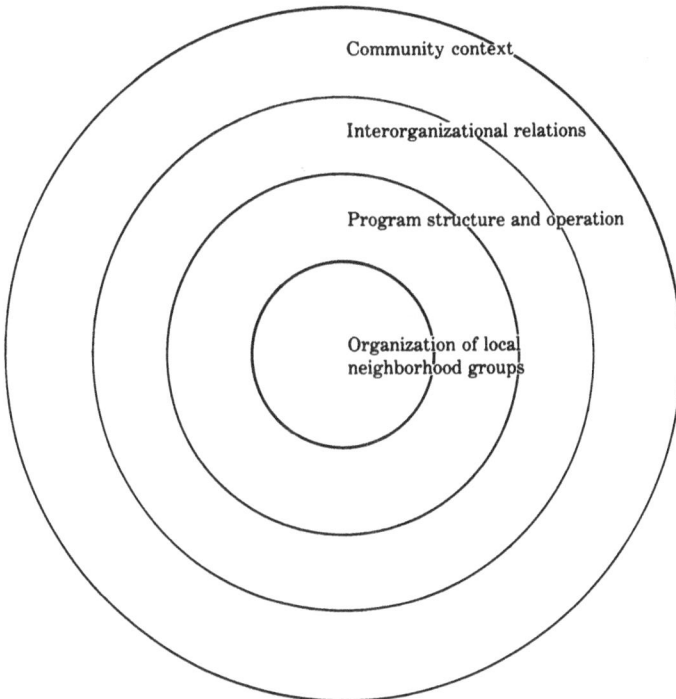

Figure 4.1. Elements of Neighborhood Planning Programs and Their Contexts.

The Organization of Local Neighborhood Groups

The organization or involvement of neighborhood groups is central to neighborhood planning. The manner in which neighborhoods are defined, local groups are organized or involved, and neighborhood representatives are selected varies among, and sometimes within, cities and may influence both program accomplishments and problems.

One of the initial steps in creating a neighborhood planning program is defining neighborhood areas. In the programs surveyed, the methods of accomplishing this varied considerably. Some programs focus on the physical dimensions of neighborhoods, while others emphasize the social or political dimensions of neighborhoods. A basic distinction also exists between methods that directly involve the community and those which do not. In most instances, however, a combination of techniques is utilized. The methods employed and their frequency are presented in Table 4.1.

The most frequent method of defining neighborhoods is through an analysis of physical boundaries. Seventy-five percent of the programs rely on physical boundaries to define neighborhood areas. Typically, maps and windshield surveys are used to identify railroad tracks, major arterial streets, and large institutional sites which create physically bounded residential areas. The second most frequently employed technique is analysis of socioeconomic data. Data on race, housing value, housing type, income, and other measures of economic status are used to identify relatively homogeneous areas. In some instances, statistical procedures, such as cluster analysis, are used to identify socially homogeneous areas. In others, a visual inspection of mapped data is employed. The third and fourth most frequently employed methods are surveys of citizens and community leaders. These surveys assess individual conceptions of neighborhoods, and the data are aggregated to reveal commonly held conceptions of local neighborhoods. In light of the emphasis on citizen participation in most programs, it is interesting to note that these two participatory techniques are employed less frequently than the nonparticipatory techniques. Finally, the least frequently used method of defining neighborhoods is to rely on preexisting political

Method	Frequency	Percent[1]
Physical boundaries	37	75.5
Analysis of socioeconomic data	28	54.9
Survey of citizens	16	31.4
Survey of neighborhood leaders	15	29.4
Preexisting political boundaries	13	25.5

1. Percent does not add up to 100 since respondents were able to choose more than one method.

boundaries. Twenty-six percent of the programs used council districts or wards to define neighborhood districts. These neighborhood boundaries were intentionally drawn to coincide with council districts so that the neighborhood organizations would have a councilman to advocate their positions.

Most programs, however, rely on a combination of techniques. Often the planning staff develops an initial proposal for neighborhood boundaries based on physical or socioeconomic conditions. This is then reviewed by community groups or community leaders and adjustments are made to reflect citizen perceptions. The revised boundaries are then adopted. In most instances neighborhoods are discrete geographic areas and cover the entire city. A few programs, however—including Portland and Cincinnati—allow overlapping boundaries and do not assure that all areas of the city are included in an officially recognized neighborhood. As we shall see in chapter 7, this can lead to problems.

Once neighborhood areas are defined, the next step is to organize neighborhood groups. Typically, the amendment, ordinance, or agreement establishing the program contains general guidelines for establishing local groups. The actual process of starting a local group, however, varies. Table 4.2 indicates that the most frequent method is to allow indigenous community leaders to organize groups in each neighborhood. In some instances, leaders are specifically identified and asked to initiate the organizing effort. In others, indigenous leaders emerge once the program is announced.

The second most frequent technique is to incorporate existing community organizations into the program. This may

Table 4.2. Organizers of Neighborhood Groups

Organizer	Frequency	Percent[1]
Community leaders	36	70.6
Existing community organizations	35	68.6
Planning Staff	23	45.1
Other	8	15.7

1. Percent does not add up to 100 because respondents were able to choose more than one method.

involve designating a particular neighborhood group to represent an area or establishing a new group composed of representatives from the existing service clubs, civic associations,
churches, and business organizations in the area. Although
this method has the advantage of relying on existing organizations, which are likely to have credibility in the community, it
may also lead to problems. In particular, many existing organizations may not represent the entire neighborhood and their
leaders may resent any limitations placed on their operations
and activities, such as a prohibition on the endorsement of political candidates.

The third most common method of organizing groups is to
have staff act as organizers. In less than 50 percent of the programs, however, was the planning staff directly involved in
organizing neighborhood groups. This may reflect the desire of
many program directors to avoid direct involvement in an area
as politically sensitive as community organizing.

Again, these techniques are often used in combination. Initial responsibility for organizing groups is often left to community leaders, although the planning staff may become involved
in organizing areas where groups are not organized. When
planners are involved in organizing, they typically employ non-
confrontational tactics, stressing the opportunities offered by
the program, rather than use strategies that might bring them
into conflict with city officials. Staff involvement, however,
seems to be the method of last resort.

Once groups are formed, representatives must be chosen.
The method of selecting representatives varies not only across
cities but, in many instances, within cities. Many programs
leave the method of selecting representatives, as well as other

Table 4.3. Methods of Selecting
Neighborhood Representatives

Method	Frequency	Percent[1]
Election by a committee	18	35.3
Election by neighborhood residents	16	31.4
Volunteers are solicited	13	25.5
No set method	11	21.6
No official representatives	5	9.8
Appointment by mayor or council	3	5.9
Other	3	5.9

1. Percent does not add up to 100 since respondents were able to select more than one method.

aspects of the operation, up to the discretion of local groups. Table 4.3 presents the methods used to select local representatives and their frequencies.

The most commonly employed method of selecting representatives is by a vote of members of the neighborhood group. This election typically takes place at an annual meeting. In some instances, St. Paul for example, neighborhood group members elect a local council which, in turn, elects a chairperson, vice chairperson, and other officers. In other cities the chairperson and other officers are elected directly by members of the organization. The second most common method of selecting representatives is by a vote of the entire neighborhood. In these cases it is not necessary to be a member of the organization in order to vote. In most instances, the voting takes place at a neighborhood meeting, but, in a few cities, neighborhood residents vote for a representative at polling places during general elections. A less frequent method of selecting representatives is simply to ask for volunteers. In many instances elections are unnecessary, since there is no competition for these positions. Twenty-two percent of the cities have no set method of selecting representatives. There the selection method is left to the discretion of local neighborhood groups, and often, as in Atlanta, a wide variety of selection processes is employed in one city. As we shall see later, however, this can lead to problems in assuring the representativeness of these groups. Finally, 10 percent of the programs do not designate official representatives, 6 percent of the programs have representatives appointed by the mayor or council, and 6 percent rely on other methods.

Program Structure

The overall structure of programs is also of concern. Structure refers to specific program elements. The method of program sanction, the administering agency, the number of program tiers, the practice of recognizing neighborhood groups, and the type of support offered to neighborhood groups will be discussed here.

One of the most important structural elements of a neighborhood planning program is its sanction or legal basis. The method of sanction, to a large extent, determines the authority and the responsibilities of the neighborhood groups, as well as the responsibilities of other parties involved in the program. It also determines how readily the program can be abolished. A council resolution, for example, is much easier to revoke than a city charter amendment.

Table 4.4 lists the most common means of program sanction. The most frequent by far is a council resolution. Almost half of the programs used this approach. The advantages of a council resolution as a method of sanction are that it is expeditious and assures maximum council involvement in the program. This involvement helps secure support for the program once initiated. Council resolutions typically recognize neighborhood organizations as official advisory bodies for their areas and establish general operating procedures for the program. (See appendix C for examples of council resolutions establishing neighborhood planning programs.) The next highest percentage of programs has no official sanction. A full 20 percent have no formal basis of authority. These programs appear to be in a tenuous position. The lack of sanction may limit the program's influence and reduce the credibility of the program in the eyes of neighborhood residents. Approximately 18 percent of the programs are sanctioned by an informal agreement between the council or mayor and the planning department. This method grants no formal authority to the program or the neighborhood groups. An even less frequently employed method of sanction is through an executive order. Executive orders instruct line agencies to initiate a neighborhood planning pro-

Table 4.4. Means of Program Sanction

Means	Frequency	Percent
Council resolution	24	47.1
None	10	19.6
Agreement	9	17.6
Executive order	4	7.8
City charter	3·	5.9
Other	1	2.0

gram. This method of sanction is typically reserved for strong-mayor forms of government and has the advantage of assuring support for the program by the chief executive of the city. The least frequent, yet most permanent, method of sanction is by a city charter amendment. Approximately 6 percent, or three programs, were sanctioned by city charter amendments. The process of charter amendment varies among states, but usually involves the formation of a charter commission to develop a proposal for a revised charter which is ultimately voted on by the public. Although it is often a long process, it provides the most firm legal basis for neighborhood planning programs. Furthermore, because it does not rely on the approval of the city council, the powers granted to neighborhood groups may be more extensive.

A second aspect of program structure is the administering agency. Programs are likely to have different orientations depending on what type of agency—for example, planning, housing, community development—is responsible for their administration. The scope and type of issues addressed and the type of assistance provided are likely to be influenced by the nature of the administering agency. A program is typically placed in a particular agency based on the initial rationale for creating the program and the initial source of impetus. Table 4.5 presents the agencies that administer programs and the relative frequency of occurrence.

Slightly more than 50 percent of the programs are administered by planning agencies, and another quarter are administered by community development agencies. A review of program documentation shows that programs administered by these agencies tend to emphasize the development of neigh-

Table 4.5. Administering Agencies

Agency	Frequency	Percent
Planning	26	51.0
Community development	13	25.5
City manager	5	9.8
Mayor/council/borough president	3	5.9
Housing	2	3.9
Independent	2	3.9

borhood plans and improvement of physical neighborhood conditions rather than the evaluation of city services, solving social problems, or other concerns. The programs administered
by the community development departments tend to have a
stronger emphasis on project development and implementation, owing to their direct access to federal funding for neighborhood improvement. Programs administered by the city
manager's office or by an independent department are more
likely to emphasize the evaluation of city services and general
neighborhood problem solving. Dayton's independent Department of Neighborhood Affairs, for example, administers a program in which mid-level managers from each of the city agencies meet with each district council on a regular basis to discuss
service delivery problems. Programs administered by the city
manager's office have the advantage of being better able to
achieve the cooperation of other city agencies. Finally, approximately 6 percent of the programs are administered by mayors, councils, or borough presidents and 4 percent by housing
agencies. As will be illustrated in the description of the case
study programs, some programs have been shifted from one
administrative unit to another. The program in Cincinnati, for
example, began in the planning department and was later
shifted to the city manager's office.

The number of program tiers is a third important aspect of
program structure. Programs are either one, two, or three
tiered. One-tiered programs simply involve local neighborhood groups. Two-tiered programs have local groups and city-
wide boards composed of representatives from each of the
local groups. In three-tiered programs local neighborhood
groups send representatives to a district group which, in turn,

sends representatives to a city-wide group. Sixty-nine percent of the programs surveyed are one tiered, 25 percent are two tiered, and 6 percent are three tiered.

City-wide groups are intended to serve several purposes. First, they provide neighborhood representatives with an opportunity to discuss common problems and share experiences. Second, they give representatives a chance to comment on the proposals and activities of other neighborhood groups. City-wide groups can act as forums for resolving conflicts that may arise between neighborhood groups. Finally, city-wide boards are a convenient means of disseminating information. One presentation to the city-wide group can inform representatives from all neighborhood groups, and public officials can be informed of neighborhood problems throughout the city.

The official recognition process of neighborhood groups within the program is also an important structural characteristic. Thirty-seven percent of the programs work only with groups that have been officially recognized, 45 percent work with groups that have received no formal recognition, and 18 percent work with both officially recognized and unrecognized groups.

Programs that formally recognize groups tend to have a greater concern for including neighborhood organizations in local decision making. Official recognition of neighborhood groups helps to assure that they are representative of the entire area and that their operating procedures are not discriminatory. It also assures that only one group represents a particular area. Furthermore, mayors and councils in these cities rely on these groups to represent the needs and concerns of the area. Neighborhood groups often review and comment on city-initiated proposals, prepare plans for neighborhood development, and hold informal hearings on requests for zoning changes. Given this formal advisory role, it becomes necessary to limit the number and type of organizations involved. The number of groups must be kept to a manageable number, and their operating procedures must assure at least a minimum level of representation. The formal recognition process is a way of meeting these requirements.

Programs that involve unrecognized groups, on the other hand, place greater emphasis on encouraging self-help activities. Their major objective is to provide technical assistance to groups involved in neighborhood improvement projects. Technical assistance may include workshops on specific topics, assistance in writing proposals, provision of planning data, or other assistance. Furthermore, these programs are typically less concerned with the representativeness of neighborhood groups, since they are not "speaking for the area."

Finally, some programs involve both officially recognized and unrecognized groups. Cincinnati, for example, officially recognizes a limited number of neighborhood groups for advisory purposes and for the receipt of program funds, but also provides technical assistance to some nonrecognized neighborhood organizations.

Another important structural element is the support provided to participating neighborhood groups. Some of the main activities of neighborhood planning program staff are aiding neighborhood organizations in developing plans, commenting on city-initiated plans and public services, and developing self-help projects. Most programs at least provide access to public information, and some provide a range of support including staff and financial assistance. Table 4.6 presents the types of support offered and their relative frequencies.

The most frequent form of support is the provision of information or data. The type of information often requested by neighborhood groups includes zoning maps, traffic counts, copies of housing codes and other city ordinances, and information on specific development projects with potential impact on their areas. Seventy-eight percent of the programs also assign city staff to provide technical assistance in plan and project development and act as liaisons between city politicians, staff, and neighborhood organizations. In some cities, staff are also responsible for administrative activities, such as recording and distributing minutes and revising mailing lists. Sixty percent of the programs provide neighborhood groups with materials including maps, informational booklets, and paper. Financial assistance is provided by 55 percent of the programs. In most instances, however, the financial assistance is for implementing projects initiated by neighborhood groups, not for operating expenses, and the funds are not actually administered by the neighborhood organizations. Rather, they are administered by a city agency. There are exceptions, however. Cincinnati, for example, has recently begun to allocate money directly to neighborhood organizations for both operating expenses and capital improvements in the neighborhood.

Table 4.6. Support to Participating Neighborhood Groups

Means of Support	Frequency	Percent [1]
Information or data	48	94.1
Staff	40	78.4
Materials	31	60.8
Financial	28	54.9
Other	7	13.7

1. Percent does not add up to 100 since respondents were able to select more than one means.

Program Operation

Characteristics of program operation are also important. Variables in this category are funding source, the roles of the planners and citizen groups, and the scope of planning activities.

Funding for neighborhood planning programs, the first important variable of program operation, comes from local, state, and federal government sources, although the most frequent source of funding is the federal government. Eighty-two percent of the programs surveyed rely on federal monies obtained through the Community Development Block Grant (CDBG) program. In many cities the neighborhood planning program fulfills the citizen participation requirements of the CDBG program; thus, a large part, if not all, of the administrative costs are covered by the program. Similarly, many of the projects initiated by the neighborhood organizations are eligible for CDBG funds. Sixty-nine percent of the programs also use local funds to support the program. Again, these funds are used for both operating and capital expenses. Often projects which are not eligible for CDBG funds are supported by local funds. Finally, 26 percent of the programs are partially supported by state funds.

The role of neighborhood planners is a second important operating variable. The major roles are presented in Table 4.7. The most frequent role specified is that of technical assistant. Planners provide technical assistance in all but one of the programs surveyed. The specific form of technical assistance, however, differs among programs. In Raleigh, for example, planners are responsible for updating mailing lists, sending out notices of upcoming meetings, and other administrative tasks. In Cincinnati and Houston planners provide community groups with assistance in developing organizational skills, including record keeping and accounting, membership recruiting, and fundraising. In St. Paul technical assistance primarily involves aiding the development of comprehensive neighborhood plans.

Acting as a liaison is the second most frequent role of neighborhood planners. This role involves informing neighborhood groups of publicly and privately initiated plans that may affect their areas and informing public officials of the concerns and desires of neighborhood groups. Planners also teach members of neighborhood organizations about the operation of city government. They explain city budgeting procedures, local, state, and federal program requirements, and agency operating procedures and constraints. In general, they inform citizens how to be influential in civic affairs.

Community organizing is the next most frequent role of the neighborhood planners. As reported earlier, 46 percent of the directors surveyed reported that the planning staff was involved in the initial organization of the neighborhood groups. The organizer may engage in a wide range of activities, including developing interest in the formation of neighborhood groups, identifying local leaders, and providing assistance to newly forming groups. Neighborhood planners often provide information on bylaws, rules of procedure, membership recruitment, and chairing meetings. Unlike many community organizers who leave after an organization has been established, neighborhood planners often aid ongoing groups in maintaining their organizations.

Acting as an advocate and a mediator are the next most frequent roles assumed by neighborhood planners. Planners are charged with the responsibility of furthering the objectives of their assigned neighborhood groups through persuasion and other traditional political mechanisms. They may also be asked by the mayor or council members to explain the position of a neighborhood. Finally, the role of mediator may involve bringing conflicting parties together to discuss issues and promote compromise and reconciliation.

The roles that the neighborhood groups play in the programs also vary. Table 4.8 presents these roles and their frequency. In all programs, neighborhood groups are involved in

Table 4.7. Roles of Neighborhood Planners

Role	Frequency	Percent[1]
Technical assistant	50	98.0
Liaison	46	90.2
Educator	33	64.7
Organizer	23	45.1
Mediator	21	41.2
Advocate	21	41.2
Other	2	3.9

1. Percent does not add up to 100 since respondents were able to choose more than one role.

problem identification. Local groups are responsible for assessing and communicating the needs and problems of their communities. This can involve a systematic survey of existing conditions or identification of problems through discussions at neighborhood meetings.

A second role frequently assigned to neighborhood groups is plan review. Public plans for future development are reviewed and commented on by groups representing potentially affected areas. In some programs only plans developed by the sponsoring planning or community development agency are reviewed, while in others the plans of all municipal agencies are reviewed. A third role often assumed by neighborhood groups is plan development. Groups may be involved in developing comprehensive neighborhood plans or more specific project plans.

Another common role is self-help. Groups engage in a wide variety of self-help activities ranging from cleanup programs to housing rehabilitation. (Specific examples are described in chapter 5.)

Fewer programs involve neighborhood groups in monitoring program or project implementation, although some neighborhood groups are involved in periodic reviews of improvement projects being implemented in their areas. This list of roles adopted by neighborhood groups illustrates the advisory nature of their involvement. Neighborhood planning groups generally do not become involved in the direct provision of services. Instead they try to improve or expand the services provided by municipal governments.

Table 4.8. Roles of Neighborhood Groups

Role	Frequency	Percent[1]
Identify problems	51	100.0
Review plans	46	90.2
Develop plans	41	80.4
Self-help	39	76.5
Monitor projects	34	66.7
Other	2	3.9

1. Percent does not add up to 100 since respondents were able to choose more than one role.

The final operating variable is program scope. Scope refers to the range of concerns addressed by neighborhood groups in the program. In some programs, groups are primarily involved in land-use issues, while others address issues of service delivery and social planning. Involvement in these three areas was assessed on a five-point scale. A value of one indicated no involvement and a value of five indicated great involvement. The greatest level of involvement was in land-use issues (mean involvement = 3.9), followed by service delivery (mean involvement = 3.4). The least involvement was in social planning issues (mean involvement = 2.8).

Interorganizational Relationships

The next group of variables concerns the relationship between the program and its political environment. Neighborhood planning programs are embedded in a larger political context and, therefore, must maintain political support to be effective. Variables discussed below are the impetus for program initiation, sources of program opposition, the relationship between the comprehensive and neighborhood planning programs, the means that neighborhood groups use to influence political decisions, and the support provided to the program by the mayor, council, city manager, city agencies, and residents.

The first factor to be examined here is the source of initial support for starting the program. Impetus for initiating a program can come from a variety of sources and often involves a collaboration of individuals. Table 4.9 presents the various

sources and their frequency. Planning directors are the most 85
frequent source of impetus for neighborhood planning pro-   Description
grams. Cities in which the planning directors provided the major impetus include Washington, Trenton, St. Louis, Chicago,
Battle Creek, Oakland, and Omaha. Citizen groups are the
second most frequent source of impetus. Cities where citizen
groups are particularly influential include Portland, Pittsburgh, Fond du Lac, and Tacoma. The mayors are the third
most frequently mentioned initial supporters. They were particularly active in Houston, New Orleans, and Atlanta. Many
mayors find the support of these programs to be an attractive
campaign plank. Planning staffs were credited as the fourth
most frequent source of program initiation. They played a particularly significant role in Madison and Toledo. City councilmen were the fifth most frequently mentioned source of impetus, and city managers were the least frequently mentioned
source of impetus. In well over half the cases, however, more
than one source of impetus was mentioned. Although the idea
of starting a program may be introduced by one person it appears that multiple sources of support are important for the
adoption of a program.

Table 4.10 examines sources of opposition to starting programs. Council persons were mentioned most frequently, followed by other city agencies. Yet, the overall percentages are
low. Council persons tend to be protective of their power, and
community councils may be seen as a threat to this power.
There is some reason for them to feel threatened, as the direc-

Table 4.9. Sources of Initial Program Support

Source	Frequency	Percent[1]
Planning director	27	52.9
Citizen groups	17	33.3
Mayor	15	29.4
Planning staff	12	23.5
Councilperson	9	17.6
City manager	5	9.8
Other	7	13.7

1. Percent does not add up to 100 since respondents were able to choose
more than one source.

Table 4.10. Sources of Initial Program Opposition

Source	Frequency	Percent[1]
None	30	58.8
Councilperson	7	13.7
City agencies	3	5.9
Planning director	1	2.0
Citizen group	1	2.0
City manager	1	2.0
Mayor	1	2.0
Other	5	9.8

1. Percent does not add up to 100 since respondents were able to choose more than one source.

tors of community councils often go on to seek political office. City agencies are also interested in protecting their turf and do not always appreciate having their operations scrutinized by citizens' groups. Mayors, city managers, planning directors, and citizens' groups, however, rarely opposed the adoption of these programs. Moreover, in 59 percent of the cases there was no major opposition to the program.

Present levels of support for programs were also assessed. Respondents were asked to rate current levels of support on a five-point scale, where one represents no support and five represents total support. Overall, the support provided by mayors was rated highest (mean = 3.8), followed by the support of councils (mean = 3.6), and citizens (mean = 3.6). City managers and other city departments received the lowest ratings of support (means = 3.4 and 3.2, respectively). It is interesting to note that the ratings of support by city councils are higher than would be expected given that they were one of the main groups that opposed the creation of the programs. This seems to indicate that once programs are established, city councils find them less threatening and more useful than they had expected. City managers, however, are less supportive than would be expected, and city departments continue to be relatively unsupportive of these programs.

The relationship between the comprehensive planning process and neighborhood planning programs was also assessed. Some neighborhood planning programs are linked directly to

the comprehensive planning process, while others are independent. The influence of the comprehensive plan in guiding zoning and other decisions made by the city government
makes such a connection desirable. Seventy-eight percent of
the programs are directly linked to the comprehensive planning process, while 22 percent have no direct connection.

The final interorganizational factor to be discussed is the variety of methods used by neighborhood groups to influence the
decisions of city officials. Table 4.11 presents the range of tactics and their frequency. The most common tactic is to attend
council meetings and voice concerns. As representatives of
neighborhood groups, citizen leaders ostensibly have more influence than private individuals since they are speaking for the
neighborhood, not simply for themselves. In many instances
the views expressed by neighborhood leaders are reinforced
by a showing of support by neighborhood group members who
also attend these meetings. Working through personal contacts with the mayor or members of the council is a second frequently utilized method. These contacts are likely to develop
over time, as neighborhood group leaders seek out politicians
to discuss local issues. Using the media to present their position to the citizenry is the third most frequently employed tactic. Because of their roles as neighborhood leaders they have
the necessary standing to be taken seriously by the press.
Many leaders have also learned how to prepare press releases
and court representatives of the media. Citizen protests follow
as the fourth most commonly used tactic. These protests tend,
however, to be of a relatively subdued nature, including pack-
ing council meetings and forming a delegation to speak with
the mayor. Finally, voting as a block is practiced by groups in a
relatively small number of programs. This would seem to reflect their tendency to avoid endorsing specific candidates or
becoming directly involved in partisan politics.

Community Context

The last group of variables describes the characteristics of cities that have adopted neighborhood planning programs. These
characteristics vary greatly and may have an important influence on program performance. Variables used to describe the
community context include city size, region, form of government, median income, percentage of persons below the pov-

Table 4.11. Methods of Influencing City Officials

Method	Frequency	Percent[1]
Speaking at meetings	45	88.2
Personal contacts	44	86.2
Use of the media	30	58.8
Organized protest	25	49.0
Voting as a bloc	6	11.8
Other	11	21.6

1. Percent does not add up to 100 since respondents were able to choose more than one method.

erty level, percentage of single-family dwelling units, and percentage of owner-occupied units.

Table 4.12 shows that neighborhood planning programs have primarily been adopted in larger cities. Only two percent of the programs in the sample are sponsored by cities with a population of under 50,000, 12 percent are in cities with a population between 50,000 and 100,000, and 25 percent are in cities with a population between 100,000 and 250,000. Finally, 23 percent are in cities between 250,000 and 500,000, and the largest percentage are in cities with populations over 500,000.

Neighborhood planning programs exist in all regions of the United States. Table 4.13 indicates that the Midwest has the largest number of programs, followed by the Southeast, North and Northwest, and Southwest and Northeast. These percentages are influenced by the number of cities in each area and should not be interpreted as indicators of the relative proportion of cities in each area having neighborhood planning programs. They do indicate, however, that these programs are operating throughout the United States.

Programs have been adopted in cities with both mayor-council and council-manager forms of government. Fifty-five percent of the programs in our survey were in cities with a mayor-council form, while 45 percent were in cities with a council-manager form.

Neighborhood planning programs are also found in cities that differ widely in economic and housing conditions. The percentage of persons with incomes below the poverty level in cities with programs ranges from 3.3 percent to 21.6 percent. The percentage of single-family dwelling units varies from 11.9

Table 4.12. Size of Cities with Neighborhood
Planning Programs

City Size	Frequency	Percent
Under 50,000	3	5.9
50,000–100,000	6	11.8
100,001–250,000	13	25.5
250,001–500,000	12	23.5
500,000 +	17	33.3

Table 4.13. Geographic Distribution of Cities
with Neighborhood Planning Programs

U.S. Region	Frequency	Percent
Northeast	6	11.8
Southeast	8	15.7
Midwest	17	33.3
Southwest	6	11.8
Northwest	7	13.7
West	7	13.7

percent to 81.3 percent. Finally, the percentage of owner-occupied units varies between 14.1 percent and 73.1 percent.

Case Study Programs

The following descriptions provide a more in-depth and comprehensive view of the organization and operation of six neighborhood planning programs. Dimensions of these programs, such as the official recognition of neighborhood groups and the number of program tiers, vary, illustrating the diversity of approaches that have been adopted in cities around the country.

Neighborhood Planning in Houston

During the last decade, Houston has been one of the fastest-growing cities in the United States. Its population in 1980 was approximately 1.6 million, which represents a 29 percent increase from 1970. The median family income of the population is $21,881, with 10 percent of families below the poverty level. Fifty-three percent of the housing units in Houston are single family, and 48 percent are owner occupied. The city has adopted a strong mayor form of government and is known for its lack of zoning regulations.

Houston's neighborhood planning program was established in 1979 to aid neighborhood groups in revitalizing and conserving their areas. The major impetus for the program came from the mayor and planning staff, and the program was established within the planning department by an executive order.

The program is designed to provide technical assistance to established neighborhood groups and to organize groups where they do not exist, with particular emphasis on low-income areas. It is staffed by seven professional planners and support personnel. The neighborhood planners provide a wide range of technical assistance to community groups on a first-come, first-served basis. Specifically, they organize workshops on such topics as deed restrictions, attaining nonprofit status, organizational capacity building, and fundraising. They also provide groups with information and data, maintain a resource file of persons, agencies, and programs available to assist groups, and help write proposals and develop neighborhood plans. The staff also organizes citizen groups in previously unorganized areas and publishes a monthly newsletter describing the activities of neighborhood groups within the city. The annual budget in 1979 was approximately $780,000.

The role of community groups in the program is to take advantage of the services offered by the staff to develop self-help projects. The groups also suggest topics for workshops and rely on the staff for consultation. The community groups define their own boundaries and develop their own operating procedures. There are no stipulations on the location or the type of groups that can participate in the program, yet extra effort is focused on low-income areas.

The neighborhood groups are not involved in formal review of city plans and are not given special status in the political process. They interact with the mayor and the council through traditional channels of communication, including speaking at council meetings and writing letters. Although there is a coalition of neighborhood groups in Houston, it has no formal ties to the neighborhood planning program.

Wilmington is North Carolina's major port city. Unlike Houston, it has experienced a slight drop in population during the last decade. The current population is approximately 44,000, which represents a 5 percent decline since 1970. Sixty-seven percent of the dwelling units are single family, and 47 percent are owner occupied. The median family income of the population is $13,517, with 20 percent below the poverty line. Wilmington has a council-manager form of government consisting of seven council members who are elected by district in nonpartisan elections.

The neighborhood planning program in Wilmington was initiated in 1974 to fulfill the citizen participation requirements for the Community Development Block Grant Program and to provide a general, city-wide mechanism for citizen participation. The program involves seventeen formally recognized local assemblies. The specific goals of the program are to provide a mechanism for citizen participation in the Community Development budgeting process, to provide citizens with a mechanism to express their views on city-initiated plans and projects, to educate citizens on the operation of city government, and to encourage self-help projects. The city manager provided the initial impetus for the program, and it was supported by the city council and local neighborhood groups. The program is sanctioned by a council resolution and operated under the direction of the planning department.

Wilmington's program has a two-tiered structure composed of seventeen formally recognized local assemblies and a city-wide Community Development Committee. The local assemblies were defined on the basis of a sample survey eliciting perceived neighborhood boundaries. Citizens within each area were then encouraged, through a media campaign and personal contacts, to organize an "assembly," or neighborhood organization. The planning department drew up bylaws which govern certain aspects of program operation. All groups must have a chairperson and a vice-chairperson, and individuals in these positions can serve only one-year terms. Furthermore, the bylaws specify that all those attending assembly meetings must also be able to vote on resolutions and other items brought to the floor. Most assemblies meet once a month to discuss neighborhood problems and react to city proposals.

Some have developed and implemented their own projects. As formally recognized groups, the assemblies enjoy a special relationship with the council. The minutes of assembly meetings are sent to council members and assembly representatives are consulted on projects affecting their areas. The assemblies have not, however, been involved in developing comprehensive neighborhood plans.

The chairpersons of the local assemblies are also members of the city-wide Community Development Committee. Five representatives from a coalition of civic groups, including the League of Women Voters, the Kiwanis Club, and others, also sit on this committee. Its primary function is to develop the city's CDBG budget and to facilitate communication between neighborhood leaders.

In 1981 the program was staffed by one full-time neighborhood planner and four student interns. The role of the staff is to assist neighborhoods in organizing and maintaining participation, provide groups with information on city actions that affect their areas, provide technical assistance, and facilitate communication between citizen groups, city council, and city departments. The operating budget of the program for 1981 was $34,000.

Neighborhood Planning in Cincinnati

Of all the case study cities, Cincinnati has experienced the largest decrease in population during the last decade. The 1980 population was approximately 385,000, which represents a 15 percent decline from 1970. Thirty-five percent of the housing stock is single family, and 38 percent is owner occupied. Median family income in 1980 was $16,800, and 16 percent of the population was below the poverty line. Cincinnati has a council-manager form of government in which nine council members are elected at-large.

This program has undergone significant change since it was initiated in 1971. The major impetus for the original program came from the city manager, who wanted to address the concerns raised by active community groups. The program, which was sanctioned by a council resolution, was originally administered by the Planning Commission. In 1976, however, it was transferred to the new Division of Community Assistance, directly under the authority of the city manager. This division

has the responsibility of planning social service delivery and
acts as the city government's liaison to neighborhood groups. The major goals of the Community Assistance Program are to assist formally recognized community councils in formulating community plans and community work programs, to provide neighborhood groups—whether formally recognized or not— with information and general technical assistance, and to facilitate community involvement in city decision making, particularly budgeting decisions. The 1981 program budget was approximately $600,000, the majority of which was CDBG money.

Cincinnati's neighborhood planning program works with both formally recognized neighborhood councils and nonrecognized groups. Most of the forty-seven formally recognized councils existed as independent neighborhood groups before the program was initiated; however, some have been organized since its inception. These councils submit yearly work programs to the manager's office for inclusion in the budget, develop self-help projects, prepare comprehensive neighborhood plans, and react to city proposals. Their reactions to proposals, however, are not actively sought by the city, and the legitimacy of their role as spokesgroups for their neighborhoods is not firmly established. The councils draw their own boundaries, which has resulted in some overlap and some exclusion of geographic areas. Although there is no set format for organization, most councils are composed of representatives elected at general meetings of neighborhood residents. Some councils have attained nonprofit status.

The Division of Community Assistance applied for a grant from the Charles Stewart Mott Foundation which initially provided each community council with three thousand dollars for operating and program costs. Matching grants of lesser amounts were given for three successive years. Many councils used this money to hire part-time staff members. The city decided to continue this practice by providing councils up to eight thousand dollars for program and operating expenses.

A number of neighborhood development corporations also exist in Cincinnati. Some receive operating subsidies from the city, while others are self-sufficient. Many of these corporations started as subcommittees of the community councils and then spun off to become independent entities. These too receive technical assistance from the Division of Community Assistance, but are not formally involved in the budgeting process. The Congress of Neighborhood Groups, an umbrella organization, also exists in Cincinnati, but is not formally associated with the neighborhood planning program.

The program is staffed by sixteen professionals organized into four Community Assistance Teams (CAT). Each team includes a team leader, a human services planner, a land-use planner, and a technician. Each team is responsible for working with the community groups in one quadrant of the city. They provide groups with information, advise them of opportunities and city projects that may affect them, and assist in the development of comprehensive and project plans. They also assist each community council with a yearly work plan which, after review and negotiation with appropriate city departments, is included in the budget process.

Neighborhood Planning in St. Paul

St. Paul has experienced a decline in population during the last decade. The 1980 population of approximately 270,000 people represents a 12.8 percent drop from 1970. Fifty-three percent of the units are single family, and 56 percent are owner occupied. The median family income of the population is $20,743, with only 8 percent below the poverty line. At the time the case study was conducted, St. Paul had a mayor-council form of government in which the seven-member council was elected at-large. A new charter has changed this, however, to a five-member council elected by district.

The neighborhood planning program in St. Paul is single tiered with formally recognized district councils. The program was built on the foundation established by the federal community action programs of the sixties, with initial impetus coming from the planning director and a task force convened to develop a citizen participation component for the CDBG program. The resulting program was sanctioned by a city council resolution in 1975. Its operating budget for 1980 was approximately $250,000.

The program has three major goals. The first is to facilitate two-way communication so that districts have input into city-wide plans. The second is to encourage and assist district councils in developing plans that promote the best interests of their neighborhoods. The third is to encourage district councils to develop and implement specific project proposals. These proposals are submitted to the city budgeting process and to other funding sources.

Seventeen districts are involved in St. Paul's district planning process. District boundaries, which were recommended by a task force, include several historic neighborhoods. In some districts strong neighborhood groups existed prior to the program. In others, groups formed to take advantage of program opportunities. A citizen participation coordinator assisted in the organization of unorganized areas. Each group developed its own bylaws, yet most elect council members at yearly meetings open to all neighborhood residents. All groups were required to hold a public hearing in the neighborhood and formally petition the city council for approval and formal recognition. Groups must demonstrate that they are broadly representative. In at least one instance, recognition was revoked because of a lack of representation.

The district councils act as the official representatives of the neighborhoods. They are responsible for developing and implementing neighborhood plans and commenting on city-initiated plans, a responsibility aided by an early notification system requiring all city departments to notify district councils of any proposals that might affect their areas at least thirty days prior to any formal action. Copies of city-initiated plans and proposals, applications for zoning changes, and minutes of city council and board meetings are routinely sent to district councils.

The neighborhood plans developed by the district councils undergo a formal recognition process. Once complete, the plans are reviewed by the Department of Planning and Economic Development and by the Planning Commission. These reviewers note objections to specific recommendations in the plans and send them on to city council for formal approval. The plans are then used as a basis for budget requests that are submitted to a budget committee composed of representatives from each district council. The budget committee, in turn, submits a recommended budget to the mayor's budget committee for final action. This budgeting process involves both the CDBG budget and the general municipal budget.

Each district council receives funds for operating expenses. The amount varies, however, depending on the socioeconomic status of the area represented. Most councils have hired at least a part-time community organizer and many staff an office in their districts. The organizers are primarily responsible for handling the paperwork and the day-to-day affairs of the district council. In 1981 the planning department hired five neighborhood planners to assist in the development of neighborhood plans, provide general technical assistance on planning issues, and inform other agency planners of the positions of the councils on specific issues.

Neighborhood Planning in Raleigh

Raleigh, the capital of North Carolina, is a rapidly-growing Sun Belt city with a 1980 population of approximately 150,000. This population has grown by 22 percent within the last decade. Sixty percent of the population live in single-family dwelling units, and 49 percent are homeowners. The median family income of the population is $21,769, with a high percentage of white-collar employment. Eight percent of the population is below the poverty level. Raleigh has a council-manager form of government in which three councilpersons are elected at-large and five by district.

Raleigh's neighborhood planning program, the Citizens Advisory Council, is a two-tiered program composed of formally recognized neighborhood groups. Established in 1973, to meet CDBG citizen participation requirements, its purpose is to educate residents about government plans, policies, and regulations and to establish a dialogue between neighborhood residents and city government. The program was originally developed by the planning department staff and is sanctioned by a council resolution.

The two tiers include local neighborhood organizations and a city-wide advisory council. Eighteen neighborhood areas were defined on the basis of census tract boundaries, major geographic boundaries, historic communities, and citizen perceptions. New neighborhood organizations were developed in each of these areas by publicizing local meetings and inviting members of existing neighborhood organizations such as church groups, garden clubs, and civic associations. The program requires chairpersons and vice-chairpersons to be elected at meetings on a yearly basis and limits their terms to one year. The local advisory councils are responsible for assessing local needs, developing recommendations for improving local

services, and evaluating proposed development. City plans
and proposals, as well as requests for zoning changes, are reviewed by local councils, and their comments are sent to the
city council. They also undertake self-help projects but receive
no funds directly from the city and have no special link to the
budgeting process. They also have not been involved in developing neighborhood plans.

Chairpersons of the local advisory councils also serve on a
city-wide advisory council. This group is responsible for assessing city-wide needs and evaluating city-wide development
projects. They also comment on proposals made by the local
advisory committees. Both the local groups and the city-wide
group have a committee structure to address specific areas
such as land use, transportation, and crime prevention.

The role of the staff is to facilitate communication by informing groups of impending decisions that may affect their areas.
They also provide technical assistance by interpreting the implications of plans and projects for citizens and assisting in
project development. Furthermore, the planners have administrative responsibilities such as mailings, reproduction of
minutes, and publicity for meetings. In 1981 the staff consisted
of two planners from the planning department and one from
the Department of Human Resources. The Human Resources
staff member was assigned to work with the lower-income
areas while the planning staff was assigned to middle- and
upper-income areas. The total budget for 1981 was approximately $60,000.

Neighborhood Planning in Atlanta

Although the Atlanta Metropolitan Statistical Area has experienced significant growth within the last decade, the city
itself has lost population. The 1980 population was approximately 420,000, which is a 14 percent decrease from the 1970
figure. Forty-five percent of the units are single family and
41 percent are owner occupied. The median family income is
$13,594, and 24 percent of the residents are below the poverty
line. Atlanta has a mayor-council form of government involving both district and at-large members.

Atlanta's program was initiated in 1974 as a result of a city
charter amendment requiring the Department of Budget and
Planning to prepare one-, five-, and fifteen-year comprehen-

sive development plans on a city-wide and geographic subarea basis. The program is three tiered with officially recognized community councils. The operating procedures were further defined in an ordinance approved by the council and the mayor. The program is designed to encourage citizen involvement in planning and budgeting, educate citizens as to the operations and constraints of the city government, and encourage the development of self-help projects. The original impetus for the program came from the mayor and from several councilpersons.

Atlanta's program organizes 186 neighborhood areas into 24 neighborhood planning units. A city-wide group, composed of representatives from the 24 councils, has also been established. The 186 neighborhoods were originally defined by the planning staff based on geographic boundaries and socioeconomic characteristics. Because the large number of neighborhoods would have been unwieldy, they were combined into planning units. These planning units establish their own bylaws. Some are composed of representatives of the local neighborhood groups, while others are run like New England town meetings. Neighborhood planning units are responsible for recommending actions, policies, and specific projects that will improve the viability of their areas and for assisting in the development of neighborhood plans. Once developed, the neighborhood plans are reviewed by the planner to avoid contradictions with city policies. Plans are then officially adopted, printed, and circulated. They are also linked to the city-wide comprehensive development plan, which is the basis for planning decisions and capital budgeting.

Representatives from each of the 24 neighborhood planning units make up the city-wide advisory board. This board allows local representatives to share concerns and information about their activities. They identify city-wide problems and bring information back to the neighborhood groups. All neighborhood planning units meet on a monthly basis and have subcommittees to address specific problems.

The staff's role in the program is to provide technical assistance to neighborhood groups, particularly in developing neighborhood plans and project proposals. They guide the groups in developing the neighborhood plans and are responsible for providing them with timely information on projects or

proposals with potential impacts on their local areas. In 1981   99
there were a total of six full-time neighborhood planners work-   Description
ing with the program.

Conclusion

It is clear from the elements described in this chapter that
there is diversity in all aspects of neighborhood planning programs. Survey and case study results demonstrate that programs use a wide variety of methods to define neighborhoods
and organize neighborhood groups. In defining neighborhoods,
cities such as Wilmington have relied heavily on citizen perceptions, while others have relied exclusively on physical
boundaries. The contrast between Houston and Atlanta illustrates the range of approaches to organizing neighborhood
groups. In Houston, at the onset of the program, no organizing effort took place. Preexisting local groups were simply informed about the available services offered by the program.
At the other extreme, in Atlanta a concerted effort was made
to organize all areas within the city and establish bylaws tai-
lored to the needs of each district.

Overall program structure also varies. Generally, programs
are officially sanctioned by council resolutions; yet a large proportion do not have a legal bases for their authority. Most programs are administered by planning agencies and tend to emphasize improvement of local physical conditions, but others
are administered by community development or other agencies, or by the mayor's office. Two-thirds of the programs are
one tiered; however, one quarter are two tiered and several
are three tiered. Programs also vary with respect to involvement of officially recognized neighborhood groups or unofficial
groups, although nearly a fifth work with both types of groups.
Finally, programs surveyed primarily provide staff support
and information to local groups. Some, however, also provide
material and financial support.

Case study programs provide examples of each type of program structure. The St. Paul, Raleigh, Wilmington, and Cincinnati programs, for example, are all sanctioned by council
resolutions; the Houston program is sanctioned by an executive order, and the Atlanta program is sanctioned by a council

amendment. All of the case study programs are administered by planning departments except for Cincinnati's which is administered by an independent department in the city manager's office. The programs in St. Paul, Houston, and Cincinnati are examples of one-tiered programs, those in Raleigh and Wilmington are examples of two-tiered programs, and Atlanta is an example of a three-tiered program. Case study programs also have varying requirements relating to formal recognition of neighborhood groups. The programs in Atlanta, Raleigh, St. Paul, and Wilmington require formal recognition, while the program in Houston does not. The Cincinnati program works with both formally recognized groups and nonrecognized groups. Finally, the types of assistance offered by programs differ. St. Paul and Cincinnati are examples of cities that provide funds directly to local groups to hire staff and fund projects. Houston emphasizes technical assistance through workshops, a newsletter, and consultation. Atlanta, Raleigh, and Wilmington all provide staff assistance in organizing, developing local plans, and analyzing development proposals.

The roles of the neighborhood planners and the neighborhood groups also differ among programs. Survey results show that planners most frequently act as technical assistants. Planners, however, were also expected to act as liaisons between other city officials and citizens, mediators of conflicts between the city administration and neighborhood groups, educators, and organizers. Neighborhood groups tend to play an advisory role, commenting on and reviewing city plans. Some, however, develop their own plans and engage in self-help activities.

Case study programs reveal the entire range of roles. In Houston planners are predominantly involved in technical assistance and the main activities of neighborhood groups are self-help projects. They are not involved in the review of city-initiated plans or budgets. In Wilmington and Raleigh planners provide organizational assistance and citizens review city plans and participate in some self-help activities. They do not, however, develop their own neighborhood plans or have a formal mechanism for influencing the comprehensive planning process. In Cincinnati planners provide technical assistance in developing plans and projects and local groups develop their neighborhood plans and have input on the budgeting process. In Atlanta and St. Paul a formal process for including local

plans in the comprehensive plan exists. There the neighborhood planners are primarily involved in plan development.

Considerable variation also exists in the level of support
given to the neighborhood planning programs by politicians
and other city administrators. Typically, mayors are most supportive, and city managers and other city departments least
supportive.

Finally, the survey results show that neighborhood planning
programs are found in cities throughout the United States.
Most programs, however, are found in larger cities. They are
also found in both mayor-council and council-manager forms of
governance, although they appear to be slightly more prevalent in cities with mayor-council forms of government, possibly because larger cities are more likely to adopt this form of
government. Cities that have adopted these programs also
vary widely in the percent of the population below the poverty
line, percent of single-family housing, and percent of home-
ownership.

In chapter 6 the relationship between these program elements and program accomplishments will be explored—the
ultimate goal being the identification of programs elements associated with program effectiveness. Before we do this, however, we will assess the accomplishments of neighborhood planning programs.

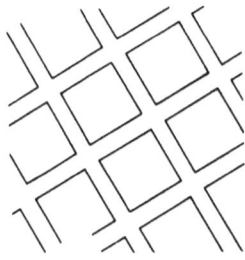

5 Program Accomplishments

This chapter presents evidence on the accomplishments of neighborhood planning programs which, along with findings reported in other chapters, will be used to evaluate the validity of the propositions presented in chapter 3. Information on program accomplishments was obtained from the survey of program directors, case study interviews, and program documentation.

The survey included an open-ended question which asked, "What are the major accomplishments of your program?" and a series of closed-ended questions asking about specific accomplishments, including the program's influence on physical conditions, local services, citizen-government relations, project implementation, and citizen ability to influence city officials. The case study interviews with program directors, neighborhood planners, and citizen representatives included the same open- and closed-ended questions, with the addition of a specific question on the program's influence on the distribution of public resources.

Many accomplishments were mentioned by both survey and case study respondents, and, generally, the most frequently mentioned accomplishments were the same for both groups. The discussion of accomplishments follows the ordering in Table 5.1, which presents the rank order of accomplishments as mentioned by survey respondents in response to the open-ended question. These are followed by a discussion of other accomplishments as identified by closed-ended survey questions and case study interviews.

Table 5.1. Program Accomplishments as Identified by
Survey Respondents

Accomplishment	Frequency	Percent[1]
Project initiation and improved physical conditions	28	54.9
Increased community awareness and competence	20	39.2
Increased citizen influence on city officials	13	25.5
Increased citizen participation in planning	12	23.5
Improved communication between neighborhoods and city officials	12	23.5
Improved local services	4	8.2

1. Percentages add up to greater than 100 since multiple answers were allowed.

Project Initiation and Improved Local Physical Conditions

The most frequent response to the open-ended survey question on program accomplishments was neighborhood improvement projects and improved local physical conditions. Almost 55 percent of the respondents freely offered this as an accomplishment. A more specific question on physical improvements attributable to the program sheds light on the nature of these improvements. Respondents were presented a list of physical elements and asked to identify which have been improved by the neighborhood planning program. The results are presented in Table 5.2.

The most frequently cited physical improvement was in housing conditions, followed by streets, curbs and sidewalks, recreation facilities, neighborhood cleanliness, street lighting, and traffic controls. Over two-thirds of the respondents identified five or more physical elements that had been improved, indicating that neighborhood groups within the program were involved in a wide range of activities.

Table 5.2. Improved Physical Elements Identified by
Survey Respondents

Improved Physical Elements	Frequency	Percent[1]
Housing	46	90.2
Streets, curbs, sidewalks	45	88.2
Recreation facilities	45	88.2
Neighborhood cleanliness	41	80.4
Street lights	31	60.8
Traffic signals	27	52.9
Other	8	15.7
None	1	2.0

1. Percentages add up to greater than 100 since multiple answers were allowed.

Case study respondents and program documentation provide more specific examples of improvements. Housing rehabilitation was a frequently mentioned accomplishment among neighborhood planners and citizen representatives in every case study city except Wilmington. One citizen representative in St. Paul commented: "We have been able to accomplish real improvements in the community. We have turned the community around in terms of deteriorating housing." A more specific example comes from Raleigh. There several inner-city task forces initiated a neighborhood maintenance program in which local youth were hired to paint and do minor repairs on the homes of elderly, handicapped, and poor residents of the area. Donations from local businesses and a stipend from Community Development Block Grant funds were used to support the program. In Cincinnati local development corporations have spun off from district councils and have become directly involved in major housing renovations. Entire blocks of abandoned housing have been refurbished through these efforts. The city has also established a sweat equity housing grant program to encourage groups to become involved in housing rehabilitation. In Atlanta a neighborhood planning unit applied for and received an Urban Development Action Grant to undertake a housing rehabilitation and neighborhood clean-up program. In addition to becoming directly involved in housing rehabilitation programs, two cities—St. Paul and Cincinnati—have involved their community councils in the siting of new subsidized housing developments.

Transportation improvements were also frequently mentioned by those interviewed in the case studies and were cited in program documentation. These typically resulted from groups lobbying the city government to make the necessary repairs, improvements, or changes. In Cincinnati, for example, program staff aided a number of district councils in analyzing their traffic problems and facilitated meetings with the Highway Maintenance Division. According to program documentation most of the street improvements recommended by these councils were implemented. In Wilmington dirt streets in low-income areas were a problem. The district councils in these areas made street paving a priority issue and were able to secure CDBG funds for this purpose. Almost all the streets have now been paved. Public transportation scheduling was an issue in Raleigh, and several community councils successfully lobbied for scheduling changes to better serve non-work-related trips by local residents.

A large number of improvements in recreation facilities were also attributed to the program. Some of these improvements were a result of lobbying efforts and some were self-help projects. In St. Paul a neighborhood council was successful in lobbying the council to build a park on an island that was originally intended for sale to private developers. The neighborhood representative felt that the neighborhood plan, which identified a lack of recreation facilities in the area, was instrumental in this victory. In Cincinnati a number of neighborhood councils have received grants from the city (through the Mott Foundation) to renovate old schools as community recreation centers. Once renovated, the communities will fund and manage their own recreation and social programs in these facilities. The city has not committed itself to operating funds. The Community Chest has, however, offered to provide a proportion of the operating costs for these centers. In Atlanta one neighborhood council fought for the improvement of a neighborhood park. Though a combination of self-help and city-implemented improvements, what was once perceived as a dangerous, underutilized park was transformed into a major neighborhood activity center. Greenways have been the focus of attention in Raleigh, as a number of the councils have been involved in maintaining and improving their condition.

Most of the neighborhood groups involved in these programs also sponsor neighborhood beautification and clean-up programs. In Houston the city has established a "rent-a-truck" program, which enables neighborhood groups to rent, for a small fee, a city-owned dump truck to carry away debris. Many of the neighborhood groups have taken regular advantage of this by scheduling periodic clean-ups of vacant lots and other properties. The neighborhood planning staff assists in organizing these events. In Wilmington the clean-up and restoration of a historic black cemetery was accomplished by a neighborhood council, which used city-owned equipment and volunteer labor. Similar beautification activities were sponsored by neighborhood groups in the other case study cities.

These are but a handful of the physical improvements credited to the neighborhood planning programs in the study. They do, however, exemplify the types of projects taken on by neighborhood groups in these programs.

Increased Community Awareness and Competence

The next most frequently cited accomplishment was increased community awareness and competence. This was mentioned by approximately 40 percent of the respondents, who said that citizens were better informed of both public and private projects affecting their neighborhoods and better able to take constructive action to maintain or improve neighborhood conditions.

The case studies provide a deeper understanding of this accomplishment. Citizens, planners and directors alike, felt that the programs provided citizens with important information on existing and proposed city plans, current physical and social conditions, and city operating procedures. In Raleigh, for example, one annual report stated: "In terms of educating members about the effects of governmental plans, all task forces have been acquainted with the proposed Land Use and Public Services elements of the Comprehensive Plan, the proposed Thoroughfare Plan, zoning amendments and Board of Adjustment requests, procedures for petitioning the City and crime trends and prevention techniques." In Atlanta, Raleigh, and

St. Paul, participating neighborhood groups are notified of all zoning change requests in their areas. These are often discussed at monthly meetings, where positions for or against the requests are adopted and sent on to the city council. Several citizen representatives reported that developers came to these meetings and, in many instances, altered their projects to win the support of the neighborhood group. All three of these cities also routinely notify neighborhood groups of plans and proposals that might affect their areas. In Houston the emphasis is on providing information on such topics as incorporation procedures, restrictive covenants, and grant writing. Citizen representatives found this information to be extremely useful. In Cincinnati and Wilmington information on the municipal or CDBG budgeting process is provided to local groups, and the neighborhood planners routinely inform groups of impending actions with potential effects on their areas. One citizen representative in Wilmington commented: "When people get educated about city government, they learn how to get things done."

Programs were also credited with helping citizens learn how to analyze issues, develop effective strategies for neighborhood improvement, and increase organizational capacity. Citizen representatives in Atlanta, Cincinnati, St. Paul, and Raleigh all felt that the neighborhood planners had been helpful in pointing out the potential costs and benefits of proposed projects and in suggesting ways to address specific concerns. In Raleigh, for example, one community council had intended to support a zoning change request based on the developer's site plans. The neighborhood planner, however, informed the citizens that, once rezoned, the developer could develop the property at maximum density and not be held to the site plans. This changed the citizens' view of the proposal.

In Atlanta, Houston, and Cincinnati neighborhood planners worked with local neighborhood groups in developing action plans and grant proposals for addressing local problems. The citizen representatives felt that this taught them how to develop plans and proposals to "get something done in the neighborhood." A specific example from Cincinnati involved the renovation of a vacant recreation building. The staff stressed the need to develop a balance sheet of expected income and expenses to ensure maintenance of the building, helped structure a work plan detailing the steps necessary for successful completion of the project, and identified who would be responsible for specific aspects of the project. The project was recommended for funding in the 1980 capital improvement budget for seventy thousand dollars.

Programs in Cincinnati have placed great emphasis on organizational capacity building. The Community Assistance Teams have prepared an organizational analysis of each community council and used this to help community groups to function more effectively. In the Pendleton area, for example, the staff helped the existing Thirteenth Street Tenant Organization and a newly formed group unite into one more broadly based council. In the Mohawk area staff met with the area council and disgruntled residents to resolve concerns about the council's representativeness of the total neighborhood. The staff helped develop bylaws and a constitution, monitored the selection of officers, and organized leadership training workshops.

Overall, these programs increase the vertical integration of communities into the larger governing structure. They provide local community groups with the knowledge and contacts to work effectively through the central administration.

Increased Citizen Influence on City Officials

Over 25 percent of the survey respondents mentioned increased citizen influence on city officials as an accomplishment of their neighborhood planning programs. Given that these responses were to an open-ended question and that the respondents were program directors, this percentage seems particularly high. More revealing, perhaps, is the response to a more specific question: "How do you rate the effectiveness of the program in influencing the decisions of city officials?" As shown in Table 5.3, over 60 percent of the respondents felt their neighborhood programs were fairly to very effective in influencing city officials, and only 14 percent rated their programs as either fairly or very ineffective.

Case study data provide further evidence that these programs offer a means for citizen influence and help to clarify the nature of that influence. Increased citizen influence was mentioned as an accomplishment by respondents in all case study cities. The following general comments are typical of the responses:

Rating of Influence	Frequency	Percent
Very effective	10	19.6
Fairly effective	21	41.2
Moderately effective	13	25.5
Fairly ineffective	6	11.8
Very ineffective	1	2.0

I think the program has been very effective. I am not saying that they [the council] have always done what we asked, but there has been a new responsiveness on the part of elected officials. When they have made decisions contrary to our decisions they have tended to be more of a compromise. (Citizen representative, St. Paul.)

[Through the program] the citizens have tremendous influence. The city is built on neighborhoods. The mayor is alert to the power of the citizen. (Neighborhood planner, Atlanta.)

The citizens have a feeling, a sense of influencing the city government. This has led to increased satisfaction and increased self-confidence. (Neighborhood planner, Raleigh.)

Citizens are running the government. I feel that the city council has given us a taste of the candy and you can't take that away. (Citizen representative, St. Paul.)

Budgeting and city expenditures, zoning, and plan preparation were the most frequently mentioned areas in which influence was exerted through the program. Respondents in St. Paul, Cincinnati, and Wilmington emphasized the importance of citizen influence on budgeting and city expenditures. In St. Paul, for example, one citizen commented: "On the east side they [the city] wanted to take an old hospital site and put some townhouses there. The city was really pushing saying, 'Hey, we need the tax base,' but the community said, 'No, we don't want that; we want a park' and they got what they wanted." In this example, the community, through lobbying and presentations at council meetings, was able to convince council members to forgo extra tax revenues from residential development and provide funds to develop a park. Records kept on the number and outcome of budget requests by district councils in St. Paul indicate that over 80 percent of the neighborhood projects were, in fact, funded. Some St. Paul planners were actually expressing concern that too much money was being spent on neighborhood projects and not enough on city-wide projects such as improvements to the sewer system.

In Cincinnati citizen representatives and neighborhood planners alike offered the neighborhood support program as evidence of citizens' ability to influence budgeting. In the words of a neighborhood planner: "They [the neighborhoods] have had influence. For example, they have lobbied for [and received] the neighborhood improvement program and the neighborhood support program. Neighborhood action has also resulted in much money being channeled into housing programs." The neighborhood support program provides neighborhood councils with funds to hire part-time workers or undertake self-help projects. The community work plans developed by neighborhood councils also add neighborhood projects to the city budget. According to one neighborhood planner, between 30 and 60 percent of the projects requested are actually funded. In Wilmington influence on budgeting was also offered as a major program accomplishment. A community representative commented: "I held meetings to get more information when asked to help plan the [community development] budget. Then, some of my ideas were incorporated into the plan and I am just one person." This participation, however, unlike that in St. Paul and Cincinnati, is confined to the CDBG budget. In the remaining three cities—Atlanta, Houston, and Raleigh—there was little mention or evidence that citizens were substantially influencing budgeting or the expenditure of city funds. The programs in these cities also lacked any direct mechanism for neighborhood group involvement in budgeting. The programs in Houston and Raleigh had no link at all. In Atlanta the program had a tenuous link through the neighborhood plans, but there was little opportunity for neighborhood groups to monitor the progress of their proposed projects.

The second area of influence concerns zoning decisions and public facility siting. Examples of citizens influencing the outcomes of zoning decisions were widespread in Raleigh, At-

lanta, and St. Paul. In Raleigh citizen representatives held local hearings on zoning change requests and fought what were
considered to be undesirable proposals. In one program year,
the annual report indicates that local task forces had taken
stands on nine zoning amendment cases before the planning
commission and the city council, and appeared eight times before the board of adjustment to voice their opinions on pending
appeals. According to one citizen representative, developers
have begun to work with the local task forces before submitting proposals to the council.

Similarly, in Atlanta neighborhood groups appear to have
had considerable influence in rezoning decisions. One citizen
representative expresses it this way: "Credibility in the zoning process is our biggest plus. Our credibility came from
responsible recommendations and building a rapport with developers and the council." Other representatives in Atlanta
expressed similar sentiments. In St. Paul one of the routine
tasks of a neighborhood organizer who works for an individual
district council is to screen zoning variance requests and bring
those in the local area to the attention of the district council.
The district council then takes a stand on the proposed variance and sends a representative to the hearings. In Wilmington local assemblies have had a major influence on the place-
ment of public facilities. In one instance the public works
department proposed the expansion of a garage for city vehicles with Economic Development Administration funds. The
local assembly, however, fought the proposal, which they considered disruptive, and was able to stop the project. According to several citizen representatives, this created a new attitude toward the local assemblies. Zoning changes did not
seem to be an area of concern in Cincinnati, and in Houston the
focus was on maintaining deed restrictions, since zoning is not
practiced.

The third area of influence was in affecting city plans. Citizen representatives in Atlanta, Cincinnati, Raleigh, and St.
Paul felt that they had had a substantial influence in altering
the nature of the cities' comprehensive plans, as well as other
expressions of official policy. In St. Paul, for example, neighborhood plans developed by district councils become part of
the official comprehensive plan for the city. Neighborhood
groups have also been involved in the development of a housing development plan for the city which identifies sites for new

subsidized housing developments. In Raleigh local councils have been extensively involved in revising the city's comprehensive plan and both its transportation and human services plans. One neighborhood planner commented that the local councils "have pretty good influence with the council. They have input on the comprehensive plan and have gotten a lot more people involved." In Cincinnati community plans were cited as a particularly powerful tool to influence the council. One citizen representative comments: "Good comprehensive community plans helped the city accept the community groups as partners in the planning process." There was little evidence of an influence on city plans, however, in Wilmington and Houston.

Increased Citizen Participation in Planning

A fourth accomplishment mentioned by 25 percent of the survey respondents was increased citizen participation in planning and governance. These respondents credited the programs with involving more people in planning and governance than other conventional citizen participation programs.

Responses from those interviewed in the case studies support this finding. Increased citizen participation was mentioned by respondents as an accomplishment in all cities except Houston. A citizen representative from St. Paul comments: "More citizens are interested in government than before. It's not a large group, but it's significant. The program draws people into the government process." Similarly, an Atlanta citizen suggests that the program "draws more people into the planning process by getting them interested in pressing local problems."

Unfortunately, figures on attendance are not routinely kept; so the actual numbers of participants in each of the programs are generally not available. In Cincinnati, however, figures were kept for the 1979 program year. They show that the average attendance per meeting was 38 and that a total of 1,607 volunteers actively participated in doing community projects.

The citizen representatives interviewed provide another source of information on this topic. They reported that the average attendance ranged from between 15 and 40 people. Although this number is not large—typically representing far less than 1 percent of the population in the area—when multiplied by 20 to 40 individual neighborhood groups in each city, it represents 300 to 1,600 residents participating on a monthly basis. This number is undoubtedly large compared to other methods of citizen participation.

Furthermore, most citizen representatives reported that when "hot" issues were being discussed, participation increased dramatically. Many residents, it seems, are willing to let the community council representatives handle the more routine issues, but become directly involved in the major issues. The ongoing nature of the participation must also be considered in evaluating the benefits of these programs. Presumably, participation by those who are familiar with the issues and the context is more effective than that by those who participate infrequently.

Improved Communication

A fifth accomplishment mentioned by approximately 25 percent of the survey respondents is improved communication between neighborhood groups and between neighborhood groups and city officials. This differs from increased community awareness in that respondents were referring to the two-way communication of views and the face-to-face meetings between citizens and government officials facilitated by these programs. Citizens highlighted the importance of letting council members and department heads know what they wanted and why, while council members and department heads pointed to the opportunity to educate citizens on the constraints under which the local government operates and on operating procedures. In St. Paul, for example, a citizen representative commented that "[through the program] city officials have become less formidable to the community. Now the community is not afraid to talk with these people. Also, city officials come out to the community to hold hearings." A citizen representative in Cincinnati commented that the program has "carried neighborhood concerns to city departments and have gotten them [department heads] out in the neighborhoods." In Atlanta and Raleigh citizens and planners commented that the city-wide groups composed of neighborhood representatives were responsible for improving communication. These groups provided a convenient mechanism for council members and department heads to discuss issues with neighborhood leaders.

Planners in Raleigh, Atlanta, and St. Paul also credited their programs with increasing their knowledge of community problems and perspectives. This knowledge, they suggested, assisted them in other planning activities in which they were involved, such as developing comprehensive plans and housing plans. They also reported that they shared these citizen concerns with others on the planning staff, thereby increasing the degree to which local plans were responsive to citizen concerns.

Local meetings and newsletters sponsored by participating neighborhood groups were also credited with improving communication within and between neighborhoods. The monthly meetings held by most neighborhood groups were said to provide opportunities for the exchange of information and ideas and generally to facilitate communication between local residents. Citizen representatives in some case study cities also credited their newsletters with improving communication. In St. Paul citizen representatives felt that their newsletter kept local residents informed of local events and concerns. In the words of one representative: "Increased communication is the result of our paper. We are publicizing the things that are happening and providing an information center." Several respondents in Cincinnati also credited their newsletters with improving local communication and with increasing participation in the groups' activities. In Houston communication within the neighborhoods was facilitated by local newsletters, while communication between neighborhoods was facilitated by a newsletter published by the planning department. Citizen leaders stressed the importance of learning what other neighborhood groups in the city were doing and of being exposed to examples of successful programs and approaches to local problems.

Improved Local Services

Only 8 percent of the survey respondents mentioned improved local services in response to the open-ended question on accomplishments. Answers to a direct question asking about specific services affected by the program, however, reveal a much greater impact on public services. As shown in Table 5.4, approximately 52 percent of the respondents indicated

Table 5.4. Improved Local Services Mentioned by Survey
Respondents

Improved Local Services	Frequency	Percent[1]
Human services	25	52.1
Public transportation	18	37.5
Police	15	31.3
Sanitation	14	29.2
Rodent control	11	22.9
Fire	7	14.6
None	13	27.1
Other	14	29.2

1. Percentages add up to greater than 100 since multiple answers were allowed.

that the delivery of human services had been improved, followed by public transportation, police, sanitation, rodent control, and fire protection. However, 27 percent of the respondents reported that none of the local services mentioned had been improved. Apparently, many programs do not involve service delivery evaluation as one of their goals or activities.

The case study data provide specific examples of improvements. When asked if they felt the program had led to the improvement of local services, an overwhelming majority of the case study respondents felt that it had. The Cincinnati program was particularly active in the area of human services. A youth employment program, for example, was developed in the Madisonville area in connection with a large amusement park. A neighborhood planner helped the community council in negotiations, fund-raising, and arranging transportation for this program. A child-care program was established in the Winston Hills area after a needs assessment sponsored by the community council identified this as an unmet need. Program staff assisted the committee in developing the needs assessment, designing the program, and writing the grant application. Programs to provide meals, housing, counseling, and recreational services for over fifteen hundred elderly residents were also established in eight council areas. These projects were funded through a combination of Community Chest, Council on Aging, and CDBG funds.

The program in Raleigh has also had an impact on human service delivery. Each of the local task forces was involved in a needs assessment project, and the results were used to direct the efforts of existing programs and to help develop new ones. In St. Paul one district council started a drug education and counseling program for local youth and their parents, and another established a day-care cooperative to serve the needs of working mothers. In Houston groups started a tutoring program for elementary school children and sponsored a youth recreation program. In St. Paul a neighborhood which lacked nearby emergency medical facilities lobbied for and received a paramedic unit in its district. Another district council identified a multiservice center as its top priority and lobbied for and received funding from the city budget.

Case study respondents also mentioned improvements in police services. In all case study cities, neighborhood groups were involved in crime prevention programs. In most instances this involvement took the form of neighborhood watch programs, but other approaches were also used. In Atlanta, for example, one neighborhood planning unit started a witness assistance program and received a federal grant to continue the program. In the interviews community representatives often made mention of inviting police officials to meetings where residents could express their concerns about local crime and become more familiar with local patrol officers. In Cincinnati a district council initiated a twelve-member neighborhood dispute board to address local conflicts and minor criminal acts, such as vandalism. The board hears disputes and passes judgments. Another council has established a youth federation to provide counseling services and to advocate for youth needs. In St. Paul one district council created a crime task force to address the problem of delinquency by instituting counseling programs and other activities. Overall, community crime prevention programs were a major activity of community groups involved in neighborhood planning programs.

Improvements in recreation services were also mentioned by respondents in Raleigh and Cincinnati. In Raleigh community councils were involved in establishing local recreation programs for adults and youth. In Cincinnati a number of councils have raised funding through street fairs and block parties for recreation programs in recently rehabilitated local recreation centers.

Table 5.5. Ratings of Program Influence on
Citizen-Government Relations

Rating	Frequency	Percent
Greatly improved relations	13	25.5
Moderately improved relations	33	64.7
No influence on relations	4	7.8
Moderately impaired relations	1	2.0
Greatly impaired relations	0	0.0

Respondents in Raleigh and Atlanta also mentioned improvements in public transportation services. In these cities, pressure from community councils resulted in improvements in bus scheduling and signalization. In Raleigh community council activity also aided in establishing a shared-ride taxi service for the elderly and handicapped.

Nearly all the groups sponsor some sort of neighborhood clean-up or beautification program. In some instances these are organized yearly, while in others they are much more frequent. Sanitation vehicles are usually supplied by the city to support these activities. Citizen respondents felt that these activities not only improved local physical conditions but also helped to promote familiarity between neighbors and increase the sense of community.

Improved Citizen-Government Relations

Although survey respondents did not freely offer improved citizen-government relations as a program accomplishment in response to the open-ended question, when directly asked if citizen-government relations had improved as a result of the neighborhood planning program, over 80 percent of the survey respondents judged the relationship between citizens and government to have moderately or greatly improved. These results are presented in Table 5.5.

Many case study respondents mentioned improved citizen-government relations in response to an open-ended question on program accomplishments. This response was particularly common in Cincinnati, St. Paul, and Raleigh. Respondents emphasized the programs' positive influence on the citizens' perceptions of the cooperation and responsiveness shown by city officials. A citizen representative from St. Paul commented: "I believe there is a little more trust in government. Less conflict. Less of an advisory role or position. Citizens understand and are more supportive of city government." In Wilmington the planning director identified a new attitude among city officials. "City government has been more responsive to citizen needs and viewpoints. For example, the director of public works now asks if an idea has been checked out with the neighborhoods. That never happened five years ago." In Cincinnati citizen representatives and the program director agreed that the program had facilitated a cooperative attitude and involved citizens in more directive rather than reactive action. This, they suggested, was well received by the city council.

The responses of case study respondents to a direct question on the programs' influence on citizen-government relations, however, were more mixed. In fact, the majority of respondents in Atlanta felt that the program had worsened relations between the citizens and government. Some suggested that the heightened expectations created by the program were being frustrated by government officials who, after asking for citizen input on decisions, were not giving it serious weight. Others felt that the government was incapable of helping them with some of the more serious problems like housing deterioration. In Cincinnati, St. Paul, and Wilmington the responses were decidedly mixed. Some citizen representatives in Cincinnati, for example, felt the program "caused more people to complain." In St. Paul the typical response was a qualified yes. One citizen representative commented that the relationship between citizens and government is "considerably better than what it was. Yet, there is still a feeling of suspicion." Moreover, a neighborhood planner answered, "Yes and no; the program has allowed people to understand [the government process], but every now and then the program reinforces the negative feelings between the citizens and government." Similarly, in Wilmington a citizen representative commented that, "to a certain extent, citizens are still afraid or do not want to be bothered because they think the council will not listen." A neighborhood planner felt that "the relations between citizens and government are the same or have improved a little. Citizens still doubt government or anyone who works for government." In Houston and Raleigh, however, a clear majority felt that citizen-government relations had improved as a result of the program.

Decreased Resistance to Project Initiation

Although survey respondents did not mention this as an accomplishment in response to the open-ended question, some did when they were specifically asked about it in a closed-ended question. As shown in Table 5.6, 17.6 percent of the respondents indicated their program had greatly decreased resistance, and a large 70.6 percent indicated that their program had led to a moderate decrease in citizen resistance to the implementation of planning projects. Only 11.7 percent of the respondents indicated that the program had either no effect or moderately increased resistance. This decreased resistance appears to be the result of early participation in the planning process, which allows citizens to "weed out" projects that are considered objectionable

When neighborhood planners and program directors in the case study cities were asked about decreased community resistance, they overwhelmingly responded that their programs were successful in this regard. A planner in St. Paul, for example, said the program had "broken down the 'them versus us' attitude" and replaced it with a give-and-take attitude about development projects. In Houston a planner commented that "educating the communities about city-wide concerns aids in the implementation of city-wide projects." Finally, a planner in Wilmington commented that there was less resistance because "many of the projects are the result of a need expressed in the community." Only two planners in all the case study cities felt that resistance to city-initiated projects had not substantially decreased.

Leadership Training and the Development of Local Organizations

The open-ended question on accomplishments in the case study interviews elicited a number of responses indicating that these programs have been effective in developing local neighborhood

Table 5.6. Ratings of Program Influence on
Resistance to Project Implementation

Rating	Frequency	Percent
Greatly decreased resistance	9	17.6
Moderately decreased resistance	36	70.6
Had no effect	4	7.8
Moderately increased resistance	2	3.9
Greatly increased resistance	0	0.0

leadership and in helping both to form new neighborhood organizations and to strengthen existing ones. Leadership training in particular was cited frequently by citizen representatives, neighborhood planners, and program directors in Atlanta, Cincinnati, Raleigh, and St. Paul. In Atlanta one citizen representative said the program had led to the "development of community activists which has allowed things to get done," while another said, "People have gotten leadership training and development." In Cincinnati the program was thought to be particularly good for helping new groups get organized and training new leaders. The Community Assistance Teams have routinely provided leadership training to new district council leaders. In St. Paul one citizen representative commented that the program had led to "the identification of good leadership within the community," and the program director commented that "the program brought out a whole new leadership in neighborhoods." In Raleigh the program was seen as a "great new stepping-stone" for residents to become involved in politics. It was a "place to develop political leadership."

This notion of neighborhood planning programs serving as a training ground for future political leaders was supported by examples of individuals starting as neighborhood group leaders and going on to hold political office. In Raleigh the former mayor had begun as a community council president. In Wilmington one of the council members started as a district council chairperson. Similarly, in Atlanta at least two recent council members had begun as heads of neighborhood planning units and one went on to become the director of budget and planning for the city. This is convincing evidence that these programs do, in fact, help to develop new political leadership.

Case study respondents in Cincinnati, Houston, St. Paul,

and Wilmington also emphasized the programs' role in creating new organizations and in strengthening existing ones. In
Cincinnati the prospect of receiving a grant of Mott Foundation money was used as an incentive to encourage the formation of district councils in areas where they did not exist. The
Community Assistance Teams also conducted confidential organizational assessments for district councils and provided assistance in improving organizational efficiency. In Houston respondents credited the program with direct responsibility for
the organization of eight civic clubs and increasing organizational capacity by assisting them in obtaining tax-exempt status, securing grants from local corporations, and handling such
technical matters as restrictive covenants. In St. Paul citizen
representatives emphasized the importance of the community
organizers funded through the program. They took responsibility for the managerial duties involved in running the organization, enabling the citizen representatives to focus on policy
issues. This increased the organizational capacity of the district councils. The programs in Wilmington, Atlanta, and Raleigh were also credited with creating a number of neighborhood organizations throughout the city.

More Equitable Distribution of Public Resources

Although it was not possible to assess quantitatively the effect
the programs had on the distribution of public resources, several questions provide some evidence on this issue. A survey
question asked, "What types of neighborhoods participated
the most in the neighborhood planning program?" Assuming
that participation is necessary for program benefits, this question provides an indication of who is receiving the benefits. As
shown in Table 5.7, slightly more than 47 percent of the respondents indicated that middle-income neighborhoods were
most likely to participate in these programs; 31 percent indicated that low-income neighborhoods participated the most;
and only 6 percent indicated that high-income neighborhoods
participated the most. This suggests that middle-income neighborhoods are most likely to benefit from these programs.
    Respondents in the case studies were also directly asked if
the programs had led to a more equitable distribution of public
resources. Overall the results are mixed. In Atlanta respondents were about equally split in their answers. One neighbor-

Table 5.7. Ratings of Neighborhood Type
Most Active in the Program

Neighborhood Type	Frequency	Percent[1]
Low income	16	31.4
Middle income	24	47.1
High income	3	5.9
Equal activity level	7	13.7
Other	1	2.0

1. Percentages add up to greater than 100 since multiple answers were allowed.

hood planner commented, "The pendulum has swung far the other way [toward poorer neighborhoods]. For example, all the new public pools have been built in the low-income areas." But others felt the more vocal middle-class areas were benefiting the most and that any move toward a more equitable distribution of public resources was the result of the CDBG program and its targeting requirements, rather than of the local neighborhood planning program. In Raleigh respondents generally felt that the program had resulted in more parks and recreation services in poorer areas, but had not greatly affected the distribution of other public resources. In St. Paul the responses were also mixed. Respondents felt that neighborhoods were the beneficiaries of more public improvements but they were unclear as to whether the program resulted in a more equitable distribution among neighborhoods. In Houston the majority of respondents felt the program had done little to influence the distribution of public resources. Respondents felt that any improvements in distribution were the result of the CDBG program or that "the squeaky wheel got the oil," which left out the relatively quiet poorer neighborhoods. Only in Cincinnati and Wilmington did most respondents feel that the programs were responsible for a more equitable distribution of public resources. In Wilmington, however, most of the examples provided to substantiate this claim were projects funded with CDBG money. Overall, the evidence supporting a more equitable distribution of public resources as a program accomplishment, is weak.

Conclusion

The data from both the survey and the case study interviews indicate that these programs can be credited with a number of important accomplishments. The initiation of neighborhood improvement projects and improved physical conditions was the most frequently cited accomplishment by survey respondents, and this was substantiated by the numerous examples in the case studies. In particular, these programs resulted in a considerable number of improvements in housing, transportation facilities, recreation facilities, and neighborhood cleanliness.

The respondents also credited neighborhood planning programs with increasing community awareness and competence. Local residents were said to be better educated on existing and proposed plans, on physical conditions in their areas, and on how to get things done through the city administration. According to the data, these programs also resulted in increased citizen influence on city officials, particularly in the area of budgeting, zoning, and plan preparation. Again these claims were substantiated by a number of specific examples of citizen pressure leading to changes in policy, funding decisions, and other matters under the control of the city administration.

The data also indicated that neighborhood planning programs led to increased citizen participation in planning. The programs were said to draw people into the planning process by getting them involved in pressing local problems. The rough estimates of the numbers of people participating in these programs are considerably greater than the numbers achieved with other traditional participation methods. Participation in neighborhood planning programs has the added advantage of being continuous.

Another frequently cited accomplishment was improved communications between residents and city officials. Citizens were better able to inform council members and department heads of what they wanted, and council members and department heads were better able to inform citizens of the constraints and operating procedures of local government. Planners were better informed of community problems and neighborhoods were better informed of common problems in other areas.

According to the responses, some programs also resulted in improvements in local services. Although slightly more than one-quarter of the survey respondents indicated no improvement in local service delivery, others attributed improvements in human services, public transportation, police, and sanitation to the neighborhood planning program. A comparison of these findings with the findings on improved physical conditions indicates that neighborhood planning programs have had more success in influencing changes in physical conditions than they have in influencing improvements in public services.

There was some indication that neighborhood planning programs led to improved citizen-government relations. In some instances, citizens were said to feel that public officials were more responsive to their needs. Other responses, however, indicated that these programs raised expectations which were then not fulfilled.

Decreased resistance to project implementation was consistently cited as a program accomplishment. Neighborhood planning programs were said to help break down the "them-versus-us" attitude and to facilitate negotiation. Residents were also said to be better informed of community-wide needs.

Respondents also credited neighborhood planning programs with providing leadership training and developing new local organizations. Serving as the chairperson of a neighborhood organization provides training in leadership skills, which are often supplemented by more formal training offered by the neighborhood planning program. A number of these chairpersons have gone on to hold elected or appointed offices in the city. In this sense, these programs offer an alternate means of assuming political office. Neighborhood planning programs have also established many new neighborhood organizations in areas where they did not exist.

Finally, there is some evidence that these programs lead to a more equitable distribution of public resources. There are many examples of poorer neighborhoods receiving major improvements, but this may be due to the targeting requirements of the CDBG program, which funds many of the activities carried out within local neighborhood planning programs, rather the neighborhood planning program itself. In fact, the data indicate that middle-income neighborhoods seem to be most actively involved in these programs.

In conclusion, it is clear that neighborhood planning programs have led to a number of important improvements in the quality of life in local neighborhoods. These improvements include direct physical improvements as well as improvements in communication, trust, competence, and influence. The following chapter addresses the relationship between the characteristics of neighborhood planning programs and selected program accomplishments.

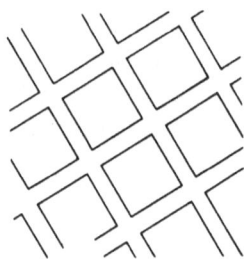

6 Factors Related to Program Accomplishments

In chapter 4 the characteristics of contemporary neighborhood planning programs were described, focusing on the organization of local groups, program structure, program operation, interorganizational relationships, and the characteristics of the community. In the preceding chapter the accomplishments of these programs were presented. The purpose of this chapter is to identify program and program context factors that are particularly important in achieving these accomplishments. The basic question to be explored is: What factors have been instrumental in the effectiveness of neighborhood planning programs?

Although some research has been done on the key elements of effective neighborhood development organizations, it is limited in two ways. First, the research has focused primarily on independent neighborhood organizations rather than on organizations associated with a larger city-wide program. It may not be possible to generalize from findings on independent groups to allow one to make conclusions about city-affiliated groups. Second, existing research has focused on the characteristics of the local groups themselves, rather than considering contextual factors, such as the support of city officials and the characteristics of the city in which the program operates. For example, effectiveness has been variously described as a function of the ability of local groups to exert political influence (Hallman, 1977; Mayer and Blake, 1981), to define goals and responsibilities clearly (Mayer and Blake, 1980), to establish connections with umbrella organizations (Schoenberg and Rosenbaum, 1980; Warren, 1963; Warren and Warren, 1977), to develop effective local leaders (Ahlbrandt and Cunningham, 1979; Mayer and Blake, 1981), to maintain active citizen participation (Hallman, 1977; Yin et al., 1973), to maintain the support of the community (Cole, 1974; Hallman, 1977; Mayer and

Blake, 1981; Yin et al., 1973), and to hire competent staff members (Hallman, 1977; Mayer and Blake, 1981; Ross, 1979; Yin et
al., 1973). In the analysis here, the community context, the relationship between the program and city officials, and attributes of program operation and structure are also considered.

Again both survey and case study data were used to identify
factors associated with program effectiveness. Case study respondents were asked two open-ended questions on important
program elements: "Can you identify any aspects or components of the program as major factors in the accomplishments
of the neighborhood planning program?" and "Are there characteristics of this city, that is, aspects of the physical, social,
political or economic make-up of the city, that you feel contribute to the effectiveness of the program?" These general questions allowed respondents to offer what they considered to be
the most important factors in the program's success.

The survey data were used in a regression analysis to identify the factors associated with two more specific measures of
program success. These measures of success were chosen to
represent the objectives of the citizens and of the planners.
The first measure, of particular interest to citizens, is, "How
do you rate the effectiveness of the program in influencing the
decisions of city officials?" The frequency distribution for responses to this question was presented in Table 5.5. The second measure, of particular interest to planners, is, "How has
the neighborhood planning program affected the implementation of planning projects?" The frequency distribution of responses to this question was presented in Table 5.6. These two
measures were used as the dependent variables in a series of
regression equations.

The independent variables in the regression analysis are the
characteristics reviewed in chapter 4, which were grouped into
five categories: the organization of local groups, program structure, program operation, interorganizational relationships,
and community context. Due to the large number of variables,
however, a data reduction strategy was necessary. This involved three steps.

The first step was to calculate a simple correlation matrix
between all independent variables within each of the five categories mentioned above. This was done to help avoid potential
multicollinearity in the subsequent regression analyses. Where
two variables were correlated at .7 or greater, one of the vari-

ables was dropped. Although this procedure does not totally rule out autocorrelation problems, it assures that obvious violations are detected. Other warning signs of multicollinearity (including large regression coefficients which are statistically nonsignificant and big changes in regression coefficients when other variables were added to the equation) were also checked in the subsequent regression analyses. No problems were detected. Most of the program variables were entered as dichotomous values. In these instances zero represented the absence of the characteristic and one represented the presence of the characteristic. Furthermore, several variables had little or no variation, and these were dropped from the analysis.

The second step of the analysis was to enter the program characteristics into five regression equations for each of the two measures of effectiveness. Five equations were necessary since there were too many variables for a single regression equation. Each of the equations contained all of the variables in one of the five categories of independent variables (see Tables D1–D5, appendix D). That is, all the variables describing the organization of local groups were entered into one equation, all the variables describing program structure were entered into another, and so forth.

The final step involved entering all program elements with a standardized regression coefficient of .20 or greater in step two into one equation for each measure of success. This procedure controls across categories for the influence of all program characteristics with moderately strong relationships to the measures of success. A standardized regression coefficient, rather than the significance level, was used to select variables for inclusion in this overall model since it is population data. The .20 value was chosen as a criterion for including variables because it represents the threshold of what is generally recognized as a moderate relationship. The simple correlations of the variables entered into these two equations were checked to guard against multicollinearity. These are presented in Tables D6 and D7 in appendix D.

In the final regression equations, a standardized regression coefficient of .25 was selected as a criterion for practical significance. This indicates that at least 6.25 percent of the variation in the measure of program success is explained by the particular program element after controlling for other variables in the equation. The selection of increasingly stringent criterion levels for practical significance reflects a desire to be conservative and to focus on the most important program characteristics.

In the sections that follow the results from the analysis of survey data and the responses from the case study interviews are presented. The sections are organized by the five categories of program elements. For ease of presentation, the regression coefficients for each category of program characteristics are presented in separate tables. These coefficients, however, come from one regression equation for each dependent variable. The adjusted R^2 for the equation predicting citizen influence of government officials is .40, and the adjusted R^2 for the equation predicting decreased resistance to project implementation is .71.

In the following discussion, the survey and case study data on each program characteristic are discussed together. In some instances the survey data indicated that a particular program characteristic is not strongly associated with either measure of effectiveness but case study respondents identified that characteristic as important. This should be expected, since the survey analysis involves two very specific measures of accomplishment while the case study responses concern more general assessments. A program characteristic may not be important in influencing the degree of influence that citizens have on city officials, for example, but still be important for other aspects of the program's success.

The Characteristics of Local Organizations

Three groupings of variables described the characteristics of local organizations: the methods of defining neighborhoods, the person or group responsible for organizing neighborhoods, and the method of selecting representatives. The analysis presented in Table 6.1 indicates that the method used to define neighborhoods does not significantly affect the program's influence on the decisions of city officials or citizen resistance to project implementation. The dashes indicate that the standardized regression coefficient for a program characteristic was less than .20 in the second step of the analysis. Thus, it was not entered into the final model.

Case study results, however, suggest effectiveness is dependent on two aspects of neighborhood definition. First, the exis-

Table 6.1. The Influence of Local Organization
on Program Effectiveness

Program Element	Increased Influence on City Officials [1]	Decreased Resistance to Implementation [1]
Neighborhood definition		
Citizen perceptions	—	—
Socioeconomic data	—	—
Preexisting districts	—	—
Physical boundaries	—	—
Organizers		
Planning staff	—	.017
Existing local groups	—	—
Local leaders	—	—
Method of representative selection		
Elected by community	—	—
Appointed	−.237	−.031
Elected by committee	—	—
Voluntary	.118	—
No official representatives	—	—
No set method	−.061	—

1. Numbers are beta weights from overall regression model. A "—" indicates that in the second step of the analysis, the standardized regression coefficient was less than .20.

tence of clearly defined neighborhoods was mentioned as an important factor in the success of the program by respondents in Atlanta, Cincinnati, St. Paul, and Wilmington. As stated by one citizen representative in St. Paul, "We have identifiable neighborhoods with a sense of who we are." Respondents talked of the importance of clearly defined neighborhoods in providing citizens with a sense of place and avoiding conflict between neighborhood groups. The existence of clearly defined neighborhoods was also said to aid in the formation and acceptance of the program. Thus, considering both the survey and case study results, program success does not appear to be influenced by *how* neighborhoods are defined, but rather by whether they are clearly defined or not.

Second, the directors and some citizen representatives in Raleigh and Atlanta felt that establishing neighborhood boundaries that did not coincide with political boundaries was an important factor in program success. Neighborhood districts in these cities typically overlapped two or sometimes three political districts. In both Atlanta and Raleigh respondents felt that noncontiguous political district and neighborhood boundaries kept the program from becoming overly involved in partisan politics. The result was more bipartisan support for the program. This sentiment was not unanimous, however. Some citizen representatives expressed frustration at not having a strong advocate on the council.

The analysis of the survey data also shows that the measures of effectiveness are not dramatically affected by who organizes the neighborhoods. That is, effectiveness is not substantially different for neighborhoods organized by the planning staff, by local leaders, or by existing local groups (see Table 6.1). Similarly, case study respondents did not identify the persons or groups responsible for organizing the neighborhoods as an important factor affecting program effectiveness.

The method of selecting representatives was also not found to contribute substantially to program performance. The survey results do, however, show some indication that representatives who are appointed by the council are less effective in influencing the decisions of city officials (beta = .237). This may be because councils appoint neighborhood representatives who do not have credibility in the community or who are not aggressive in advocating the interests of the neighborhood.

Case study respondents also did not indicate any one method of selecting representatives as contributing to program effectiveness. Many respondents, however, did comment that flexibility in the rules for deciding how to select representatives was a positive program characteristic. Neighborhood planners and citizen representatives in Atlanta and Wilmington felt that the lack of specific guidelines for representation allowed local groups to adopt the method most suited to their particular needs. A citizen representative in Atlanta described the advantages of this flexibility: "[In Atlanta] you have the whole spectrum of types of participation, from New England town meetings to elected councils. If people can't participate in the way they feel comfortable, then the process won't work." Therefore, the particular method appears to be less important than allowing participating neighborhood organizations to choose their own method of representation. As we shall see in chapter 7, however, there are also problems associated with allowing groups to work out their own method of representation.

The publication of local newspapers was also mentioned by citizen representatives in St. Paul and Cincinnati as an important activity of local organizations. In St. Paul, for example, many of the district councils publish community newspapers that keep residents informed of their activities, publicize local events, and provide information of general interest. These papers were said to provide an important channel of communication that greatly contributed to the success of the program. One citizen representative commented that "the community newspaper is a necessity." Respondents credited the newspapers with helping to develop a sense of community and generate support for the program among neighborhood residents. It keeps those who do not actively participate on a regular basis informed of the group's activities.

In sum, program effectiveness is enhanced when neighborhoods have been clearly defined, the method of selecting representatives is determined by the local organizations, and newspapers are used to communicate with residents of the community.

Program Structure

Five groupings of variables were used to describe program structure: the method of program sanction, the administering agency, the number of tiers, the official recognition of local groups, and the support provided to participating groups. The results of the analysis of survey data show that when neighborhood planning programs are sanctioned by council resolutions, ratings of the influence that citizens had on the decisions of city officials increased (see Table 6.2). The other methods of sanction—including city charter amendment, executive order, and informal agreement—showed only weak associations to either measure of effectiveness. Council sanction may assure a certain level of commitment by council members to the program and to citizen involvement. Since they originally authorized the program, they are less likely to feel threatened by it. Sanction by council resolution may also help to legitimize the program in the eyes of other public officials (for example, agency personnel), helping to foster greater cooperation. The method of program sanction, however, does not significantly influence citizen resistance to project implementation. Similarly, case study respondents did not cite the method of program sanction as an important factor, but given that this variable did not vary within programs, this is not surprising.

Table 6.2 also indicates that the administering agency is related to ratings of citizen resistance to project implementation but not to ratings of citizen influence on city officials. Programs administered by planning departments were rated as being less effective in reducing the resistance to projects, and programs administered by housing departments were rated as being more effective in reducing resistance. This may be a function of the type of project typically administered by these departments. Often the planning department is involved in projects that bring large-scale physical changes, such as new roads or rezonings, which are likely to generate considerable community resistance. Housing departments, on the other hand, often confine their projects to specific sites which may not generate as much community-wide resistance. A more narrow focus on housing, as opposed to general planning issues, may also limit the range of projects considered.

The only mention of the importance of the administering agency by the case study respondents was in Cincinnati. There the director and neighborhood planners felt that being a branch of the city manager's office put the program in a better position to influence the decisions of other city departments and to influence municipal budgeting. Furthermore, it made the program more visible and indicated a commitment by the city to neighborhood planning.

The number of program tiers showed a moderate association with ratings of the degree to which citizens were able to influence the decisions of city officials, yet the regression coefficient fell slightly short of the criterion level of .25. The number of program tiers was not found to be related to decreased resistance to planning projects. Yet the case study results indicate that a tiered organizational structure is an important program element. Respondents in all three case study cities which had a tiered organizational structure (Atlanta, Raleigh, and Wilmington) identified it as a major contributor to program success. Respondents explained that city-wide groups composed of representatives from the local organizations are effective in

Table 6.2. The Influence of Program Structure on Program Effectiveness

Program Element	Increased Influence on City Officials [1]	Decreased Resistance to Implementation [1]
Method of sanction		
City charter	.024	−.157
Executive order	—	—
Council resolution	.322 [2]	.093
Informal agreement	—	—
No sanction	—	.097
Administering agency		
Planning	−.105	−.267 [2]
Community development	−.044	−.178
Independent	—	—
Housing	−.016	.266 [2]
Mayor/council	—	—
City manager	—	—
Number of tiers	.200	—
Recognition of local groups	—	.153
Support to local groups		
Financial	.286 [2]	—
Staff	—	.244
Materials	—	—
Information	—	.046

1. Numbers are beta weights from overall regression model. A "—" indicates that in the second step of the analysis, the standardized regression coefficient was less than .20.

2. Meets criterion for practically significant association.

fostering a city-wide perspective on problems. One neighborhood planner in Atlanta comments: "The city-wide group is good. It enables neighborhood leaders to put their neighborhood planning unit in the context of the whole city. Everyone must contend with the needs of other areas."

The planning director in Atlanta also felt that the city-wide group provided an efficient means for council members and administrators to communicate with neighborhood representatives. They could attend one meeting and talk with representatives from all neighborhoods. From the citizens' perspective, the city-wide group was an effective means for "talking with the administration." Citizen representatives in Raleigh felt that proposals carried more weight when they were submitted and backed by the city-wide group. Thus, neighborhood representatives actively sought the support of the city-wide council. From the council members' perspective, support by the city-wide group helped assure them that there was community-wide support for a project and that the project was not going to be fought by surrounding neighborhoods. Overall, a tiered structure appears to facilitate communication between all those involved in neighborhood planning programs.

Table 6.2 also indicates that there is no significant difference in the ratings of citizen influence or decreased project resistance between programs that formally recognize groups and those that do not. Case study respondents also failed to mention this as an important program aspect.

The type of support provided to local groups, however, is associated with measures of program performance. The survey results show that financial support to local groups significantly increases the effectiveness of the program in influencing the decisions of city officials. Financial support often enables community groups to hire community workers or undertake independent studies, which appears to increase the influence of these groups. Resources to obtain adequate information through surveys and other primary data collection techniques may also help to increase citizen credibility and clout. Further, the results show that, when controlling for financial support, the program's influence on city officials is not significantly affected by the amount of staffing, materials, or information. Thus, financial support appears to be the most important type of support provided.

Case study respondents reinforce this finding of the importance of financial support to neighborhood groups. Two types of financial support were mentioned: direct funding of neighborhood organizations and access to the budgeting process. Direct funding of neighborhood groups was mentioned as a major factor in a program's accomplishments by the planning directors, neighborhood planners, and citizen representatives

in both cities that provided it: Cincinnati and St. Paul. Respondents viewed direct funding as a sign of commitment to
the program and a factor contributing to increased citizen participation and citizen competence. In Cincinnati, where Mott
Foundation money has been given to neighborhood groups
to fund locally initiated projects, one neighborhood planner
comments: "The funding of neighborhood groups has had a
profound impact on the program. Money is given directly to
the community councils. This has made the community aware
of how to manage money, leverage and initiate their own
projects."

Funding was considered important because it enabled community councils to hire staff, which helped to remove the
heavy administrative burden from council presidents and resulted in more effective organizations. For example, in St.
Paul a combination of Community Development and municipal
funds is used to allow district councils to hire a "community
organizer." Citizen representatives considered their groups to
be more effective because the organizer had time to attend
meetings during the day and review documents sent as part of
the early notification procedure.

Financial support to neighborhood groups is also provided
through the budgeting process. Case study respondents in Atlanta, Cincinnati, St. Paul, and Wilmington mentioned access
to the budgeting process as an important element in program
effectiveness. This link was seen as particularly important in
implementing neighborhood-initiated projects. The St. Paul
planning director reflects on the process: "In St. Paul you get
certain points in the capital budgeting scheme if your project
is part of a plan. This gives them [district councils] something
to strive for and they know if they put it in there, it is going to
have some impact on the decisions that the city makes. I think
that it is critical. It's like any planning process: unless you
have a way to impact day to day decisions that the city makes
the plans are useless."

Thus, financial support to local groups influences program
effectiveness and appears to enable citizens to obtain other
types of support. The survey results show that influence on
city officials is influenced by financial support, and case study
results suggest that direct funding to local groups improves
other aspects of program effectiveness, including increased
participation, increased citizen competency, and increased initiation of local projects.

Case study respondents also talked about the importance of the city providing information to local groups. In particular, they identified information on city plans or proposals and data on neighborhood trends—such as crime rates, housing abandonment, and the like—as extremely useful in program planning. Although some groups had the capacity to collect their own information, the majority relied on the central administrations for their information.

Respondents also emphasized the importance of receiving information in a timely manner. Early notification procedures requiring city agencies to inform neighborhood groups of city-initiated plans or proposals well before they are considered for final approval were mentioned as particularly important by respondents in Atlanta and St. Paul. City agencies in these cities are required to notify community groups of plans or proposals that may affect their area at least thirty days before the proposal is scheduled to be voted on by the city council. This kept groups informed and afforded them the time to study proposals and develop a response. Atlanta's planning director comments: "The early notification system is a very important part of the program. There is a chance [for communities] to respond before a public hearing on a list of recommended projects." Respondents also saw early notification as important in maintaining trust in city agencies and in the overall program. Without it, groups often do not find out about a project until the last minute, which leads them to conclude that the sponsoring agency was intentionally trying to exclude them from participation.

Finally, case study respondents mentioned program flexibility as a structural element influencing effectiveness. Flexibility, they said, allowed groups to form subcommittees to address specific areas of interest to the local community. The lack of restriction on the issues addressed permits local groups to focus on the problems they feel are most pressing. They are not restricted to dealing with land use, housing, or other issues, but can address a wide range of issues including schools, physical development, and public and human services. Thus, flexibility in program structure, like flexibility in the organization of local groups, enables the program to better fit the specific needs of an area.

In sum, a number of structural characteristics influence program effectiveness. Most important appears to be financial support to local groups. Both survey and case study respondents cited funding as playing a major role in program effectiveness. Case study respondents went on to emphasize the importance of providing timely information. The type of administering agency, the method of sanction, the number of tiers, and the flexibility of program guidelines also appear to contribute to program effectiveness. The results suggest that effectiveness is enhanced when the program is administered directly by the city manager; officially sanctioned by the council; multitiered to allow easier communication with public officials; and flexible in allowing local groups to address the full range of local problems.

Program Operation

Seven categories of variables were used to describe program operation: the role of the planners, the role of the citizens, the planners' training, program scope, the number of planners, the age of the program, and the source of the program funds. As presented in Table 6.3, in programs where planners are assigned the roles of educator and advocate, ratings of citizen influence on city officials are lower. These somewhat counter-intuitive results may be explained by the need for planners to adopt these roles in programs in which citizen groups are relatively unskilled or uninvolved and not effective in influencing the decisions of city officials. The planners may be trying to compensate for weaknesses in the citizen organizations. Furthermore, in programs where planners are assigned the role of educator, ratings of the decreased resistance to project implementation were lower. There planners may be helping citizens to critically analyze proposed projects, resulting in less of a decrease in resistance to planning projects. Finally, the results indicate that in programs in which planners adopted an organizer role, there was a large decrease in resistance to project implementation. Again, this association may be the result of planners having to adopt an organizer role because groups have not been active. Groups organized by the planning staff may also work more closely with city officials in developing and reviewing plans, resulting in less resistance at the time of implementation.

The role of citizens in the program, as shown in Table 6.3, is also associated with program effectiveness. The programs that

Table 6.3. The Influence of Program Operation on Program Effectiveness

Program Element	Increased Influence on City Officials[1]	Decreased Resistance to Implementation[1]
Role of planners		
Advocate	−.271[2]	—
Educator	−.373[2]	−.355[2]
Liaison	—	−.082
Mediator	—	−.088
Organizer	—	.272[2]
Role of citizens		
Review plans	.278[2]	—
Develop plans	.395[2]	.044
Monitor projects	—	—
Self-help	—	—
Number of planners	.409[2]	−.283[2]
Program scope		
Land use	—	—
Socioeconomic	—	—
Service delivery	—	—
Planners' training	—	—
Year initiated	—	—

1. Numbers are beta weights from overall regression model. A "—" indicates that in the second step of the analysis, the standardized regression coefficient was less than .20.

2. Meets criterion for a practically significant association.

involved citizens in the development and review of plans were rated as more effective in influencing the decisions of city officials. Apparently, the review and development of plans provide mechanisms for citizens to express their concerns and have an effect.

This view was shared by case study respondents. Citizen representatives in St. Paul, Atlanta, and Cincinnati identified the development of local plans as an important educational experience. It helped them understand local conditions and develop a comprehensive program for improving or maintaining the neighborhood. They also saw those plans as important in establishing credibility with the city council and in supporting various decisions adopted by local groups. In St. Paul formal adoption of local plans by the planning board and city council was also mentioned as an important aspect of the program. Formal adoption gave them more credibility and made them more useful in influencing the decisions of city officials.

The number of neighborhood planners is also associated with measures of program performance. It is positively associated with citizen influence on the decisions of city officials and with increased citizen resistance to project implementation. Higher levels of staffing may help citizens in obtaining information, analyzing programs and projects, and developing effective strategies for influencing city officials. Staff also provide support services—such as maintaining mailing lists and providing technical assistance—which are important in maintaining an effective organization.

Finally, the results show no significant relationship between training received by planners, the scope of the program (that is, land use, social planning, or service delivery orientation), or the age of the program and either measure of program effectiveness. These factors were also not mentioned by case study respondents.

Overall, the important operational characteristics of neighborhood planning programs are the involvement of citizens in plan preparation and review and the levels of program staffing. Although some roles of the planner are negatively associated with measures of program performance, these seem to be the result of a reaction to poorly organized citizen groups.

Interorganizational Relations

The analysis of interorganizational relations took in three categories of variables: the support of the mayor, council, city agencies, and residents; the relationship of the program to the comprehensive planning process; and the means citizens use to put pressure on city officials. The analysis of survey results presented in Table 6.4 indicates that the support of city agen-

Table 6.4. The Influence of Interorganizational Relations on Program Effectiveness

Program Element	Increased Influence on City Officials[1]	Decreased Resistance to Implementation[1]
Current support		
Mayor	—	−.247
Council	—	—
Other agencies	.252[2]	.170
Residents	—	—
Tie to comprehensive planning program	−.005	.436[2]
Means of citizen pressure		
Speaking at council	—	−.351[2]
Media	—	.206
Voting as a bloc	—	−.304[2]
Personal contacts	—	.307[2]
Protests	—	—

1. Numbers are beta weights from overall regression model. A "—" indicates that in the second step of the analysis, the standardized regression coefficient was less than .20.

2. Meets criterion for a practically significant association.

cies is positively associated with ratings of citizen influence on the decisions of city officials. The importance of support from city agencies was also emphasized by case study respondents in Atlanta, Wilmington, and Cincinnati.

Support for the program often entailed the direct involvement of agency heads. The importance of agency heads attending neighborhood meetings was emphasized by citizen representatives and neighborhood planners. Their presence at meetings, respondents said, facilitated effective communication and created a sense of mutual respect. A planner in Wilmington comments: "An important part of the program is that the department heads are directly involved. They come to meetings and deal directly with the citizens. This provides them with first-hand information on the problems and concerns of the community." Respondents in Atlanta and Cincinnati expressed similar sentiments.

As indicated in Table 6.4, the link to the comprehensive planning process is the second interorganizational factor associated with one of the measures of program performance. In programs that feed into the comprehensive planning process, citizen resistance to project implementation is lower. The conclusion one could draw here is that the opportunity to influence the content of the comprehensive plan lessens resistance to development guided by it. As intended, the involvement of citizens early on in the planning process results in less resistance during the implementation phase.

The means that citizens use to exert pressure on city officials are also associated with ratings of program performance. As might be expected, speaking at council meetings and voting as a bloc were negatively associated with ratings of decreased resistance to project implementation. These forms of citizen influence may be viewed as outgrowths of citizen dissatisfaction; therefore, it is not surprising that they are associated with increased resistance. The use of personal contacts by citizens, on the other hand, is positively associated with decreasing citizen resistance to projects. It appears that face-to-face interaction may improve communication and understanding and help to reduce citizen opposition to projects.

In sum, the support of city agencies, a direct link to the comprehensive planning process, and several means of citizen pressure on public officials are associated with program effectiveness.

The Community Context

Four variables were used to describe the community context of neighborhood planning programs: city size, type of government, median income of residents, and percent of owner-occupied dwelling units. The analysis presented in Table 6.5 indicates that none of these variables was associated with either rating of program effectiveness at or above the criterion level. The median income of residents and the percent of owner-occupied dwelling units show positive associations, but the coefficients are below the .25 level.

Table 6.5. The Influence of Community Context
on Program Effectiveness

Resistance to Element	Increased Influence on City Officials[1]	Decreased Resistance to Implementation[1]
City size	—	—
Type of government	—	—
Median income	.010	—
Percentage owner occupied	.103	—

1. Numbers are beta weights from overall regression model. A "—" indicates that in the second step of the analysis, the standardized regression coefficient was less than .20.

When case study respondents, however, were asked about the characteristics of their cities that contributed to the effectiveness of the program, they were able to identify a number of aspects. The most frequently mentioned characteristic was the predominance of single-family residential neighborhoods. Respondents in Atlanta, Cincinnati, Houston, and St. Paul mentioned this and suggested that single-family neighborhoods are more conducive to the development of a sense of community and to a concern for the physical appearance of the local area.

The natural existence of physically distinct neighborhoods was also offered as a characteristic of the city that contributes to the effectiveness of the program by respondents in Cincinnati and St. Paul. In Cincinnati, a number of respondents emphasized the natural topographical features that created distinct neighborhoods and encouraged a sense of community. Several others mentioned that many neighborhoods were once separate communities that had been annexed over time. In St. Paul respondents felt that the pattern of development in the city was conducive to defining distinct neighborhood areas. This minimized initial conflict over where the neighborhood boundaries should be drawn.

The existence of well-organized neighborhoods was also mentioned by respondents in Cincinnati and Atlanta as a characteristic of the city that influenced program success. Neighborhood planners in both cities identified this as important in generating initial support for the program and maintaining active group participation. Beginning the program with neighborhood groups already in existence also made the job of organizing neighborhoods easier. The planners could concentrate their efforts in the unorganized areas, rather than have to organize all areas in the city.

A council elected at large was identified as an important characteristic in Cincinnati and St. Paul. At-large councils, respondents suggested, are less likely to be threatened by neighborhood leaders and are more likely to be supportive of the program. They are more likely to appreciate the special perspective of neighborhood groups.

Several other characteristics of the cities judged important were unique to individual cities. In Houston respondents talked of the importance of a good economy and the involvement of the business community. In Cincinnati those surveyed credited a strong planning tradition with contributing to the program's effectiveness. Finally, in Raleigh respondents cited the city's high socioeconomic level and highly educated population as contributing to the success of the program.

Conclusion

The data from the survey and the case studies identified a number of program and contextual characteristics to be associated with program effectiveness. At the level of the local neighborhood organizations, having clearly defined neighborhoods was seen as an important aspect of a successful program. It was not important how neighborhoods were defined; only that their boundaries were clear. It also did not seem to matter who organized the neighborhood groups; only that they were organized. The majority of case study respondents also felt that neighborhood boundaries should cut across political districts to avoid excessive involvement in partisan politics. Restrictions on endorsement by neighborhood groups of political candidates serve a similar function. Analysis of the survey data indicates that ratings of the influence of citizens on the decisions of public officials were higher when neighborhood group representatives were not chosen by council members. The case study respondents did not identify a preferred method of selecting citizen representatives, but rather stressed the importance of allowing each neighborhood to determine its own method of representation. Finally, the publication of local newspapers was seen as an important means of keeping neighborhood residents involved, developing a sense of community, and generating support for the organizations and their activities.

A number of structural characteristics also showed some association with program effectiveness. Respondents from programs that were sanctioned by council resolution, rather than by executive order, charter amendment, or informal agreement, gave higher ratings of citizen influence on public officials. This means of sanction would seem to assure council support for the program (at least at the time of its inception) and greater cooperation from other public officials responsible to the council. The type of administering agency also affected one measure of effectiveness. Programs administered by the planning department were less likely to decrease resistance to planning projects, and programs administered by housing departments were more likely to decrease resistance. Furthermore, programs with two- or three-tiered organizational structures (where local representatives form the membership of area and city-wide parent organizations) were found to be more effective in developing a city-wide, rather than parochial, perspective among group leaders and in fostering communication between neighborhood groups and city officials.

The financial support of neighborhood organizations, including both direct support and access to the budgetary process, was found to be important in program effectiveness. Respondents saw financial support as giving a clear sign of government commitment to the program, increasing participation, and improving citizen competence and effectiveness. They also linked this support to increases in the number of improvement projects being undertaken. Finally, they saw the provision of information and the adoption of an early-notification system to inform neighborhood groups of proposals that affected their areas as important aspects of successful programs. These notification systems provided citizen groups with the necessary information for effective participation.

Several operational characteristics were also found to be important. In particular, citizen group involvement in the development and review of plans was positively associated with citizen influence. According to the respondents, the development of neighborhood plans by citizens was an important educational experience and one which helped establish credibility with public officials. The number of neighborhood planners assigned to work with neighborhood groups also affected performance: the greater the number of planners, the higher the ratings of citizen influence and the more the neighborhood group resistance to planning projects. More technical assistance appears to aid citizens in developing effective strategies for influencing city officials.

Interorganizational relations also influenced program effectiveness. The results indicate that the support of other city agencies is particularly important to successful programs. In many instances these other city agencies are responsible for implementing the plans developed by neighborhood groups. Without the support of these agencies the projects or policy changes advocated by local groups may not be implemented. Linking the neighborhood planning program to the comprehensive planning program also decreased resistance to planning projects. Neighborhood group involvement in comprehensive planning appears to smooth the way for implementation. Finally, several means of exerting influence on city officials are also associated with measures of program performance. Speaking at council meetings and voting as a bloc were positively associated with increased resistance to project implementation. These two means of influence would appear to be expressions of dissatisfaction with public projects or policies, which explains that association. Use of personal contacts is negatively associated with resistance to project implementation. Personal contacts may result in compromises that would reduce citizen resistance to proposed projects.

The statistical analysis did not uncover any strong relationships between the characteristics of cities and the measures of effectiveness. More specifically, city size, median income, type of government, and the percent of owner-occupied dwelling units failed to show strong associations with either measure of effectiveness. Respondents in the case study cities, however, mentioned several factors they considered important to the success of their programs. A high proportion of single-family neighborhoods was mentioned as important in four of the six case study cities. Single-family neighborhoods were considered more conducive to a sense of community. Physi-

cally distinct and well-organized neighborhoods were also considered an important ingredient of success. These characteristics helped provide support for the inception of programs and
made the task of organizing communities much easier. Finally,
respondents mentioned the importance of at-large councils in
several cities. Under an at-large system, councilpersons were
less likely to be threatened by neighborhood leaders.

In conclusion, this chapter has presented a number of program characteristics that appear to be important components
of successful programs. These characteristics should be considered in the design of new neighborhood programs and in the
revision of existing programs. This information will be used to
develop a set of specific recommendations in chapter 8.

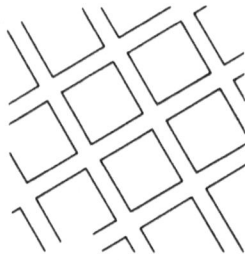

7 Program Problems

In the preceding two chapters the accomplishments of neighborhood planning programs have been discussed. These, however, are only half of the picture. Neighborhood planning programs also experience a number of problems, which have inhibited their effectiveness. The purpose of this chapter is to present the most common problems facing neighborhood planning programs. This analysis of program problems will be used in the conclusion to develop recommendations for improving program effectiveness.

The data on program problems come from the survey and case study respondents who were asked in open-ended questions about the major problems with the neighborhood planning program. Over 90 percent of the survey respondents identified one or more problems. Similarly, case study respondents had little difficulty in identifying problems that inhibited program effectiveness.

The problems mentioned by both case study and survey respondents fall into nine categories: inadequate project implementation; low rates of citizen participation; lack of citizen competence; lack of support for the program; staffing problems; inadequate representation; poor communication; unclear program goals; and interneighborhood conflicts. Each of these is discussed below.

Inadequate Project Implementation

The problem most frequently mentioned by survey respondents was inadequate project implementation. As shown in Table 7.1, over 35 percent of the respondents cited this as a problem. In some instances, they blamed a slow planning

Table 7.1. Problems with Neighborhood Planning Programs Identified by Survey Respondents

Problem	Frequency	Percent [1]
Inadequate project implementation	18	35.3
Low rates of citizen participation	12	25.0
Lack of citizen competence	11	22.9
Lack of support	10	19.6
Staffing problems	7	14.6
Inadequate representation	6	12.5
Poor communication	5	10.4
Unclear program goals and procedures	4	8.3
Interneighborhood conflicts	4	8.3

1. Percentages add up to greater than 100 since multiple answers were allowed.

process for the failure to implement neighborhood-initiated projects. In others, they faulted the lack of a direct link to the capital budgeting process or simply a lack of funds for implementing citizen proposals. Citizen groups were developing projects, but adequate funding was not available for their implementation.

Problems in implementation were mentioned by case study respondents in all cities except St. Paul. In Cincinnati, in spite of the Mott Foundation grants to neighborhood groups, the neighborhood planners were particularly critical of the lack of funding for community projects. They felt that little discretionary money was available and that community groups had not been aggressive enough in assuring that their projects were included in the budget requests of city departments. In fact, they saw having to work through city departments, rather than having a direct channel to the budgeting process, as partially to blame for the lack of project funding. As might be expected, department heads were giving high priority to their own budget requests and low priority to the neighborhood-initiated requests.

In Atlanta it was the citizen representatives who commented on the lack of funding for neighborhood projects. One representative commented, "We are not very successful in getting the council to fund projects." Even when the city council had set aside money for neighborhood projects, problems still occurred. As one representative explains: "The city is short on implementation. The council takes money allocated for projects developed by the neighborhood planning units and uses it for their own projects. The set asides are there on paper, but they disappear. No one keeps track of the money set aside for the neighborhood planning unit projects."

A system for tracking projects through the bureaucracy and greater accountability for the expenditure of set-aside monies were suggested by neighborhood planners as partial solutions to this problem. The planning director in Atlanta, however, felt that citizen complaints about inadequate project implementation could be traced to the unrealistic expectations held by local groups. According to the director, groups should be concentrating on one or two priority issues rather than submitting "wish lists" and should be more active in seeking funding from other sources, including federal and foundation programs. Clearly, there were discrepancies between the expectations of neighborhood groups and those of the city administration.

In Wilmington projects that qualified for CDBG monies were often funded, but local assemblies had no influence on the regular municipal budgeting process. If a project did not qualify for CDBG funds, no local alternative sources of funding were available. Thus the middle- and upper-income neighborhoods, which were generally ineligible for CDBG funds, saw no strong reason for participating. Citizen representatives expressed a desire to have a greater role in the municipal budgeting process.

In Houston respondents were also concerned with project implementation, as the program provided no direct funds for local projects and offered no unique opportunity to influence the capital budgeting process. Moreover, because the CDBG program was administered by a separate department, the neighborhood planning program could not offer increased influence over the expenditure of CDBG funds. In fact, several planners commented on the lack of cooperation between the neighborhood planning program and the Community Development Department. Both the neighborhood planners and citizen representatives considered this lack of funding for local projects to be a major drawback of the program.

Similarly, in Raleigh citizen representatives commented that the lack of funds for implementing local improvement projects was a major problem with the program. The program offered no direct funding of projects undertaken by community councils, nor did it substantially increase influence over the budgeting process. Citizen representatives felt that much more could have been accomplished if small amounts of money had been available to support neighborhood-initiated projects.

Low Rates of Citizen Participation

Even though increased participation was a frequently mentioned program accomplishment, many respondents still felt that citizen participation rates were too low. As shown in Table 7.1, 25 percent of the survey respondents mentioned participation as a problem. Maintaining interest among community residents in the absence of a major threat to the area was said to be extremely difficult.

Respondents in all case study cities except Cincinnati also mentioned problems in maintaining citizen participation. More specifically, two problems with participation were cited: the failure of groups to organize in some areas of the city and poor attendance at neighborhood group meetings.

In Wilmington, Raleigh, and St. Paul some areas of the city were not represented by neighborhood groups. In Wilmington many upper-income areas did not participate since the program did not offer them a means of funding local projects. In Raleigh the organizations in some of the more stable middle- and upper-income neighborhoods had become inactive. Typically, these areas were fully developed and relatively stable. The neighborhood planners there complained of not having enough time to "pump up groups that do not show interest." In St. Paul some indigenous neighborhood organizations refused to become a part of the program. The reluctant organizations did not want to conform to the requirements of the program and were concerned about being co-opted.

Poor attendance at monthly meetings was also mentioned

as a problem by neighborhood planners and citizen representatives. The reasons given for poor participation, however, varied. General citizen apathy was the reason given by some respondents in Raleigh, St. Paul, and Wilmington. As one, somewhat frustrated, citizen representative in Wilmington commented: "If help is free and someone else is doing the fighting, then they are all for it. Otherwise, no action. They won't come to meetings. There are people out there, but they just don't have that backbone."

Others attributed poor participation to leadership "burnout." Respondents in Houston, St. Paul, and Raleigh felt that the excessive demands placed on leaders resulted in rapid turnover, which hampered efforts to develop stable organizations. These same demands also inhibited leaders from spending enough time on efforts to increase participation. Still others felt that elements of program operation and structure were responsible for discouraging participation. In Wilmington, the planning director commented: "We have taken one mechanism to fit seventeen areas. There has been good participation in some areas and poor in others. We cannot make it fit specific areas. If we could work directly to fit their needs, we would have better participation."

Similarly, in Atlanta a citizen representative commented that some local organizational structures discouraged participation by having rules that limit voting rights and even speaking privileges. One neighborhood group was said to be run on the "big daddy" model, in which one powerful leader controlled the meetings. In another, once the neighborhood council was elected, they made all the decisions and limited the participation of others attending the meetings. Finally, respondents in Houston, Atlanta, and Raleigh attributed low rates of participation to a lack of awareness of the program among the general populace. Many people were simply ignorant of the existence of the program and even of their local neighborhood organizations. Poor publicity was blamed for this lack of awareness.

Both the lack of organizations representing certain areas of the city and low turnout at neighborhood group meetings are closely related to another problem: that of poor representation. Low rates of participation bring the representativeness of the neighborhood groups into question. This will be discussed in further detail later on in this chapter.

Lack of Citizen Competence

Twenty-three percent of the survey respondents mentioned lack of citizen competence as a problem. Excessive citizen demands, inadequate citizen leadership, and parochial attitudes among citizens were the most frequently mentioned problems in this general category.

The case study results indicate similar problems. In all cities except Raleigh, either neighborhood planners or citizen representatives felt that citizen groups had not been aggressive or active enough. Many citizen groups, they suggested, had difficulty developing and implementing local projects. Instead they were satisfied to react to the plans and projects of planners and developers. This was often attributed to poor leadership. A citizen representative in Atlanta comments: "The leadership is inconsistent. They are always making last-minute changes. Chairpersons do not keep up with things and on top of things. They are not aggressive enough."

A related complaint heard from neighborhood planners in Wilmington, Cincinnati, and Raleigh was that citizen groups relied too heavily on technical assistance and "hand-holding" from the planners. They needed, it was felt, to be more self-sufficient. One Wilmington planner, for example, commented, "If I had a magic wand, I'd take away the neighborhood planning program then ask the people what was the next step. They wouldn't have one." Similarly, a planner in Cincinnati commented, "The neighborhood groups need more training. They have to be more self-sufficient." In general, the feeling was that citizen groups needed to accept more responsibility and be more independent.

Others identified citizens' lack of familiarity with local plans, policies, and procedures as contributing to their ineffectiveness. Citizen leaders did not take the time, respondents said, to study existing plans and procedures. A Raleigh planner, for example, described the result of a poor understanding of the zoning ordinance: "Builders and realtors have influenced the neighborhood groups on zoning cases. It's easy to snow these people with fancy graphics of a proposed development. The builder then gets up in front of the city council and says he has the committee's support. But once the zoning is changed they can change their plan and develop to the maximum allowable densities. The community can, and sometimes does, get fooled." In Wilmington and Atlanta planners complained that citizens had not learned how to work through administrative channels to get action on their proposals. They had not learned whom to contact when they had problems.

Finally, neighborhood planners in Atlanta felt that citizens were making excessive demands on the city. The citizens, they suggested, had not developed an understanding of the practical limitations of city government. One planner commented, "People are very vocal about their needs and expect them to be satisfied immediately. They don't realize that the city can't deal financially with all the demands. They don't realize the city's limits." Planners also felt that many of the citizens attended meetings only to complain and were unwilling to take the necessary action to solve their problems.

Lack of Support

Over 19 percent of the survey respondents mentioned lack of support for the program as a problem. In general, respondents singled out city departments, city councils, and city managers as being particularly uncooperative and at times antagonistic to neighborhood groups involved in the program. They saw them as reluctant to allow neighborhood groups to play an active role in decision making. This finding is supported by the ratings of support reported in chapter 4. City departments were rated as least supportive, followed by city managers and city councils.

Case study respondents had similar views. Respondents from all cities except Houston mentioned lack of support by city officials as a problem and identified city councils and city departments as particularly uncooperative. In general, they saw city councils as wanting to involve neighborhood groups in decisions only selectively. A citizen representative in Atlanta commented: "All things need to be approved by the NPUs [Neighborhood Planning Units] . . . but the NPUs are used by council. Council waffles back and forth between listening to the NPU and ignoring them. If council wants something it will try to get the NPU approval but if the NPU wants something, the council says they don't need to listen because the NPU is only advisory."

This perspective was also shared by planners and planning

directors. St. Paul's planning director observed: "The politicians tend to use the district councils. Every once in a while
there is an issue that the city council does not want to deal
with, and they will shift the burden onto them [the district
councils]. Other issues they keep to themselves. Politically,
they cannot afford to oppose the district councils but politicians don't like giving up responsibility to groups like that."

The most frequent explanation for this lack of support from
city councils was that they were threatened by the prospect
of losing some of their power to neighborhood group leaders.
One planning director observed that "the council felt the citizen chairs were in competition with the councilpersons' role."
Some councilpersons felt that if citizens had a problem they
should come directly to them and not to the head of neighborhood organizations. They felt that the program tended to un-
dermine their political support.

The attitude of many city deparments was viewed similarly.
Respondents in all cities except Houston mentioned problems
in securing the cooperation of city departments. The planning
director in Cincinnati commented: "There is an inability of line
departments to accept neighborhood participation, particularly in budgeting." A neighborhood planner in Wilmington re-
counted similar problems: "I have trouble with department
heads. For example, the new manager changed the format to
deal with department heads such that I could not directly meet
with the heads. I had to meet with the planning director and
the manager to get this changed. I don't get information the
way I want to. . . . I hear stuff second hand. If I don't get
tipped, then I know last minute like the citizens. This under-
mines my credibility."

Many department heads saw the program as belonging to
the city planning or community development department and
were unwilling to cooperate unless ordered to do so by the
manager, council, or mayor. In general, the public works and
transportation departments were mentioned as the least cooperative, and the planning and police departments were seen
as most cooperative. The police departments were rated particularly high, as they used the neighborhood councils to establish rapport and to organize community crime prevention
programs.

City managers were generally seen as unsupportive, although there were some exceptions. A neighborhood planner

in Raleigh commented: "There is a philosophical problem . . . the neighborhood interest versus the government. The city manager wants more control in the decision-making process, but the community advisory councils are not responsive to him." Managers, respondents suggested, have not been taught to appreciate the importance of involving citizens in public decision making.

Staffing Problems

Approximately 15 percent of the survey respondents mentioned program staffing as a problem. The two most frequently mentioned staffing problems were understaffing and excessive work loads for the planners. Many planners suffered from "burnout" and low morale because they were laboring under heavy work loads.

At least one respondent from each case study city also felt that his or her program was understaffed. Respondents from Atlanta and Cincinnati were particularly vocal on this issue. A planner from Atlanta, for example, comments: "Having one planner for four NPUs is unrealistic. The planner cannot provide all the necessary services. There is not enough time to be versed in the happenings of each neighborhood." From the perspective of the citizens, the lack of staff had the following consequences: "We've had two planners. The first one I never saw. The second I saw rarely until recently" (citizen representative, Atlanta); "You have to ask them to do things that we shouldn't have to ask for because they are so understaffed" (citizen representative, Cincinnati); "Because the staff is overworked, notices didn't go out on time and promises were not kept" (citizen representative, Raleigh).

Predictably, in programs considered to be understaffed, planners felt overworked and talked of burnout. In Atlanta, Cincinnati, Raleigh, and St. Paul planners generally complained of too much work. Atlanta and Raleigh respondents further explained that the lack of support services was one major reason planners were overworked. A Raleigh planner commented: "I'm bogged down in clerical work. There is one secretary for 13 people, and we send out over 4,000 pieces of mail per month!" In Atlanta planners and citizens called for more support services to allow neighborhood planners to attend to what they saw as the more important aspects of their jobs, such as helping to increase participation and providing technical assistance on substantive issues. The requirement that planners attend a large number of night meetings also contributed to burnout. Their job requires them not only to attend the regularly scheduled meetings of neighborhood organizations to which they are assigned but also to attend the meetings of neighborhood group subcommittees and the city council. Together this often means three or four night meetings a week and sometimes several meetings in one evening.

Beyond their work with neighborhoods, planners in Atlanta and St. Paul were further burdened with responsibilities for other projects. A planner in Atlanta commented on this problem: "There is some conflict due to the availability of time to do what is necessary. The department is project-oriented but the planner is busy communicating and working with the neighborhood, plus working on the project. It's a tremendous work load." A planner from St. Paul voiced a similar problem: "It's hard to be a neighborhood planner from the planning department because of other demands on my time. I can't be out as much as I would like to be because I have to be here to do paperwork or other equally important projects."

The problem in Atlanta is exacerbated by the fact that job advancement is based on the general project work and not on neighborhood project work. Neighborhood planning is viewed by the planning director as the "breaking-in," low-level position in the department: "Neighborhood planning is a good place to get your feet wet—to enter into working with other programs like CDBG. Its hard to attract neighborhood planners because of the pay scale. So its a good place to break in. . . . Neighborhood planning is not an end point for planners. . . . There is a ladder in the department so they don't get stuck in neighborhood planning." Clearly, this creates conflict for the neighborhood planners. The incentive within the department is to work on the substantive projects unrelated to neighborhood planning; yet the demands of neighborhood groups are great, requiring the devotion of considerable amounts of time and energy. Moreover, neighborhood planning is considered a low-status position from which one wants to move as quickly as possible.

Finally, citizen representatives in Raleigh, Cincinnati, and Atlanta mentioned a lack of staff competence. In most instances the problem was a mismatch between the skills of the planners and the needs of the neighborhood groups. In Raleigh, for example, citizen representatives of neighborhoods to which a human services planner was assigned felt their needs were more appropriate for the skills of a physical planner. In Cincinnati several citizen representatives felt that the staff was not providing adequate technical assistance in supporting the social services provided by local neighborhood groups. In Atlanta citizen representatives talked of the lack of experience of the planners assigned to them. Because the neighborhood planning positions were typically entry level, the neighborhood planners were often just out of school. They were not familiar with the local political process and were not able to provide adequate assistance in helping citizens influence the political process. Citizens wanted more experienced planners assigned to the program.

Inadequate Representation

The lack of representativeness of neighborhood groups was identified as a problem by approximately 13 percent of the survey respondents. According to these respondents, the neighborhood groups were dominated by one faction of the community and did not represent the interests of all community members. A closed-ended question also asked about the representativeness of local groups. As presented in Table 7.2 a total of 13.8 percent of the respondents indicated that neighborhood groups were either very or fairly unrepresentative, another 41 percent indicated that neighborhood groups were only moderately representative, and approximately 45 percent felt that the groups were either fairly or very representative.

Case study respondents in Atlanta, Raleigh, Cincinnati, and St. Paul also cited a lack of representativeness as a problem. In St. Paul, for example, the planning director commented: "Representation is a real problem. We sometimes wonder if we are dealing with the right interests in a neighborhood. You have to be conscious of the fact that there are other interest groups besides the district council that need to be included."

Citizen representatives and the neighborhood planners in St. Paul expressed similar concerns about representation, and

Table 7.2. Ratings of the Representativeness
of Local Groups

Rating	Frequency	Percent
Very unrepresentative	1	2.0
Fairly unrepresentative	6	11.8
Moderately representative	21	41.2
Fairly representative	19	37.3
Very representative	4	7.8

respondents in St. Paul also offered several factors contributing to the lack of representativeness. One neighborhood planner felt the problem stemmed from the autonomy created by
providing public funding to neighborhood groups. "The process tends to institutionalize neighborhood organizations. It
gives them a source of income independent from their community. In that sense they become an institution that doesn't
really have to deal with the wheelings and dealings of their
neighborhood. The result is some district councils don't have
much relationship to the people in their district." A second
planner felt that some district councils saw themselves as judicial bodies rather than advisory councils.

> Councils rule on whether you have a legitimate concern
> or whether you're a flake, or whether they're going to
> support you or not. And all you get from them is a
> vote—no discussion. When this happens, the system de
> generates. The council really doesn't have the support
> of anybody. Citizens don't support it. At council you will
> have a district organizer saying, "Everybody supports
> this," and a group of very angry citizens saying, "That's
> not true!" The decision makers begin to feel they cannot
> count on the district councils.

Furthermore, several citizen representatives observed that
district council representatives would often advocate their
personal interests rather than the interests of the community.
One district council, for example, was controlled by developers, who, as might be expected, were in favor of development.
Finally, some district councils have been controlled by one fac-

tion of the neighborhood. In one instance the recognition of a neighborhood council was withdrawn when it was discovered that the council was dominated by predominantly white residents who had only recently arrived in the area and that the predominantly black long-time residents had not been included.

Respondents in Atlanta also felt that some of the neighborhood planning units were not representative. The bylaws of some groups restricted discussion of issues to a small group of elected officers, who also held sole voting powers. Except for voting for officers at yearly meetings, the community at large had little say over the positions adopted by these councils. Moreover, the turnout at some of the meetings in which elections were held was relatively small compared to the total number of people in the neighborhood, casting further doubt on the representativeness of the leadership of some neighborhoods.

In Raleigh also respondents expressed concern over the poor turnout for elections of neighborhood chairpersons. As described by one neighborhood planner: "An effort has been made to advertise that there will be an election, but not all the people vote. In fact very few do. That makes it hard to justify that the leadership is representative." City councilmen sometimes questioned neighborhood representatives on the number of persons who attended meetings at which elections were held and specific positions were adopted, and often the answers to these questions were used to discredit the positions of the neighborhood leaders.

One other problem with the representativeness of local groups surfaced in Cincinnati. There respondents charged that some neighborhood group leaders were more concerned with issues as defined by the national neighborhood movement than with issues of concern to the local neighborhood. As a citizen representative explains: "In some neighborhoods there are professional neighborhood spokesmen. These people are not representative. They relate to the national neighborhood movement; not their local neighborhoods. I am worried about parochialism and a neighborhood stance for the neighborhood movement's sake." The lack of turnout for the elections of neighborhood representatives was also a concern of a number of respondents in Cincinnati.

Poor Communication

Slightly over 10 percent of the survey respondents mentioned poor communication between citizen groups and city officials as a problem. The main complaints were that the activities of city departments and city councils were not being communicated to neighborhood organizations, and neighborhood leaders were having a difficult time gaining access to city officials.

Poor communication was also mentioned as a problem by respondents in all of the case study cities. They often talked of the need to know more about what was going on in city hall. As expressed by a citizen representative in Wilmington: "As far as the assemblies are concerned, the city council has to be aware that it is a two-way communication. They have to give information to the local assemblies not just get information from them. They need to give explanations." In St. Paul a citizen representative commented: "There is a real bad communication problem between the community councils and the city council. Not enough information is exchanged, and I often have trouble being able to talk to councilmen."

Respondents also commented on poor communication between city departments and between the community council and the citizens. According to one citizen representative in St. Paul: "The basic problem we have had is dealing with the bureaucracy—in terms of it not being together. The right hand does not know what the left hand is doing." This lack of communication between agencies led to unnecessary conflict and misunderstanding. A second representative from St. Paul commented on the lack of communication between the community councils and the citizens. "We need more money for communication: for getting the information out to the people through newspapers, radio, and television. We don't do it very well now."

A lack of feedback on proposals sent to the city council was the major complaint heard from citizen representatives in Atlanta and Wilmington. No one was informing them of the status of projects or their progress through the city bureaucracy. Moreover, when a proposal was altered or rejected, the rationale was not explained to the local groups. Respondents in Atlanta, Wilmington, Raleigh, and Houston also felt that the city was not doing a good job in bringing the program to the attention of the public. One citizen representative in Atlanta, for example, commented: "There is a communication problem with the neighborhood planning units. There was a long time before I found out about them. I was on the school board and so I should have heard of it. But, the program was not publicized." Similarly, in Houston citizen representatives talked of not knowing what services were available through the program. Overall, the program had not been adequately publicized, and many people were still unaware of its existence or of the specific opportunities and services offered.

Unclear Program Goals and Procedures

Slightly more than 8 percent of the survey respondents mentioned unclear program goals or procedures as a problem. In the case studies, however, this was one of the most frequently mentioned problems in all cities except Houston. Unclear program goals seemed to be a particularly salient problem in Cincinnati. There virtually everyone interviewed felt that program goals were either not clearly defined or poorly understood. As one neighborhood planner commented: "Some Community Assistance Team members are not sure what they're supposed to be doing. There is a lack of direction in the program. It's never been given a clear charge or mandate." This lack of clarity caused misunderstandings between the citizens and the planners and unnecessary confusion.

Respondents in St. Paul, Wilmington, Atlanta, and Houston pointed to problems caused by unclear definitions of the roles of each of the groups involved in the program. The planning director in Wilmington, for example, observed: "There is no clear roles of the three groups: city administration, council, and citizens. Department heads talk about 'getting the Community Development Councils money' and the Community Development Council talks about 'our money'. They should know better. The roles get blurred." A citizen representative in Atlanta felt that the program would be more effective if roles were clarified.

The role that seemed least well defined was that of the planner. Everyone's perception of the planner's role was said to be different, and there was no formal definition for the planners to go by. As one planner in St. Paul commented: "Other city departments have a different view of what my role should be, and they are disappointed when they don't see that. They expect me to be representing the cities' position to the neighborhoods and explaining why it is right." The community groups, on the other hand, expect planners to advocate for their positions. Many planners talked about the difficulty of balancing these two demands.

Conflict also centered around the particular roles adopted by planners. The two that caused the most controversy were planners acting as advocates and as community organizers. In Raleigh and St. Paul respondents reported conflict between planners and city officials over the advocate role. Raleigh's planning director was adamantly against advocacy planning. He confided that he purposefully understaffed the neighborhood program so planners would not be identified with one area. Planners were forced to work with many groups, and this he felt would protect against advocacy planning. A comment by Wilmington's planning director exemplifies his department's attitude toward planners adopting an organizer role: "The role of the planners has been ill-defined. There was brouhaha over their organizing activities. Organizational action is outside the bounds of appropriate activity for city employees. There is a fine line between information sharing and organizing which they shouldn't step over." The programs that did encourage planners to engage in organizing activities emphasized the use of non-confrontational, opportunity-based approaches to organizing.

Respondents in Wilmington, Atlanta, and Cincinnati identified the lack of procedures for program operation as a major cause of the lack of program direction and clarity. The planning director in Wilmington, for example, observed: "We got into the program on the basis of a council resolution two paragraphs long. That is the extent of our mutual understanding." In particular, guidelines for assuring representation and maintaining communication were lacking. An Atlanta citizen representative, for example, commented: "Bylaws must be improved—specified and clarified. They must be uniform and have clear guidelines on representation. Council had a set of guidelines but they were not introduced because of the mixed response from the neighborhoods. I didn't like that process either because the guidelines should have come from the neighborhood groups, not from council. But we need more specific guidelines for operation." Respondents in Cincinnati and Wilmington also felt that the lack of more specific guidelines weakened the operation of the program and that more clear procedures should be developed.

Interneighborhood Conflicts

Slightly over 8 percent of the survey respondents identified conflict between neighborhood groups as a problem. Similarly, neighborhood group conflict was mentioned by a small number of survey respondents in St. Paul, Raleigh, and Atlanta. In St. Paul several neighborhood groups were involved in boundary disputes, each claiming to represent the same area. In Atlanta one neighborhood group wanted to expand its boundaries to include what was originally part of another neighborhood organization. They claimed that the area was functionally connected to their area. This generated a heated battle between the two groups. Finally, in both Raleigh and St. Paul there was mention of officially designated neighborhood councils being in conflict with indigenous neighborhood organizations. In one Raleigh neighborhood, an independently organized group criticized the city-initiated group for being ineffectual and competed with the latter for membership. In St. Paul the conflict centered on the development of multifamily housing in the neighborhood. The city-recognized district council was planning for multifamily development and the independent group was against any multifamily housing. It is interesting to note that there was little mention of neighborhood groups within a program competing for limited resources. Apparently, this is not a major problem.

Conclusion

In previous chapters the accomplishments of neighborhood planning programs and the factors contributing to these accomplishments were reviewed. The intent of this chapter was to complete the picture by presenting the major problems limiting the effectiveness of neighborhood programs.

The most frequently cited problem was inadequate project implementation. Many local improvement projects were pro-

posed, but relatively few were carried out. Respondents cited
the slowness of the planning process, the lack of a direct link to
the municipal budgeting process, and a general lack of funds
for improvement projects as reasons for the lack of implementation. In fact, many programs do not provide any special
funds for improvement projects and do not give neighborhood
groups any special access to the budgeting process.

Low rates of participation were another frequently cited
problem. In many cities attempts to organize neighborhood
groups in some parts of the city were unsuccessful. Thus those
areas went unrepresented. Even where groups were present,
attendance at monthly meetings was often poor. In many instances residents were willing to turn out only when the area
faced an immediate "threat" (for example, a major road widen-
ing or development proposal). Poor publicity about the overall
program was also blamed for low rates of participation.

A number of planning directors and neighborhood planners
also mentioned a lack of citizen competence. Given the limitations of municipal government, they said, citizens made unrealistic demands. Planners also felt that many citizens clung
to parochial perspectives. The adequacy of local leadership
was also questioned. Many neighborhood leaders, they believed, relied too heavily on staff assistance and had not become acquainted with the plans, policies, and procedures of
the city.

Planners and citizens also cited lack of support for the program as a problem in many programs. City departments, city
council members, and city managers were seen as particularly
unsupportive. The most common explanation provided for this
lack of support was that those individuals or groups were
threatened by a perceived loss of power.

A number of staffing problems were cited. In particular
many respondents felt that there were too few planners for
the number of groups involved in programs and that this led to
excessive work loads and "burnout." In some cities neighborhood planning is an entry-level position. This lack of experience limits the assistance they can provide. Finally, in cities
where planners have a dual responsibility, including neighborhood planning as well as other projects, sufficient attention is not paid to the concerns and needs of neighborhood
organizations.

Another problem mentioned was inadequate representation. In some cases local neighborhood organizations were dominated by one faction of the community, in others developers had "taken control" of the organization, and in still others one particular ethnic or racial group dominated. Such situations, however, were more the exception than the rule. In cities that allowed great flexibility in how local organizations operate, some organizations had bylaws that, respondents charged, discouraged community participation once leaders were chosen.

Poor communication was also a problem. Neighborhood leaders felt that they were not being adequately informed of the activities of city departments and the city council. They wanted earlier notification of proposed projects and policies. Neighborhood leaders also complained of not knowing the status of projects submitted by them for approval and of not getting a clear explanation when a project was denied. Finally, many felt that the larger community was not well informed of the existence of the program or the activities of local groups.

The problem of unclear goals and responsibilities plagued some programs. According to those surveyed, the lack of clearly defined responsibilities for neighborhood planners and community representatives led to confusion and misunderstanding among program participants. The role of the planner in the program was particularly contentious. Participants differed in their opinions of the appropriateness of organizing and advocacy activities. Some also complained about the lack of guidelines for assuring representation and maintaining communication.

Finally, interneighborhood conflict was mentioned as a problem. Some of the case study cities had experienced boundary disputes between groups, and there were also conflicts between officially designated groups and other groups vying for membership in the same neighborhood.

The problems identified above represent limits or obstacles to reaching the full potential of neighborhood planning programs. Many of these problems can be avoided, however, through careful planning and an adequate commitment of resources. Improved cooperation and communication will also be important in addressing these problems. Specific recommendations for avoiding or solving the problems discussed above are presented in the following chapter.

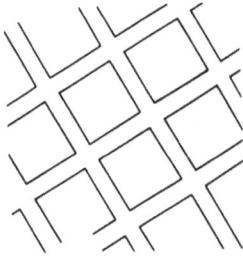

8 Conclusion

Evaluation of the Propositions

Having reviewed the characteristics, major accomplishments, factors associated with accomplishments, and major problems with neighborhood planning programs, we are now in the position to evaluate the eight propositions put forth at the end of chapter 3. What do these data indicate about the validity of the various claims made for neighborhood planning?

Proposition 1 states that neighborhood planning programs are more responsive to local characteristics, desires, and problems. The available evidence provides considerable support for this proposition. As we discussed in chapter 4, all of the neighborhood planning programs surveyed involved local neighborhood groups in identifying local problems, and an overwhelming majority also involved those groups in reviewing plans developed by city agencies and in developing their own local plans. These activities would seem to provide an opportunity for local residents to express their own, possibly unique, perspectives on the development of their neighborhoods. In particular, the development of a neighborhood plan by the local organization provides the opportunity for residents to discuss the future of the area, reach some consensus, and communicate this to city officials, developers, and other interested parties. As reported in chapter 4, 78 percent of the programs surveyed had a direct link between the neighborhood and comprehensive planning programs. That is, information generated by the neighborhood planning program was used in developing or revising the local comprehensive plan. Probably the strongest example of this connection among our case study cities was found in St. Paul. There the neighborhood plans are officially sanctioned by the planning commission and the city council and become an official part of the city's comprehensive plan. This is particularly significant, since local zoning ordinances are typically based on the comprehensive plan.

So far, however, we have only shown that the opportunity for local groups to influence planning decisions exists. What evidence is there that these groups actually had an effect? As we discussed in chapter 5, 60 percent of the survey respondents reported that their neighborhood planning programs were fairly to very effective in influencing city officials. Moreover, in the case studies, citizens also felt that they had had a substantial impact on local decisions. The evidence suggests that in many instances citizens were able to change decisions to benefit the expressed interests of the local neighborhoods. Even more convincing is the number of specific instances of citizen groups influencing decisions cited by case study respondents. These include decisions to allow or not allow specific development projects in the area, as well as decisions involving the expenditure of municipal funds. Also in chapter 5 we described numerous self-help projects undertaken by groups working with these programs, including neighborhood crime prevention programs, clean-up and beautification programs, and the like. Many groups also sponsored social activities, such as street fairs. These activities are conducive to the expression of local values and preferences.

Proposition 2 states that neighborhood planning programs will increase the number of citizens participating in municipal planning. The evidence suggests that some increase does occur, but the percentage of persons participating is still extremely low. We saw that 25 percent of the survey respondents offered increased participation as a response to our open-ended question on program accomplishments. Moreover, in response to a question in our case study interviews on attendance at monthly meetings, citizen representatives typically cited attendance figures between fifteen and forty. Multiplied by twenty to forty individual neighborhoods, these numbers indicate that between three hundred and sixteen hundred residents participate on a monthly basis. This is considerably higher than the turnout for a typical planning commission meeting or public hearing designed to elicit citizen participa-

tion, unless a particularly controversial project is being discussed. To a large extent, this increase in the number of persons participating on a regular basis appears to be a function
of a larger number of positions created by forming neighborhood groups. Each group typically has a chairperson, vice-
chairperson, secretary, and treasurer. Many groups also form
ongoing committees—such as transportation, land use, and
recreation—each with its own chairperson and appointees.
Holding these positions appears to maintain interest and a
continuing commitment to the local group.

In chapter 7, however, we saw that lack of participation was
a frequently mentioned problem by both survey and case study
respondents. The rate of continuous participation within typical neighborhoods was well under 1 percent. Case study respondents attributed this to citizen apathy, inadequate organization, "burnout," and poor publicity. Although participation
rates could undoubtedly be improved by assuring an open organizational framework (for example, something on the New
England town meeting model), citizen apathy and burnout are
more difficult to address. Being realistic, it seems very unlikely that with the best of efforts regular participation rates
could be increased much above 5 percent. The month-to-month
issues do not seem salient enough to draw people away from
other leisure activities. As long as somebody is willing to keep
the group running, most citizens seem willing to delegate responsibility to group leaders, just as in our electoral system
individuals are content to vote for representatives who then
take care of day-to-day matters. Other than voting, the overwhelming majority have had little or no experience in political
activities.

The evidence shows, however, that attendance at meetings
increased substantially when elections were being held and
when "hot" issues were being discussed. This suggests that
citizens do tend to see these organizations as representative in
an electoral sense and that the group provides a mechanism
for community mobilization to address issues of particular importance. The neighborhood group and the mechanisms for
communicating with city officials are there when issues of
more immediate concern develop. Nonetheless, the low regular participation rate does raise questions about the representativeness of local groups. This will be discussed further
below.

Beyond the numbers of persons participating, the quality of participation must also be considered. A major difference between neighborhood planning programs and most other methods of citizen participation is that many participants in neighborhood planning programs are involved on a continuing basis. They become knowledgeable about planning issues and the operation of local government. Consequently, local public officials are more open to their suggestions, and they are better able to influence decisions. This point was stressed by respondents in the case studies and was evident from our conversations with citizen representatives. The learning that comes with participation is cumulative, so that the effectiveness of the participation increases over time.

A second qualitative difference between participation in neighborhood planning programs and participation in most other forms of citizen involvement programs is that it is more likely to be active rather than reactive. Our results indicate that citizens are taking the initiative to propose projects rather than simply oppose them, although neighborhood planners would like to see citizen groups do even more of this. This is substantially different from the role citizens play in traditional forms of citizen participation.

Proposition 3 states that neighborhood planning programs would result in a planning process that is more project than policy oriented, resulting in more local physical improvements and an increase in the political constituency for planning. Although we do not have hard evidence of an actual increase in the number of local projects resulting from these programs or in the total expenditures for them, the available evidence suggests that this proposition is substantiated at least in the more active programs. Improved local physical conditions was mentioned by 27 percent of the survey respondents in the open-ended question on accomplishments. Moreover, in a closed-ended question, upwards of 88 percent of the respondents felt that the program had improved local housing, local streets, curbs and sidewalks, and local recreation facilities. Also the list of projects initiated by neighborhood groups working with these programs, reviewed in chapter 5, is convincing evidence. There are innumerable examples in the more active neighborhood planning programs of citizens initiating proposals and receiving public funding. In fact in St. Paul some planners were worried that too much of the municipal budget was being

spent on neighborhood projects and not enough on city-wide
projects, such as repairing sewer systems and the like.

Four out of the six case study programs had specific mechanisms for citizen groups to submit budget requests to the council, although there was considerable variation in the number of projects funded in each city. In St. Paul records indicate that over a one-year period approximately 80 percent of the budget requests made by local groups were funded. Programs that did not have a direct link to the budgeting process, the Houston program, for example, tended to have less success in initiating local projects. These programs relied mostly on self-help projects or on projects funded by private sources. Consequently, fewer projects were initiated. Overall, though, neighborhood planning programs have led to a more project-oriented planning process and numerous neighborhood improvements.

In addition, the results of our study provide some evidence that neighborhood planning programs have led to an increase in the political constituencies for specific plans, but little evidence that persons then generalize that interest in specific issues to a general support of local planning. Once local plans are developed, residents are concerned with seeing that the plans are implemented or adhered to. The methods that citizens use to influence the decisions of city officials include speaking at meetings, lobbying, use of the media, and organized protest. This amounts to a constituency for specific plans; citizens are actively supporting plans rather than just fighting them. As reported in chapter 5, 87 percent of the respondents stated that their neighborhood planning program had either greatly or moderately decreased resistance to the implementation of planning projects. This was most likely the result of early negotiations between planning staffs and citizen groups through the program. Planners often sought out comments from residents and used them in the development of plans. This is not to say, however, that many of the citizen representatives were not still highly critical of the planning department and their activities. A number of citizen representatives criticized their planning departments for proposing what were seen as ill-conceived projects and for not acting fast enough. In these cases a constituency supporting local planning did not emerge.

Proposition 4 states that neighborhood planning programs will result in the addressing of a wider range of problems by the planning process and an improvement in public services.

There is some evidence supporting this proposition; the paramount concern, however, was with physical development. For example, only 8 percent of the respondents freely mentioned improved services as a program accomplishment, compared to 27 percent who freely mentioned improved physical conditions. Moreover, human services was the only service mentioned by a majority of those surveyed in response to a direct question on the services improved as a result of the program. Twenty-seven percent reported no improvements in services attributable to the program. In several cities there were also complaints from citizen representatives that the school board was not involved in the program; thus, they had no direct way of addressing problems with the local educational system.

Nonetheless, some programs did seem to have an influence on service delivery. These were usually the programs that specifically emphasized the evaluation of local services. In Dayton, Ohio, for example, middle-level management from city departments meet regularly with neighborhood residents. Furthermore, a number of citizen respondents in the case studies specifically mentioned the ability to address any neighborhood issue as a contributing factor in the accomplishments of the programs. The relative lack of influence on local service delivery as perceived by respondents may simply indicate that residents are largely satisfied with the way services are currently being provided and would rather concentrate their efforts on physical development.

Proposition 5 states that there will be an increase in social interaction and a stronger sense of community in local areas. Unfortunately, our ability to draw strong conclusions on this issue is limited by the nature of our data. A resident survey would be necessary to test this proposition adequately. Our data do, however, provide some preliminary indication of how neighborhood planning influences local sense of community. Chapter 5 discussed the evidence that many of these programs have led to the development of new community organizations and have strengthened existing organizations. This can be expected to lead to some increase in social interaction and sense of community as neighborhood residents come together on a regular basis. Citizen representatives in at least one case study city felt that this had led to a greater sense of community solidarity and cohesiveness.

The low participation rates at local group meetings, how-

ever, indicate that local social interaction is increased only for
a small percentage of neighborhood residents. There is little reason to believe that the sheer existence of a group would affect the social interaction of those who do not participate in group activities. Yet through their sponsorship of street fairs, bake sales, and other community activities neighborhood groups may have some influence on local social interaction. This type of activity, however, was confined to the more active community groups. The average group did not go much beyond holding monthly meetings. The potential for increasing the local sense of community exists; yet in most instances this was not realized. It also did not seem to be a major goal of the majority of neighborhood groups participating in these programs.

Community newspapers sponsored by neighborhood groups might also be expected to increase the sense of community among local residents. Information about local events and concerns would seem to increase individual sense of belonging to an area. There is no direct evidence to support this contention, however. In addition, very few of the neighborhood groups published local newspapers. Only in St. Paul were community newspapers prevalent. In general, then, it appears there is potential for increasing local sense of community and social interaction, but because of low participation rates and a limited range of activities, this potential has not been realized.

Proposition 6 states that neighborhood planning programs will facilitate the integration of participants into the larger society and increase the vertical ties between the neighborhoods and the larger community. There is evidence that programs do in fact integrate participants into the larger society, but only for the select few in leadership positions. In chapter 4, 25 percent of the programs were reported to have two-tiered organizational structures and another 6 percent have three-tiered structures. As shown in chapter 7, tiered organizational structures facilitated the integration of neighborhood leaders into the larger political realm. In addition, the roles of group leaders take them into frequent contact with local public officials, and personal relationships often develop.

In the sense that the neighborhood leader is better integrated into the local political establishment then, the local area is better integrated into the larger community. Issues raised at local meetings or by local residents can be communicated directly to public officials. The increased integration of neighborhood leaders is also evident in the tendency for neighborhood leaders to move into mainstream politics. In three of the case study cities neighborhood leaders have gone on to become members of the city council or mayors. Thus, neighborhood planning programs provide an alternative mechanism for accessing the municipal political system. According to our findings, they provide interested local residents with opportunities to gain leadership training, knowledge of local issues, and political connections, all of which are necessary for running a successful campaign for city council or mayor.

There is little evidence, however, that these programs aid in integrating new residents or others not directly involved with the program into the community. None of the programs in our study provides services that were specifically oriented toward integrating newcomers into the local neighborhood or the larger community. For example, there was no mention of educational programs such as those sponsored by settlement houses. Possibly because they focus on the physical dimensions of city planning rather than on social services, they seem to ignore this social function.

Proposition 7 states that neighborhood planning programs will increase citizen trust in local government. The evidence on this proposition is mixed. Although a majority of respondents felt that the programs have improved citizen-government relations and trust in public officials, a substantial minority felt that the programs had not helped or had worsened relations. Those that felt that their program had improved relations emphasized the importance of better information dissemination and communication between citizens and public officials. Municipal agency heads or their representatives and elected officials often attended local meetings, and this was seen as instrumental to improved relations.

The proportion of local proposals or recommendations that were accepted by the local government also appeared to influence citizens' feelings of trust in government. Citizen representatives who were effective in their attempts to influence local officials tended to say relations had improved. Those who were not felt the program had not led to improved citizen-government relations.

Those who felt that their program had not led to improved citizen-government relations often cited breakdowns in the process of approving local projects or the lack of a true commitment to the program on the part of public officials. Agency heads, for example, were only selectively notifying local groups of projects that might affect their area, or local groups were not being notified early enough to develop effective arguments. This created some ill-will among residents. Some programs also raised expectations without providing funding to follow through. Citizens were asked to develop projects, but funds for those projects were not forthcoming. In these situations the programs tended to worsen citizen trust in local government, rather than improve it. Thus, the degree to which a program improves citizen trust in government appears to be a function of how well the program operates and the degree of commitment on the part of local officials.

Proposition 8 states that neighborhood planning programs would result in a more equal distribution of public goods. As reported in chapter 5 the majority of case study respondents were found to feel that the program had achieved a more equal distribution of public goods. In supporting these conclusions they often cited improvements in the poorer areas of the city that were attributable to the programs. It is unclear, however, whether the poorer areas actually received a higher proportion of public funds or whether there was simply an across-the-board increase in expenditures for neighborhood projects. The relative proportion of expenditures in the poorer areas may not actually have increased. In fact, evidence from both survey and case studies indicates that it was the middle-income neighborhoods that were most active in the programs. Thus, assuming that the amount of activity is directly related to the benefits received, the middle-income neighborhoods would benefit the most. Furthermore, where significant improvements were made in low-income areas, they tended to be funded through the Community Development Block Grant Program. The majority of these funds must be spent in low-income areas. If these monies had not been available, it is unlikely that local funds would have been committed. Thus, the programs can not be fully credited with these improvements.

In conclusion, although neighborhood planning programs provide an opportunity for poorer areas to influence local public expenditures, their lack of participation and inadequate representation within the mainstream governing structure have limited their achievements in this area. Poorer areas are competing with middle-class areas, which tend to be better organized and better connected to the political leadership. Furthermore, middle-class areas typically have higher voter turnout rates, which are likely to influence political decisions in their favor. Thus, it seems unlikely that neighborhood planning programs by themselves can do much to alter the distribution of public goods. More fundamental changes in attitudes and in the political system are necessary to accomplish this goal.

To summarize, neighborhood planning programs do appear to live up to many of our expectations. They do seem to result in a planning process which is more responsive to local values and preferences, more local improvements, a modest increase in participation, and an increase in the political constituency for specific plans. In addition, there appears to be some improvement in service delivery—particularly in human services, public safety, and public transportation—but most programs remained focused on physical development.

Other expectations, however, were unfulfilled. In particular, the expectations concerning enhanced social cohesion and sense of community were not borne out. Except for those leaders who were most active, neighborhood planning programs did not significantly increase local social interaction or integrate citizens into the larger community. Furthermore, there was little evidence that these programs led to a more equal distribution of public goods. Monies spent in lower-income areas were primarily those provided by the CDBG program and would have probably been spent there regardless of the local neighborhood planning program. In addition, middle-income areas were more likely to participate in these programs. Finally, the evidence on the influence of these programs on citizen-government relations was mixed. If the program ran smoothly and had the support of local public officials, relations generally improved; otherwise, relations were impaired.

Contemporary Programs in the Light of Past Programs

In chapter 2 we presented three historical approaches to neighborhood planning and suggested that each emphasized a different dimension of the neighborhood concept. The settlement house approach emphasized the social neighborhood; the neighborhood unit approach emphasized the physical neighborhood (and to some extent the social); and the community action approach emphasized the political neighborhood. Being

most directly influenced by the community action approach,
contemporary neighborhood planning primarily emphasizes the neighborhood as a political entity. As we have seen, these programs seek to develop an active political organization in each neighborhood within the city, so as to involve residents in local decision making. These programs are different from the community action approach, however, in that they seek to involve the entire city, not just specific subareas. This would help account for the strong political support among citizens for these programs. They are generally seen not as programs for special subgroups (for example, for poor blacks) but as programs that can involve and benefit all.

Another unique feature of contemporary neighborhood planning programs is the emphasis on improving communication between government officials and citizens throughout the municipality. Whereas earlier programs focused mainly on managing new growth or increasing opportunities for the disadvantaged, contemporary programs focus on facilitating communication and citizen involvement. In this sense the emphasis of contemporary programs is broader. A larger number of issues and concerns may be addressed.

Furthermore, contemporary neighborhood planning programs are sponsored by local governments, not by the federal government or by philanthropists as were earlier programs. This is not to say that federal funds and federal regulations have not influenced the initiation and operation of contemporary programs; as we have seen, they have. But these programs are designed and operated at the local level, and this appears to have a number of benefits, including flexibility and strong citizen support.

The physical dimensions of the neighborhood, however, are also emphasized in contemporary programs. Considerable effort is focused on defining neighborhood areas, and physical features play an important role in deciding neighborhood boundaries. Moreover, the major concern of groups involved with these programs is improving the physical aspects of their areas, rather than improving public services or social conditions. Yet, there is a major difference between contemporary programs and the neighborhood unit approach. Contemporary programs do not try to impose an ideal conception of neighborhood design on local areas as proponents of the neighborhood unit approach did. Rather they allow local citizens' groups to develop their own conceptions of what the physical neighborhood should be and then help them in trying to realize those conceptions.

The one dimension of the neighborhood concept that has received little direct attention in contemporary programs is the social neighborhood. Unfortunately, most programs are oriented toward the physical improvement of areas and place little emphasis on such problems as poverty, poor education, drug abuse, and the like. This lack of emphasis on the social neighborhood may be the result of the commonly held feeling that local social problems are being addressed by social welfare agencies. Undertaking social programs may also entail more responsibility than most community groups are willing to accept. Typically, these programs do not emphasize the development of a socially cohesive neighborhood characterized by frequent informal contacts and strong social control.

This is not to say, however, that contemporary neighborhood planning programs have no influence on the social neighborhood. Although the development of a social neighborhood is not stressed, it is undoubtedly strengthened by the development of a local organization. Previous research has shown that there is an association between participation in local voluntary organizations and the number of friends one has in the local area (Bell and Boat, 1957; Hunter, 1975; Wright and Hyman, 1958). In addition we have seen that some neighborhood groups sponsor local social events that bring the community together and, at a minimum, promote familiarity with neighbors. Much more could be done along these lines, however. Ahlbrandt and Cunningham (1979) have emphasized the importance of a strong social neighborhood for neighborhood viability and stability. Contemporary programs seem to have underemphasized this important aspect of neighborhoods.

It is unlikely that contemporary neighborhood planning programs will be the ultimate solution to urban problems. These programs will undoubtedly change in the future as conditions change and creative new ideas emerge. Based on recent trends, citizens are likely to play a larger role in future programs, taking on even greater responsibility for defining goals and objectives and for the actual operation of programs. In the future cities are likely to do more subcontracting with neighborhood organizations for the provision of certain services. Citizens will also be involved in more self-help activities as cutbacks in municipal responsibilities occur. This should help to strengthen

neighborhoods and give them a larger role to play in municipal affairs. The contemporary experience with neighborhood
planning should help prepare groups to take on these new
responsibilities.

Two Important Problems

Before we present our recommendations for establishing and
improving neighborhood planning programs, we should take
note of two of the most pressing problems generally encountered by neighborhood planning programs. The first is the lack
of funding for the operation of the program and for implementing projects developed within the program. If programs are
successfully to involve neighborhood groups in improvement
activities, technical assistance is a necessity. After all, most
citizens have had little experience with planning and improvement activities. Neighborhood planners are needed to help in
developing neighborhood plans, organizing communities, and
designing and developing improvement projects. This is particularly important during the initial years of the operation of
a program. This means that a sufficient number of neighborhood planners must be hired to provide such assistance. Our
interviews with neighborhood planners lead us to suggest that
a neighborhood planner should be responsible for no more than
five neighborhoods. Beyond this number, tension develops as
citizens' groups and planners alike become frustrated with the
level of assistance provided. Adequate secretarial support is
also important. Many of the neighborhood planners had to do
considerable amounts of clerical work—such as updating mailing lists and transcribing meeting minutes—which reduced
the amount of contact time with community groups and their
representatives. If neighborhood groups are to develop a capacity effectively to address local problems, the adequate
funding of technical assistance is crucial.

The efficiency of providing certain types of technical assistance can be improved by holding workshops for neighborhood
leaders on topics of common interest. This avoids duplication
of effort on the part of the planners. The neighborhood planning program in Houston, for example, successfully used this
approach. Topics of common interest might include organizational capacity building, the organization and operation of local

government, community organizing, fundraising, developing neighborhood plans, financial management, leadership skills, and others.

Beyond funding for the operations of the program, however, some funds must be made available for implementing projects developed by community groups. This provides an incentive for participation and assures that the program will have a positive influence on local physical conditions, thus providing readily observable examples of success. Money for neighborhood projects can be provided in several ways. The first is to provide neighborhood groups opportunities to participate in the municipal budgeting process. Many of the programs studied had written procedures for including neighborhood groups in the capital improvements budgeting process, but this input was often confined to the CDBG budget, organized so that projects were eliminated by department heads before the final budget, or so loose that project proposals were lost in the process.

One way to solve this problem would be to set aside a share of the capital improvements budget, say 1 to 5 percent, for neighborhood projects. A budget committee or the council could then choose among the projects submitted by neighborhood groups. This would assure that neighborhood projects were not ignored in favor of the more traditional and routine capital expenditures. This would also assure that some number of neighborhood projects were funded and thus provide an incentive for neighborhood groups to develop improvement projects.

A second method of providing project funds would be to provide each group with a small mini-grant that could be used, within general guidelines, for a range of activities, including hiring a part-time or full-time worker, as is done in St. Paul, or funding specific neighborhood projects, as is done in Cincinnati. These funds could be used as "seed money" to demonstrate the effectiveness of a program and secure funding from foundations or other sources for a larger-scale project. Moreover, these mini-grants would act as strong incentives for persons to participate. The experience of the Cincinnati program demonstrates that offering grants to local areas is a very effective way of organizing neighborhoods. It provides participants with certain minimum assurances that their effort will make a

difference and that the local government is seriously committed to the program. These grants also help to develop the
organizational capacity of local groups by providing them with
the opportunity to develop a capacity for fiscal management.

During these times of municipal fiscal crisis, however, the
sources for these funds may be difficult to locate. CDBG monies
could be used to at least partially fund the operation of these
programs. Neighborhood planning programs satisfy the citizen participation requirements of the CDBG program; thus at
least some administrative costs could be charged to them. But
this is not enough. Funding must also be available for small
grants and the support of neighborhood initiated projects. In
this foundations could help. The Mott Foundation, Ford Foundation, and others have shown considerable willingness to
fund neighborhood development projects. The Mott Foundation's support of the Cincinnati program is one example of the
type of funds available. It is doubtful, however, that the CDBG
program and contributions from private foundations can cover
the full expenses of these programs. The sponsoring cities
must be willing to contribute some money from their own
revenues.

These programs need not be expensive, however, particularly if the sources of funds discussed above are used partially
to subsidize them. Moreover, we have seen there are substantial benefits to having a set of active neighborhood organizations engaged in self-help and other neighborhood preservation activities. These programs help in maintaining the
stability and viability of neighborhoods, which in turn should
help to maintain the tax base and reduce the cost of public services. Overall, then, neighborhood planning programs appear
to be a wise investment.

Another possible source of funding is the neighborhood organizations themselves. They could solicit local businesses for
contributions and hold fundraising activities. These activities
could be further encouraged by linking them to matching
grant programs that are sensitive to the economic levels of the
neighborhoods. A formula could be established for determining the matching ratio that was based on the average family
income in an area. A low-income area, for example, might
receive five dollars for every dollar raised, while an upper-
middle-income area might receive one dollar for every dollar

raised. In-kind contributions, such as labor, might also be considered in such matching grant formulas. This type of program would help to stretch the public dollar.

The second major problem generally encountered by neighborhood planning programs is lack of participation, which is closely associated with the question of representativeness. If participation rates are low, how can public officials trust that the group is speaking for the majority of the residents or that proposed projects are acceptable to the overall community?

Based on our analysis of the case study programs, we can offer several suggestions for raising participation levels. First, the existence of the program needs to be made known to a larger proportion of the populace. Cities appear to do little to publicize their program. A city-wide publicity program utilizing a full range of media could be organized to let people know the purpose of the program and its operating procedures.

Second, participation increases as more persons are given specified roles or positions within the neighborhood organization. Certain programs, such as that in Raleigh, take advantage of this fact to improve participation, while others do not. Individuals could be appointed to special committees along substantive lines—such as transportation, housing, and the like—and to committees responsible for fundraising, publicity, recruiting, and other organizational maintenance tasks. This keeps people actively involved and has the added advantage of guarding against leader "burnout," as responsibilities are broadly delegated. Block captains could also be recruited for each block in the neighborhood. They would be responsible for encouraging others to participate, reporting local problems and concerns, and bringing information back to others on the block.

Third, a local newsletter or paper which keeps citizens informed of local issues and organization activities could also aid in maintaining and increasing participation. These newspapers could be used to generate interest in neighborhood issues and establish a greater sense of community, both of which contribute to increased participation. Many neighborhoods in St. Paul use this approach successfully.

Fourth, neighborhood groups could sponsor social events that bring neighborhood residents together. In addition to annual fairs, auctions, and the like, regular business meetings could be organized to leave time at the end for more informal

interaction. Community development activities should be fun.
That is the best way to assure adequate participation. This also means that neighborhood leaders should be encouraged to keep the business meetings moving and to limit their length. Nothing discourages participation more than meetings that run on late into the evening.

Even if these techniques were employed, however, in many instances, participation rates would not be high enough to assure adequate representation. Regulations that assure that membership is open to all, officers are duly elected, and meetings are open are also necessary. Having local district representatives can also help assure that all geographic and subcultural groups in the area are involved. Mechanisms must also be developed for handling complaints concerning nonrepresentativeness. In St. Paul, for example, the council has established guidelines that it uses to evaluate the representativeness of groups called into question. Beyond this, as long as groups have open organizational structures and mechanisms exist for addressing complaints, they must be given the benefit of the doubt. From the case studies it seems clear that the activities of these groups provided positively valued goods to the community at large, and in this sense can be said to "substantively represent" citizens in the area (Rich, 1980; Peterson, 1970).

Recommendations

The following recommendations for establishing and improving neighborhood planning programs were derived from the analyses of the accomplishments and problems of neighborhood programs and from other comments made by case study respondents. They are not meant to be rigid prescriptions, but reflect what seems to have worked, or not worked, in currently operating programs. Each city must work out a program that best suits local circumstances.

Recommendation 1: When initiating a program, involve citizen leaders, council members, mayor, city manager, and department heads in its formulation.

For a program to be most effective, the support of all these persons and groups is essential. In chapter 7 we saw that lack of support for the program was one of the most frequently mentioned problems. If any of these groups feels that it has been excluded or has not been given sufficient opportunity to help shape the program, it is likely to withhold support down the road. For example, in many instances, department heads have not been involved in formulating neighborhood programs and they are often the group which is the least cooperative. Some degree of resistance and conflict must expected while the program is being initiated. Department heads and city managers often do not like to have to involve citizens in what they see as professional matters. Thus, special attention should be focused on convincing them of the benefits of these programs and ensuring their cooperation. Once the program is established, willingness to cooperate with the program should be considered when selecting new department heads or a new city manager.

Recommendation 2: Establish a well-documented, detailed organizational structure that clearly specifies the powers and responsibilities of the various groups involved and the operating procedures to be followed. Where flexibility is desired, the range of acceptable options should be specified.

Many of the programs studied were founded on short council resolutions or other documents that lacked specificity. Perhaps those responsible for drafting the documents were trying to avoid conflict that would normally occur if more specific requirements and operational details were presented. In the long run, however, this lack of specificity generates confusion, misunderstanding, and mistrust. As discussed in chapter 7, many of the conflicts between neighborhood groups and the city administration can be traced back to differences in expectations concerning how the program would operate. Council members, for example, often expected neighborhood groups to be run on a New England town meeting style and were upset when groups adopted a style of management that used a board of directors. These misunderstandings can be avoided if more time is spent working out operational details and responsibilities during the formation of the program.

At the same time, flexibility in the system of representation and in the range of issues addressed by local organizations was found to be desirable. This allowed local groups to establish procedures that were suited to local desires and to address the full range of local problems. In order to assure that flexibility does not lead to problems, however, the range of acceptable options should be agreed upon or a set of criteria for evaluating other options should be established.

Recommendation 3: The process of defining neighborhoods should be a collaborative process between the local planning staff and community representatives.

Early in the process of initiating a neighborhood planning program neighborhood areas must be defined. The manner in which this is done can have implications for the eventual success of the program. As discussed in chapter 6, our research suggests that having clearly defined neighborhood areas helps to foster a sense of community and to avoid conflicts over turf. The neighborhood boundaries should not be imposed by planners, however; rather they should be determined through a collaborative process utilizing both objective data available to the planner and the subjective impressions of residents. Planners might initiate the process by drawing initial boundaries based on an analysis of socioeconomic characteristics, historical districts, and natural or man-made boundaries. This preliminary set of boundaries could then be discussed with neighborhood leaders and other interested citizens and changes made to accommodate their perceptions. The number of neighborhoods defined must be considered in light of the staff support available, the size of the city, and the extent to which neighborhoods have been previously identified.

As this is one of the first activities in initiating a program, it is important that citizens see that they are to play an active role. In several of the case study cities, citizens were not involved in defining the neighborhoods, and even years later this remained a source of stress. Once operative, programs should also have a formally established procedure for changing neighborhood boundaries.

Recommendation 4: The decision whether to establish new neighborhood groups or involve indigenous groups and whether to formally recognize groups should be based on the goals of the program.

If the program is concerned solely with fostering self-help efforts, working with existing groups is best and there is no need for formal recognition. This approach is exemplified in Houston's neighborhood planning program, as described in chapter 4. Indigenous groups are more likely to be self-sustaining and have a natural base of support in the community. If groups do not exist in key areas, however, staff members should become involved in creating them. As demonstrated in Cincinnati, incentives such as the offer of initial seed money can be an effective organizing tool.

If, however, the program is designed to involve neighborhood groups in an advisory capacity as spokes-organizations for their areas, working with existing groups can be problematic, and a system of formal recognition is necessary. This is the approach adopted by Cincinnati, St. Paul, Atlanta, Raleigh, and Wilmington. The major problems with involving existing groups in an advisory capacity are that they are probably not representative of the entire community and that their operating procedures may not encourage or allow widespread participation. These problems were discussed in chapter 7. To overcome them, two options are available. The first is to require indigenous groups to change their operating procedures to conform to the rules of the program. The rules should specify nondiscriminatory membership requirements and inclusionary policies to assure that all segments of the neighborhood are represented. These requirements for participation, however, are likely to cause some friction and resentment among indigenous groups. The second option is to establish new groups. The potential problem here is that a new group may be seen as competitive or be dubbed "a company shop." One way to minimize this problem is to invite leaders of indigenous organizations to play major roles in the new organizations. Even so, some friction must be expected in the formative stage of these programs regardless of the approach adopted.

Recommendation 5: Neighborhood planning programs should be formally sanctioned by a council resolution.

Our analysis indicates that a formal means of sanction is important in program performance. Sanction by a council resolution was found to be associated with greater citizen influence on the decisions of city officials. This type of formal sanction seems important in demonstrating commitment on the part of the government to the program. A city charter amendment has the advantage of being harder to rescind, typically requiring a popular vote, but is a slow and often difficult process. Sanction by executive order appears more risky, since the program may be seen by the city council as a threat to its power or as a way for the mayor to make political gains. City council amendments have the advantage of being relatively expeditious and of assuring, at least at the time of passage, that the programs have the support of local politicians.

Recommendation 6: In designing a neighborhood planning program, include a mechanism for communication between neighborhood leaders.

As discussed in chapter 6, the tiered system of program structure utilized in Raleigh, Wilmington, and Atlanta represents an important mechanism for neighborhood leaders to share experiences, discuss common problems, and develop positions on issues with implications for areas larger than individual neighborhoods. It also provides a forum for neighborhood groups to work out differences among themselves and an efficient mechanism for the dissemination of information to neighborhood leaders. There is also some evidence that participation in these city-wide organizations of neighborhood leaders helps to break down strictly parochial perspectives and engender more of a concern for city-wide issues and problems.

Recommendation 7: Local neighborhood groups should be involved in developing comprehensive neighborhood plans, reviewing plans prepared by city departments, and taking part in self-help activities.

There was some disagreement among case study respondents concerning the utility of developing comprehensive neighborhood plans. Some felt that the time and effort required to develop a comprehensive neighborhood plan could be better spent working on specific projects for neighborhood improvement. The majority of those involved in developing comprehensive neighborhood plans, however, did feel that the educational experience and the increased credibility they gained with the council were worth the effort. To guard against groups becoming bogged down in developing a plan and not moving on to specific projects, the job of developing the comprehensive plan should be delegated to a committee which can work on the plan while the group continues to address other issues. Our analysis also indicates that reviewing plans developed by city agencies is also an important activity. For citizens to be able to exert influence over the development of their neighborhoods, they must be aware of what the city agencies are planning and be able to work with them in developing acceptable projects. A specific process of notification should be established to ensure that neighborhood organizations are kept informed and involved at an early stage of the planning process.

Self-help projects are an equally important activity of neighborhood groups and one that should be encouraged and supported. Incentives can be used to entice groups to undertake self-help activities, such as requiring a certain level of self-help activity before other projects are funded. Neighborhood clean-up, community crime prevention activities, and many other self-help activities are inexpensive and can go a long way toward improving the quality of life in local neighborhoods.

Recommendation 8: Program support to local groups should include financial support and technical assistance.

As discussed above, small discretionary grants should be offered to participating neighborhood groups for the development of demonstration programs or for basic support services. As reported in chapter 6, financial assistance to neighborhood groups was positively associated with the measure of citizen influence on city officials. In addition, technical assistance should be available to help neighborhood groups organize, develop local plans, design specific improvement projects, write grant proposals, keep informed of new city plans and policies, and research and evaluate opportunities for improving their areas.

Recommendation 9: A mechanism for neighborhoods to submit proposals for inclusion in the annual capital budget should be a part of the program.

If neighborhood groups are to develop plans and projects for improving their areas, funds for implementing the more urgent projects should be provided through the municipal bud-

get. The most frequently mentioned problem in chapter 7 was
inadequate project implementation. Ideally, a certain propor- tion of the annual budget should be set aside for neighborhood group projects. This would ensure that at least some of the projects received funding. A special budget committee made up of neighborhood representatives, department personnel, and others with city-wide concerns could be responsible for recommending the most urgent projects to the council or mayor. This is similar to the way St. Paul screens budget re- quests from neighborhood organizations. It is important, how- ever, that neighborhood groups be informed of the status of their budget requests and be given a chance to explain their importance.

Recommendation 10: Establish direct lines of communication between department heads and citizen representatives, neighborhood planners and other departments, citizen representatives, and the council and mayor.

In both the survey and the case study interviews there were many complaints about poor communication or not being able to get in contact with "the right people." In certain programs requests from neighborhood groups for information and expla- nations had to be channeled through the neighborhood planner and the planning department. Neither the citizen representa- tive nor the neighborhood planner was supposed to contact other departments directly. This was seen as a cumbersome and slow method of communication. Also, neighborhood groups felt that they were not receiving important information from city departments and the city council in a timely fashion. To address such problems, some cities have instituted an "early notification process" to keep citizens informed of upcoming agenda items and other matters of potential concern to neigh- borhood groups. These are an important component of neigh- borhood planning programs.

Recommendation 11: The neighborhood and comprehensive planning programs should be coordinated.

Ideally, information on citizen desires gained while developing neighborhood plans and improvement projects should be used in the development or updating of the local comprehensive plan. The data reported in chapter 6 indicate that coordinating these two planning processes results in less citizen resistance to the implementation of planning projects. We can speculate that, after having been involved in their design, citizens find these projects more acceptable. In addition, neighborhood groups involved in the program should be allowed to comment on early drafts of the comprehensive plan.

There will, however, be times when comprehensive plans and neighborhood plans conflict, and a method for handling these conflicts must be built into the process. In St. Paul, for example, recommendations in neighborhood plans that conflict with the comprehensive plan are simply noted, with no attempt to resolve the conflict at that time. The conflict is addressed at the time that a specific project or proposal relating to that particular issue is presented. This avoids battles over aspects of the plan that may never be implemented.

An important issue related to coordinating the comprehensive and neighborhood planning programs concerns staffing. Should staff members be assigned to work with one program only or should they be involved in both? There are costs and benefits involved in each method.

Involving the same staff members in both programs has the advantage of providing each staff member with first-hand exposure to the concerns and perspectives of neighborhood residents. This should make them more sensitive to these concerns when developing the comprehensive plan. The problem with this staffing arrangement is that it does not recognize the particular strengths and weaknesses of the various staff members. Some may be particularly good in working with citizens, while others may not. Furthermore, unless sufficient staff is provided, splitting staff responsibilities may result in the staff members' giving insufficient attention to the neighborhood planning program, as they are likely to give priority to the comprehensive planning process.

The alternative, having staff assigned to one program or another, has the advantage of providing a fixed level of staff support to both programs and allows assignment based on the skill of individual staff members. The problem with this approach is that the programs are more likely to be seen as distinct entities, which may inhibit communication between staff members assigned to each program. If this staffing option is

employed, methods of information exchange should be built
into the program. These might include regularly scheduled
meetings between the staff members of each program or other
similar methods of fostering communication.

Recommendation 12: Staff the program adequately.

According to the data presented in chapter 7 many of the problems with neighborhood planning programs are the result of
overworked neighborhood planners. Based on our interviews
with neighborhood planners, individual planners should work
with no more than five neighborhood groups. Beyond this
number, staff members are unable to provide adequate assistance to individual groups. In addition, they need good clerical
support. In many cities planners spend large amounts of their
time on routine clerical work, such as updating mailing lists.

*Recommendation 13: Short training programs should be
designed for both new neighborhood planners and new
neighborhood leaders.*

Program operation could be substantially improved if new
planners and citizen representatives had short training programs to get them started. Much of the perceived lack of citizen competence discussed in chapter 7 could be avoided if
training were available. In most instances these people are
simply thrown into the water and expected to swim. A considerable amount of frustration could be avoided if basic strategies, requirements, and techniques could be presented to new
participants. Neighborhood planners need to learn how to
organize and sustain community groups, what resources are
available to neighborhood groups, the limits of their role, and
other important information. Community leaders need to learn
how to run a meeting, how to recruit new participants, how
the program operates, who to contact about certain problems,
and other important information. The effectiveness of programs should improve considerably if this sort of basic information were communicated at the beginning of one's involvement with the program.

*Recommendation 14: Legal council should be readily
available to neighborhood group leaders.*

For neighborhood groups to participate effectively in planning matters it is important that they have access to professional legal advice. They should be able to call city attorneys when they have legal questions.

Recommendation 15: A monitoring and evaluation process should be built into the program. Yearly evaluations should be done to assess accomplishments, detect problems, and suggest changes in the program's structure and operation.

Neighborhood planning programs should not be static, but change in response to changing conditions. As experience is gained with a program, ways to improve it will undoubtedly become evident. A procedure for making such changes involving the neighborhood groups themselves should be designed.

Conclusion

Many American cities are at a crossroads. One road leads to further deterioration, outmigration, and concentration of the poor. To travel this road a city needs simply to continue ignoring the problems of local residential areas and exclude citizens from participating in planning decisions that affect the quality of neighborhood life. This will ensure that residents with the means to do so will move to other locations, and the decline will continue.

The other road leads to stabilized and improved local neighborhoods that will hold existing residents and attract new ones. To travel this road a city must address the local problems experienced by residents on a day-to-day basis, which influence confidence, attachment, and commitment to an area and to the city as a whole. This is not to say that nonlocal, nonresidential problems should be ignored, but an effective planning strategy must include a mechanism for addressing the "smaller" problems of residential areas. A better balance is needed between the attention and resources focused on large-scale downtown development and that given to small-scale neighborhood development. The analysis presented here indicates that neighborhood planning programs offer a mechanism for striking this balance. They have been shown to result in a number of improvements in the physical and social conditions in local neighborhoods.

To travel this second road, citizens must also be involved in identifying problems and designing solutions. Our experience has demonstrated time and again that citizen involvement is a necessary ingredient of successful residential stabilization and revitalization projects. All the money and labor will go for naught if local residents are not involved in maintaining and protecting improvements once they are made. Citizen participation in the design and implementation of solutions raises the probability that their commitment will be strengthened and that residents will remain in their urban neighborhoods. With all the societal factors that work against this commitment, local governments should act to encourage it or, at the least, to accommodate its expression where it exists. Participation is an essential ingredient of commitment, and neighborhood planning programs are well suited for encouraging participation.

The results of this evaluation are encouraging enough to recommend that all medium-to-large-sized cities adopt a neighborhood planning program. They have the potential to solve many of the urban problems facing American cities and to help avoid future problems. To reach their full potential, however, they must receive support from both city officials and residents. Adequate funding and staffing are essential to successful programs and so is personal commitment from both city officials and residents. The potential benefits of these programs, however, seem well worth the support required.

Appendix A.
Questionnaire and
Interview Schedules

Mail Survey of Program Directors

1. Background Information

We would like to begin by asking you some background information about the neighborhood planning program in your city.

1. How large is your professional planning staff?
   _____ *number of staff positions*

2. How many staff positions are allocated to the neighborhood planning program? (Please total part-time positions, e.g., two half-time positions would equal one full-time position.)
   _____ *number of staff positions*

3. What is the approximate operating budget of your department?
   $_____

4. What is the approximate annual expenditure on your neighborhood planning program?
   $_____

5. Have funds been allocated for projects developed as a result of the neighborhood planning program? (*circle one*)
   1 No
   2 Yes
   If yes, was the source of these funds?
   1 local
   2 state
   3 federal
   4 other . . . (specify) _____

6. What year was the neighborhood planning program initiated?
   _____ *year*

7. Who provided the major impetus for starting the program? (*circle one or more*)
   1 Mayor
   2 Councilperson
   3 City manager
   4 Citizen groups
   5 Planning director
   6 Planning staff
   7 other . . . (specify) _____

8. Who were the major opponents of starting the program? (*circle one or more*)
   1 Mayor
   2 Councilperson
   3 City manager
   4 Citizen group
   5 Planning director
   6 Head of other city department (specify) _____
   7 other . . . (specify) _____

9. How was the program sanctioned? (*circle one*)
   1 City charter
   2 Executive order
   3 Ordinance or council resolution
   4 Agreement with planning department
   5 No official recognition
   6 other . . . (specify) _____

10. How were the neighborhoods defined? (*circle one or more*)
    1 Survey of community leaders
    2 Survey of citizens
    3 Analyses of socioeconomic data
    4 Use of preexisting political districts
    5 Physical boundaries
    6 other . . . (specify) _____

11. What is the range of number of people per neighborhood?
    _____

12. Are basic planning data available for neighborhoods? (*circle one*)
    1 Yes
    2 No

13. How are the neighborhood groups organized? (*circle one or more*)
    1 By planning department staff
    2 By involving existing community organization
    3 By community leaders
    4 other . . . (specify) _____

2. The Role of Neighborhood Planners and Neighborhood Groups

Next we would like to ask you about the roles of the neighborhood planners and neighborhood groups in the program.

1. What is/are the role(s) of the neighborhood planner in the program? (*circle one or more*)
   1 Liaison
   2 Advocate
   3 Technical assistant
   4 Educator
   5 Mediator
   6 Organizer
   7 other . . . (specify) _____

2. Do the neighborhood planners receive any special training for their job by your agency? (*circle one*)
    1 Yes
    2 No

3. What is/are the role(s) of the citizen groups in the neighborhood planning program? (*circle one or more*)
    1 Identifying local problems
    2 Reviewing and commenting on plans or other planning proposals
    3 Developing plans or proposals
    4 Monitoring program implementation
    5 Self-help
    6 other . . . (specify) _____

4. How do the neighborhood groups exert pressure on the mayor or council to gain support for their proposals or recommendations? (*circle one or more*)
    1 Speaking up at council meetings
    2 Using the media to publicize issues
    3 Voting as a block
    4 Through personal contacts with mayor or council
    5 Organized neighborhood protests
    6 other . . . (specify) _____

5. How are neighborhood representatives selected? (*circle one*)
    1 Elected by vote of entire neighborhood
    2 Appointed by the mayor or council
    3 Elected by members of neighborhood groups
    4 On a voluntary basis
    5 No official representative
    6 No set method
    7 other . . . (specify) _____

6. What type(s) of support are provided by the city to the neighborhood groups? (*circle one or more*)
    1 Financial
    2 Staff
    3 Materials
    4 Information or data
    5 other . . . (specify) _____

7. On each of the rating scales below how do you rate the involvement of the neighborhood groups with the following kinds of issues? (*circle the number that best corresponds to your response*)

    Land Use   1   2   3   4   5
                    not   greatly
                involved   involved
    Social
    Planning   1   2   3   4   5
                    not   greatly
                involved   involved
    Service
    Delivery   1   2   3   4   5
                    not   greatly
                involved   involved

3. Organization and Operation of the Neighborhood Planning Program

Finally, the last set of questions helps us to gain a more detailed understanding of the organization and operation of the neighborhood planning program.

1. Does the neighborhood planning process feed directly into the comprehensive planning process or are they basically independent activities? (*circle one*)
   1 Feeds directly into the comprehensive process
   2 They are basically independent

2. How do you evaluate the level of achievement of neighborhood planning program goals? (*circle one*)
   1 No achievement
   2 Low achievement
   3 Moderate achievement
   4 High achievement
   5 Complete achievement

3. Is the staffing, both clerical and professional, adequate for the neighborhood planning program? (*circle one*)
   1 Very adequate
   2 Fairly adequate
   3 Moderately adequate
   4 Fairly inadequate
   5 Very inadequate

4. What have been the major accomplishments of the neighborhood planning program? Please list general achievements, not specific projects.

5. What have been the major problems with the neighborhood planning program?

6. How do you rate the effectiveness of the program in influencing the decisions of city officials? (*circle one*)
   1 Very effective
   2 Fairly effective
   3 Moderately effective
   4 Fairly ineffective
   5 Very ineffective

7. On the rating scale below, how do you rate the level of support given the program by the following groups? (*circle the number that best corresponds to your response*)

Mayor	1	2	3	4	5
	no				great
	support				support
Council	1	2	3	4	5
	no				great
	support				support
City					
Manager	1	2	3	4	5
	no				great
	support				support

Other City
Agencies   1   2   3   4   5
          no   great
      support   support

City
Residents   1   2   3   4   5
          no   great
      support   support

8. How would you rate the overall representativeness of neighborhood groups? (*circle one*)
   1 Very unrepresentative
   2 Fairly unrepresentative
   3 Moderately representative
   4 Fairly representative
   5 Very representative

9. How has the neighborhood planning program effected implementation of planning projects? Has it . . . (*circle one*)
   1 Greatly decreased resistance
   2 Moderately decreased resistance
   3 Had no effect
   4 Moderately increased resistance
   5 Greatly increased resistance

10. Which of the following local services have been changed as a result of the neighborhood planning program? (*circle one or more*)
    1 Police
    2 Fire
    3 Sanitation
    4 Human services
    5 Public transportation
    6 Rodent control
    7 other . . . (specify) _____
    8 None

11. Which of the following local physical elements have been improved by the neighborhood planning program? (*circle one or more*)
    1 Streets, curbs, or sidewalks
    2 Housing
    3 Street lighting
    4 Recreational facilities
    5 Traffic signals
    6 Neighborhood cleanliness
    7 other . . . (specify) _____
    8 None

12. How would you rate the influence of the neighborhood planning program on the relation between citizens and government? Has it . . . (*circle one*)
    1 Greatly improved relations
    2 Moderately improved relations
    3 Had no effect
    4 Moderately impaired relations
    5 Greatly impaired relations

13. Which of the following types of neighborhoods participate the most in the neighborhood planning program? (*circle one*)
    1 Low income
    2 Middle income
    3 High income
    4 other . . . (specify) _____
    5 All the same

14. Are there special characteristics of your city—that is, elements of the physical, social, economic make-up of the city—that contribute to the effectiveness of the program?

Neighborhood Planning Study
Interview Schedules

Agency Director Questionnaire

1. I'd like to begin by asking you about your own professional experience in planning:
   a. Where else worked?
   b. How long in the field?
   c. How long with this agency?

2. Can you tell me about your staff and your annual budget?
   a. How big?
   b. What positions?
   c. Staff of the neighborhood planning program (NPP)?
   d. Women and minorities?
   e. Is number of staff assigned to NPP adequate? Rate on five-point scale.
   f. Annual budget?
   g. Annual budget of NPP?

3. O.K., now in focusing in on your neighborhood planning program, can you give me a brief history of the program?
   a. When initiated?
   b. Whose idea? (mayor, councilman, citizen group, planning director)
   c. Major supporters?
   d. Any opponents?
   e. How was program sanctioned? (city charter, executive order, ordinance or council resolution)
   f. How were neighborhoods defined?
   g. How were neighborhood groups organized?

4. What were the original goals of the NPP? Have they changed at all since the beginning of the program?

5. Do you collect data on the neighborhood level?
   a. What types? (physical, demographic, social, problems, perceptions)

6. How about the neighborhood planners? What do you see as their role in the program? What are they supposed to be doing? (liaison, technical assistant, organizer, advocate, educator, mediator, plan developer)

7. What do you look for when hiring these people? (education, experience, personality)

8. Do they receive any special training once hired?

9. O.K., now I would like to focus in on the communities' role. What is their role in the program? What are they supposed to do? (develop plans, review plans, self help, enumerate problems and priorities)
   a. How can they express desires and concerns?
   b. What means of influence do they have?
   c. Are plans officially sanctioned?
   d. How are community representatives selected?
   e. Are they expected to confine their activities to land-use issues?
   f. What else would you like to see them doing?

10. Do you offer any support to neighborhood groups? (financial, staff, materials)

11. How about the relationship between the NPP program and your comprehensive planning process? How are they coordinated?

12. What are the major accomplishments of the program?
    a. Earlier you mentioned the goals of the program. Which have been achieved and to what extent? Rate on a five-point scale.
    b. Would you say it decreased resistance to the implementation of planning projects?
    c. Led to an improvement in local services?
    d. Improved local physical conditions? Examples?
    e. Improved relations between citizens and government?
    f. Created more equal distribution of public goods?

13. Can you identify any aspects or components of the program as major factors in these accomplishments?

14. O.K., now what have been the major problems?
    a. What program changes would help avoid these problems?
    b. Any other changes you would like to see?

15. How about the effectiveness of the program in influencing the decisions of city officials? On a five-point scale, where one is not influential and five is very influential, how would you rate it?

16. How about the role of the community groups in the program? Do you think they have enough influence? How would you rate it if one was too weak, three was the right strength, and five was too strong?

17. Now I would like to ask about the level of support given to the program by a number of parties. How about the *mayor*? How supportive is he/she?
    a. On a five-point scale, where one is no support and five is great support, how would you rate his/her support?
    b. How about the *council*? How supportive are they?
    c. Rate on five-point scale?
    d. How about *other city agencies*?
    e. Rate on five-point scale?

f. How about *the community's* support?

g. How would you rate it on a five-point scale?

18. In general, how representative are the community groups? Do you think they represent the views of all subgroups in the community? (e.g., business, homeowners, renters, etc.)
    a. How would you rate their representativeness on a five-point scale, where one is nonrepresentative and five is very representative?

19. How have other city agencies reacted to the program?
    a. Any problems?
    b. How might relations be improved?

20. O.K., just a couple more questions. Are there any special characteristics of this city, that is, *physical, social, economic* or *political* aspects, that you feel contribute to the effectivness of the program?
    a. Any special characteristics that inhibit the effectiveness of the program?

21. Is there anything else that you think I should know about the program?

22. Sex of respondent _____
    Age _____
    Race _____

Neighborhood Planner Questionnaire

1. I'd like to begin by asking you about your own professional experience in planning:
    a. Where else worked?
    b. In what capacities?
    c. How long with this agency?
    d. How long a neighborhood planner?

2. O.K., now in focusing in on your neighborhood planning program, can you give me a brief history of the program?
    a. When initiated?
    b. Whose idea?
    c. Major supporters?
    d. Any opponents?
    e. How was program sanctioned?
    f. How were neighborhoods defined?
    g. How were neighborhood groups organized?
    h. How is it structured?

3. What do you see as the initial goals of the program?

4. Could you tell me something about how you perceive *your* role in the neighborhood planning program? (advocate, organizer, liaison, technical assistant, educator, mediator, plan developer)
    a. Role same as that officially defined by the agency?

b. What problems do you have in carrying out your role? What are the frustrations and how do you deal with them?

c. What are the sources of satisfaction in your work?

5. Now I'd like to ask you to describe your activities during a typical day.
   a. Other major tasks?
   b. How closely are you supervised?
   c. How do you get your work assignments?

6. O.K., now I would like to focus on the communities' role. What is their role in the program? What are they supposed to do? (develop plans, review plans, self-help, enumerate problems)
   a. Have they had difficulty in performing their role? Explain.
   b. How are community groups organized? (leader, chosen, organizational structure)
   c. How can they *express desires* and concerns?
   d. How are they able to *influence major decisions* affecting their community?
   e. Do they have enough influence?
   f. How would you rate their influence if one was too weak, three was the right strength, and five was too much?
   g. What else would you like to see them doing?

7. Have community groups been initiating projects and have they been able to obtain funding for these projects? Examples?

8. What is your relationship with the community groups?
   a. What kinds of direct assistance do you provide them?
   b. How do they view you?
   c. Have you done anything to lose their confidence?
   d. Have you had difficulty in mobilizing community support and keeping up interest?
   e. Have you tried to increase participation?

9. By what means are you able to influence major decisions that affect your community(ies)?

10. To what extent are the activities of the community groups confined to land-use issues? How do you feel about this?

11. Earlier you mentioned the goals of the program. Which have been achieved and to what extent? (Rate on a five-point scale where one equals nonachievement and five equals total achievement.)
    a. Have there been any other accomplishments of the neighborhood planning program (NPP) that decreased resistance to the implementation of planning projects?
    b. Led to an improvement in local services?
    d. Led to improved relations between citizens and government?
    e. More equal distribution of public goods?
    f. Any other benefits?

12. Can you identify any aspect or components of the program as major factors in these accomplishments?

13. Now, turning to the problems, what have been some of the major problems, and what changes are necessary to avoid them?
    a. Is there anything else you would like to see changed?

14. Now I'd like to ask about the level of support given to the program by a number of parties? How about the *mayor*?
    a. On a five-point scale, where one is no support and five is great support, how would you rate his/her support?
    b. How about the *council*?
    c. Rating
    d. City manager?
    e. Rating
    f. How about other *city agencies*?
    g. Rating
    h. How about the *communities' support*?
    i. Rating

15. How would you describe the people who make up the community councils? Are they representative?
    a. Again, on a five-point scale how would you rate their representativeness, where one is nonrepresentative and five is very representative?
    b. Are there any major internal conflicts within community groups?
    c. Any conflicts between groups?

16. Has it been difficult to balance the interests of the community and those of the planning department?

17. How supportive is the agency of your work as a neighborhood planner?
    a. Enough staff support?
    b. Rate on a five-point scale, where one is enough support and five is not enough.

18. Has the NPP affected other city agencies? How have they reacted to the program?
    a. How might relations be improved?

19. O.K., just a couple more questions. Are there any special characteristics of this city, that is, *physical, social, economic* or *political* aspects, that you feel contribute to the effectiveness of the program?

20. Did your formal education in planning prepare you well for your present job?
    a. What should neighborhood planners be exposed to in planning school? (topical areas, techniques)

21. What other questions should I be asking you about your program?

22. Sex of respondent _____
    Age _____
    Race _____

1. I would like to begin by asking you if you can tell me something about *your* history with the neighborhood planning program (NPP).
   a. How long involved? How long a representative?
   b. How got involved?
   c. Why got involved?

2. Have you been or are you now involved in other civic activities?

3. How do you see your role in the program? (leader, facilitator, organizer)
   a. What are your major duties?

4. What characteristics (traits, skills) should someone have to do your job?

5. What do you see as the overall goals of the neighborhood planning program?

6. O.K., now about your group, can you tell me something about the activities of the group?
   a. How often does it meet?
   b. What goes on in a typical meeting?
   c. Other than hold meetings, what other activities is it involved in?
   d. How do you attract new members?
   e. Do you inform other people in the community who are not directly involved in the NPP about activities of your group? How?
   f. How large is a typical turnout for community meetings?
   g. Is there a problem in obtaining community support and interest in the program?
   h. Does your group include representation from all the subgroups in the community (racial groups, business, homeowners, renters)?
   i. Where one is very representative and five is nonrepresentative, how would you rate the representativeness?

7. What have been the major issues your group has been concerned about?

8. Now, I would like to ask some questions about the operation of the NPP. How are the desires of your group *communicated* to planners and decision makers (i.e., councilmen, mayor)?
   a. How can the group *influence decision processes* of planners and decision makers?

9. Has your group initiated any projects? Which ones? Have you asked for or received funding for these projects?

10. What do you see as the major accomplishments of the program?
    a. Earlier you mentioned the goals of the program. Which of these have been achieved and to what extent? Rate on a five-point scale where one equals nonachievement and five equals total achievement.
    b. Improved local services?
    c. Improved local physical conditions?
    d. Improved the relations between citizens and government?
    e. Resulted in a more equal distribution of resources?

11. Can you identify any aspects or components of the program as major factors in these accomplishments?

12. O.K., now looking at the other side, what have been the major problems you have encountered in the NPP?
    a. What program changes would be necessary to avoid these problems?
    b. Is there anything else you would like to see changed in the NPP?

13. How effective do you think the NPP program is in influencing the decisions of city officials?
    a. On a five-point scale, where one represents not influential and five represents very influential, how would you rate the program?

14. What about the amount of citizen influence? Do you feel they have the right amount of influence?
    a. Again, on a five-point scale, where one represents not enough influence, three represents the right amount, and five too much, rate level of community influence.

15. Now I'm interested in how your group interacts with the planning agency and the planners.
    a. What kinds of support do you receive from the planners? Can you rate support on a five-point scale, where one is very adequate and five is very inadequate?
    b. How has your relationship been with the neighborhood planner? Anything more he/she could do for you? Does he/she have your interests in mind?
    c. As a citizen representative with whom do you have the most contact? (e.g., neighborhood planner, other representatives of the planning agency, other city agencies)
    d. Do you feel this arrangement works effectively for you?

16. What about the level of support by others? How about the *mayor*?
    a. On a five-point scale, where one is no support and five is great support, how would you rate his/her support?
    b. How about the *council*?
    c. Rating?
    d. The *city manager*?
    e. Rating?
    f. *Other city agencies*?
    g. Rating?

17. Has your organization been able to attain funding for projects which they initiated?

18. Do you think there are any subgroups in the community that have benefited the most from the NPP? (business, minority, ethnic group)

19. Has the NPP brought you in contact with other city agencies? How have they responded?

20. Are there characteristics of this city, that is, aspects of the physical, social, political or economic make-up of this city, that you feel contribute to the effectiveness of the program?
    a. Any special characteristics that inhibit the effectiveness?

21. Can you imagine an alternative program or organization which might be more effective in aiding your group in achieving its goals? Describe.

22. What is your occupation?

23. How many years of school have you completed?

24. What is your approximate income?

25. What else should I know about the NPP or your group's activities?

26. Personal characteristics of respondent
    a. Sex
    b. Age
    c. Race

Appendix B.
List of Programs Surveyed

Allentown, PA

Asheville, NC

Atlanta, GA

Baltimore, MD

Boston, MA

Boulder, CO

Chicago, IL

Cincinnati, OH

Columbus, OH

Dallas, TX

Dayton, OH

Denver, CO

Des Moines, IO

Detroit, MI

Eugene, OR

Flint, MI

Fort Worth, TX

Fresno, CA

Gary, ID

Honolulu, HI

Houston, TX

Independence, MO

Jacksonville, FL

Kalamazoo, MI

Kansas City, MO

Lincoln, NE

Madison, WI

Minneapolis, MN

New Orleans, LA

New York, NY

North Wilkesboro, NC

Oak Park, MI

Oakland, CA

Omaha, NE

Phoenix, AZ

Pittsburgh, PA

Portland, OR

Providence, RI

St. Louis, MO

St. Paul, MN

Salem, OR

San Antonio, TX

San Diego, CA

Seattle, WA

Spokane, WA

Tacoma, WA

Toledo, OH

Trenton, NJ

Washington, DC

Wilmington, DE

Wilmington, NC

Appendix C.
Examples of Council Resolutions
Establishing Neighborhood Planning
Programs

St. Paul, Minn.

Council Resolution

WHEREAS, the City Council fully supports the goal of improved citizen participation in the City of St. Paul, and

WHEREAS, the City Council adopted the boundaries of July 22 as amended delineating seventeen neighborhoods in the city, and

WHEREAS, the City of St. Paul has directed the Office of the Mayor to use these districts singularly or in combination as a basis for citizen input for community development programs, and

WHEREAS, the City Council has requested the Office of the Mayor to initiate an early warning communications system between the city and the neighborhoods, and

WHEREAS, the citizen participation component of the general district planning process may be found to be inadequate in some districts,

THEREFORE BE IT RESOLVED, that the Office of the Mayor is authorized to take steps to create or improve the citizen participation process when one or both of the following circumstances exist:

1. The district planning teams recognize the need for increased citizen participation in order to expeditiously bring about the completion of the general district planning process. In this case the Office of the Mayor would begin the citizen participation process by initiating whatever steps necessary to make the planning process viable.

2. The neighborhood itself may recognize the need for a broader based citizen component and request that the Office of the Mayor implement the necessary steps to strengthen the citizen participation process.

The guidelines and steps for this process are attached to this resolution and shall be considered a part thereof.

Steps to the Establishment of a Citizen Participation Process

There are some areas where difficulties are arising with the general planning process because there is no clear organization or combination of organizations that speak for residents of the area. Since planning cannot take place in a vacuum this not only hampers the plans to be developed but will probably make the legitimacy of these plans open to question when the implementation phase begins.

In these cases it would seem more logical to emphasize the development of a citizen participation process prior to the completion of the district planning process. Unfortunately, the action of the City Council of July 22, 1975, which delineated seventeen neighborhood districts, directed to the Office of the Mayor to use these districts singularly or in combination as a basis for citizen input for community development programs, allowed the initiation of an early warning communication system, and the initiation of a general district planning process, did not give the administration the authority to proceed on the development of citizen participation components where necessary. Therefore, it is necessary to provide the administration with the authority and guidelines for this process.

The citizen participation process outlined in these guidelines may be activated in one of two ways:

(1) The city planning team may recognize the need for increased citizen participation in order to promptly bring about the completion of the general district planning process. In this case the administration shall begin the citizen participation process using whatever steps necessary to make the planning process viable.

(2) The neighborhood itself may recognize the need for a broader based citizen component and request that the administration implement the necessary steps to bolster the citizen participation process.

The steps and guidelines are as follows:

Step 1. The city shall develop an inventory of community groups and organizations. This inventory shall identify all existing groups, institutions, organizations, clubs, individuals, social service agencies, churches, labor unions, fraternal organizations, and business associations.

Step 2. The city shall initiate contact with groups and individuals within the district and describe to them the citizen participation process and its relationship to community development activities and other programs. In addition to meetings with groups and individuals, the city should use, wherever possible, existing resources within the area such as community newspapers, church bulletins, or community bulletin boards in order to assure broad dissemination of information relating to the program.

Step 3. Refine designated boundaries. The citizen organizations in the districts should first make every effort to reach agreement among themselves on the boundaries. If there is a dispute, citizen groups should be given a maximum of 45 days to resolve the matter.

City Planning staff should be requested to analyze the disputed area, taking into consideration such things as natural or man-made boundaries and other appropriate planning criteria. Planning staff should then make their analysis available to the community groups, as well as to appropriate City officials.

If the community groups are unable to reach agreement on the boundaries, the City Council, or an appropriate subcommittee thereof, should schedule a public meeting with advance notice to all interested parties. After hearing the facts of the situation and making use of the planning department analysis, the final decision should be made by the full City Council. Door-to-door survey within the disputed area to elicit the opinion of the residents should be considered.

There may well be areas in which a survey could be used and reasonably valid results obtained. (Step 3 represents policy already approved by City Council.)

Appendixes

Step 4. The City shall establish a working committee to develop structure, by-laws, and functions of the district organization.

All meetings of the working committee shall be open meetings.

Each district shall determine the structure for the process of citizen participation. This may involve the creation of a new organization, recognition of an existing group, or a cooperative arrangement among existing groups. However, this structure shall be one that will ensure that the process is broadly based, democratic and nonexclusionary. The by-laws governing the process shall include: the purpose of the organization; the method of election or selection of officers; membership qualifications; duties of officers; the manner of conducting meetings; a regular meeting schedule; boundaries; and an affirmative action plan.

Step 5. Public hearings in the neighborhood on the proposed structure and by-laws shall be held. Prior to the hearing there shall be ample public notice and ample time for groups in the community to discuss the proposal at their regular meetings. The city shall provide groups and individuals with adequate material and resources to describe and explain the process.

Step 6. Following the above hearings, the working committee shall refine the proposed structure and make whatever changes necessary in the proposal.

Step 7. A public hearing in the neighborhood on the revised structure shall be held.

Step 8. The proposed structure is presented to the Mayor and City Council. The proposal is reviewed by City staff and staff makes recommendations to the Mayor and City Council.

Step 9. The City Council holds a public hearing on the proposed structure of the community organization. City Council approves, rejects, or modifies the proposal.

Step 10. The neighborhood implements structure and organization and integrates it with the district planning process.

If it is desired, the City shall assist the neighborhood in conducting any elections or community conventions required. The City shall also assist the working committee in notifying the residents and distributing election or convention materials.

Salem, Ore.

Neighborhood Program*

64.250. *Purpose of Neighborhood Program.* The purpose of the Neighborhood Organization Program is to involve citizens in local government planning and decision-making as it affects the development of their neighborhood. It is the intent of this chapter to provide an effective mechanism whereby the citizens of the city sharing common neighborhood identity, goals, and concerns may form organizations and become officially recognized as advisory bodies to the

*Excerpt from Chapter 64 Salem Revised Code.

common council to all boards and commissions engaged in community planning and development.

64.260. *Neighborhood Responsibilities.* Responsibilities of an officially recognized neighborhood organization include:

(a) Development of an organization which will maintain itself and further the intent and purpose set forth in SRC 64.250.

(b) Representation of a neighborhood opinion and concerns before public bodies and agencies.

(c) Identification of neighborhood resources.

(d) Gathering of general data concerning the neighborhood.

(e) Identification of neighborhood problems and needs.

(f) Holding of neighborhood meetings to disseminate information and determine opinions of area residents and property owners.

(g) Development of recommendations to appropriate governmental agencies.

(h) Preparation of a neighborhood plan.

(i) Assistance in implementing the adopted neighborhood plan.

(j) Any other nonprofit, community service activities in which the membership of the organization may decide to engage.

64.270. *City Responsibilities.* Once a neighborhood organization is officially recognized, it shall be accorded the following services and consideration by the city, subject to availability of resources as determined by the city administrator:

(a) A community service counselor to act as liaison with other city departments and agencies, to conduct research and provide information, and to assist the neighborhood in organizational development and maintenance and implementation of projects.

(b) Mailing, printing, clerical, graphic services to meet the needs of the neighborhood organization.

(c) Assistance of neighborhood planning team in order to prepare and update a neighborhood plan.

(d) Timely notice to the neighborhood organization of any proposals affecting the neighborhood that are to come before advisory boards and city council.

(e) Solicitation of the neighborhood organization's position and reasoning on any issue especially affecting that neighborhood.

64.280. *Standards for Recognition of Neighborhood Organizations.* A neighborhood organization shall meet and continue to maintain conformity with the following minimum standards for official recognition:

(a) That one or more well-publicized general neighborhood meetings have been held for the purpose of information and approval of boundaries, organizational objectives, and bylaws.

(b) That bylaws provide for the following:

(1) Geographic representation on executive board.

(2) When applicable, interest groups within the neighborhood shall have appropriate executive board representation.

(3) Minutes of all official board, committee, and general meetings shall be taken and preserved; one copy will be maintained by the organization and another filed with the department of community development.

(4) Participation shall be open to any resident, property owner, or business in the neighborhood.

(c) That the organization's structure is capable of providing necessary communication between the neighborhood residents and elected and appointed city officials.

(d) That the neighborhood organization has an awareness of its duties and responsibilities with respect to the neighborhood organization program.

(e) That the geographical boundaries of the neighborhood organization are set at the centerlines of arterial streets or at some other clearly defined and relatively permament natural or man-made feature.

(f) That the territory of the neighborhood is logical and represents a community of interest and identity as a neighborhood.

(g) That the neighborhood organization has met with city staff and formally requested recognition by the planning commission and city council.

64.290. *Procedure for Forming a Neighborhood Organization.* When interest has been expressed by a number of residents, a request should be made to the department of community development for city staff assistance. After information meetings with city staff and interested residents, businesses, and property owners, one or more neighborhoodwide meetings shall be held to increase awareness of the program and formally request recognition as an official neighborhood organization. The request will be considered by the planning commission and forwarded with its recommendation to the common council. Once the group has been recognized by council resolution, the common council and planning commission will look to the association as the official citizen organization for that area of the city. Bylaws and boundaries of neighborhood organizations will be approved by this process and may in the future be amended by the same procedure.

64.300. *Recognition of Existing Neighborhood Organizations.* A neighborhood organization which was officially recognized by resolution of the common council on or before the effective date of this ordinance shall be deemed recognized for purposes of this chapter without further proceedings.

64.310. *Procedures for Annual Review of Neighborhood Organization Status.*
(a) Within 60 days following an annual general meeting for electing board members, the neighborhood organization will provide the Salem Planning Commission with evidence of compliance with the standards set forth in SRC 64.280.
(b) The report will be reviewed by the planning commission and city council. If the report indicates noncompliance, the organization will be asked to take corrective action. If corrective action is found necessary by the city council and such action is not taken within 60 days following council notifying the neighborhood organization of noncompliance, recognition of the neighborhood organization will be suspended.

64.320. *Notice of Official Recognition.* Upon formal recognition by the city, the mayor shall cause a letter to be sent in his name to all property owners, residents, and businesses within the neighborhood. The mayor's letter shall include the following:
(a) A statement encouraging all property owners, residents, and businesses within the newly recognized neighborhood to participate in meetings, preparation of neighborhood plans, and other activities leading to proposals and recommendations to city government.
(b) A description of neighborhood boundaries.
(c) The names, addresses, and telephone numbers of all officers of the neighborhood organization.
(d) A list of all standing committees and a description of each.
(e) The names of persons and departments within city government who will be serving as primary contacts with the neighborhood organization.

64.330. *Notification of Neighborhood Action: City Policy.*
(a) It is the policy of the City of Salem that all affected property owners, residents, and businesses be notified of meetings, studies, and other activities of recognized neighborhood organizations.
(b) Where the city assists with the mailing of announcements of organizational

meetings prior to official recognition of the neighborhood organization, such notices shall be sent to all property owners, residents, and businesses in the area of the proposed neighborhood organization.

64.340. *Notification Procedures.*

(a) All general neighborhood meeting notices and newsletters shall be mailed to all property owners, residents, and businesses in the designated neighborhood and shall include the purpose of the meeting and agenda items.

(b) The neighborhood association shall notify all property owners, residents, and businesses of any special studies that may result in recommendations affecting the permitted use of their land. In order to afford maximum participation by individuals having interests within the affected area, notice shall be given prior to the time such studies commence.

(c) All official board and general meetings shall be listed in a calendar of neighborhood meetings published weekly through a local newspaper of general circulation.

(d) Neighborhood newsletters shall include a summary of meeting minutes, including decisions and actions resulting from those meetings.

64.350. *Newly Annexed Areas.* Whenever an area is annexed to the city, the planning commission shall, within 30 days of the effective date of the annexation, recommend to the common council one of the following alternatives:

(a) That the area be added to the territory of an existing neighborhood organization;

(b) That the area be recognized as the nucleus of a new neighborhood organization and its citizens encouraged immediately to seek recognition as a new neighborhood organization; or

(c) That the area be recognized as the nucleus of a new neighborhood organization; but because it is yet undeveloped or is of too small a size, it should be temporarily represented by another neighborhood organization. In such an event, the temporary representative organization shall function in all respects as though the area were within its boundaries except that it shall not develop any neighborhood plan for the newly annexed area.

Neighborhood Plans

64.360. *Neighborhood Plans, Generally.* A citizen plan is a plan encompassing a broad range of concerns and including the entire neighborhood area. A neighborhood plan provides for more detailed goals and policies of the neighborhood as a refinement of and consistent with the Salem Area Comprehensive Plan. It shall be considered as applying to a shorter time frame than the comprehensive plan.

64.370. *Scope of Neighborhood Plans.*

(a) A neighborhood plan should address each of the following elements:

(1) Land use.

(2) Transportation.

(3) Public facilities and services.

(4) Housing.

(5) Parks, recreation, and open spaces.

(b) In addition, the neighborhood plan may address subjects of particular concern to the neighborhood such as:

(1) Economic activity.

(2) Social services.

(3) Environmental quality.

(4) Urban design.

(c) The neighborhood plan should include such maps and diagrams as may assist in showing the application of goal and policy statements in the plan.

64.380. *Time Frame and Phasing.*

(a) Neighborhood plans, particularly maps and detailed land use statements therein, should be reviewed biennially and should focus on a time span of at least five to ten years.

(b) Within the time span of the plan, the timing or phasing of specific applications of policies may depend upon the happening of future events or may depend upon predicted growth over a particular time period. The neighborhood plan should specify the preconditions or timing of such policies and their application.

64.390. *Conformity to Other Plans.* Neighborhood plans must conform to the rest of the comprehensive plan. In addition, they should consider and accommodate as much as possible all applicable statewide planning goals.

64.400. *Elements of Neighborhood Plan Which May Be Adopted.* Only the goal and policy statements of the neighborhood plan, and any generalized land use map projecting those goals and policies, shall be considered for adoption. Specific recommendations as to zoning or public improvements shall not be adopted but should be considered and acted upon separately.

64.410. *Initiation of Neighborhood Plans.*

(a) Property owners, residents, and businesses within the neighborhood shall be afforded maximum opportunity for involvement in all phases of the preparation of a neighborhood plan. Notification of all general neighborhood and board meetings where the plan will be discussed and notification of the process by which the plan is being prepared shall be given as provided in SRC 64.330 and 64.340.

(b) Proposed neighborhood plans must be presented at a minimum of two informational neighborhood meetings. In addition to these public meetings, the neighborhood organization is encouraged to use other means of contacting citizens to obtain their input and review of the neighborhood plan. A specific effort should be made by neighborhood organizations to obtain the opinions of property owners, residents, and businesses directly affected by the plan.

(c) The final draft neighborhood plan shall be adopted by resolution of the neighborhood organization's governing board and affirmed by vote of the membership at a general neighborhood meeting. The process for official adoption of the neighborhood plan is deemed initiated upon a filing of that resolution and a copy of the neighborhood plan with the secretary of the planning commission.

64.420. *Planning Commission Action on the Neighborhood Plans.*

(a) Prior to holding public hearing as provided in SRC 64.080, the planning commission shall hold a joint work session with representatives of the neighborhood organization. The purpose of such work session shall be to give the planning commission and the neighborhood organization an opportunity to exchange comments about the neighborhood plan, to identify any areas of potential disagreement, and to give the neighborhood organization an opportunity to refine its plan prior to the public hearing. Such work session shall be held within four weeks of receipt of the draft neighborhood plan. At such work session, the neighborhood organization shall prove compliance with the provision of SRC 64.410.

(b) Based upon the work session described in subsection (a) of this session, the neighborhood organization shall, within 60 days after the work session, submit any additions, modifications, or deletions it wishes to make to its neighborhood plan or notify the planning commission that it wishes to make no changes.

(c) The planning commission shall hold the public hearing provided in SRC 64.080 within 30 days following the neighborhood organization's action described in subsection (b) of this section. The planning commission shall forward the neighborhood plan to the city recorder along with its recommendations within fifteen days thereafter unless the neighborhood organization requests a further work session as provided in subsection (d) of this section.

(d) If, after public hearing before the planning commission, the neighborhood organization so requests, the planning commission shall schedule a further joint work session to be held for the purposes and in the manner specified in subsection (a) of this section. The request shall be made within seven days of the close of the public hearing, and the work session shall be held within fourteen days of the request. Within fifteen days after the joint work session, the planning commission shall forward the neighborhood plan to the city recorder along with its recommendations.

64.430. *Council Action on Neighborhood Plan.* Following public hearing as provided in SRC 64.080, the common council shall either recommend changes to the neighborhood plan or adopt such portions thereof as are deemed appropriate under SRC 64.390. If the council recommends changes, the neighborhood organization may either revise its plan and resubmit it for adoption or it may notify the council that it declines to amend its plan further. In no event shall the council adopt any portion of a neighborhood plan which portion is in conflict with the rest of the comprehensive plan.

64.440. *Status of Neighborhood Plan.*

(a) The neighborhood plan shall be the basis for any neighborhood recommendation to any city board, commission, or agency having planning responsibilities.

(b) Every city board, commission, and agency having planning responsibilities shall consider the neighborhood plan before making any decision which would affect the neighborhood.

(c) The common council shall consider the neighborhood plan before making any final decision as to the acquisition, construction, or improvement of public facilities in the neighborhood.

Adopted by the Common Council this 15th day of November 1977.

Signed by the Mayor this 16th day of November 1977.

Minneapolis, Minn.

Resolution of the City of Minneapolis Creating a Unified Citizen Participation Plan and Process, 31 January 1979

Whereas, the Minneapolis City Council and the Mayor have declared their intention to adopt a Unified Citizen Participation Plan; and

Whereas, the City has solicited and received a variety of recommendations for a Unified Citizen Participation Plan; and

Whereas, those recommendations have been considered in context of the existing citizen participation processes; and

Whereas, the City Council is interested in further improving its citizen participation the processes on a base of successful past practices;

Now, therefore, be it resolved by the City Council of the City of Minneapolis:

That there is hereby created in the accompanying petition a Unified Citizen Participation Plan to provide opportunities for citizens to contribute in meaningful ways to each phase of the City's decision-making system; planning, programming, budgeting, monitoring and evaluation.

That the Plan be related and coordinated with City Council policy actions regarding neighborhood and community planning organization and activities and regarding Capital Improvement Program (CIP) development.

That the Plan is intended to provide a permanent citizen participation structure and process to which citizens and citizen organizations can relate.

That the Plan is not intended to replace or discourage traditional means citizens use to convey their concerns and interests to their City government, including voting, contacting elected officials, petitioning, and working through establishing or ad hoc neighborhood groups or other organizations which represent community interests such as business associations or labor unions.

That the Plan provide for the focus of citizen participation on the City's operating and capital programs rather than on any specific source of funds.

That the Plan implementation shall be the joint responsibility of the administrative agencies identified with specific tasks described in the accompanying petition; and that these agencies shall act in a cooperative and coordinated manner necessary to effectively carry out the requirements of the Plan.

That the Plan promote cooperation among citizen groups and between citizens and the City.

That this resolution supersede all previous City Council actions related to Community Development Block Grant (CDBG) citizen participation processes.

That the Plan as adopted shall be in effect until it is amended or superseded by a new plan.

That citizens shall have opportunities to advise on any revision of the Plan; such opportunities to include testimony at public hearings before the City Council and its committees, written recommendations and reports by individuals and organizations, and at other times as requested by the City Council. Any changes in the Plan shall be made by the City Council and Mayor.

That affirmative action guidelines for the City of Minneapolis shall be followed to the greatest extent possible in the organization of any citizen advisory group provided for by the Plan.

That the organization of the Unified Citizen Participation Plan and processes, as set forth in Petition No. 215726 on file in the Office of the City Clerk, is hereby made a part of this resolution.

Atlanta, Ga.

Neighborhood Planning Ordinance

Section 6-3011
Definitions

As used in this article:

(a) Neighborhood means a geographic area either with distinguishing characteristics or in which the residents have a sense of identity and a commonality of perceived interest, or both.

(b) Neighborhood planning unit, hereinafter also referred to as N.P.U., means a geographic area composed of one or more contiguous neighborhoods, which have been defined by the department of budget and planning based on criteria previously established by the department and approved by the council for the purpose of developing neighborhood plans.

(c) Atlanta Planning Advisory Board, means that board established for the purpose of advising the city on planning matters of a city-wide nature.

(d) Resident shall mean any person 18 years of age or older whose primary place of residence is within the neighborhood planning unit, or who operates or represents a corporation, organization, institution or agency which owns property or has a place of business or profession within the N.P.U.

(e) Neighborhood planning committee means a body of residents of the neighborhood planning unit organized for engaging in comprehensive planning matters affecting the livability of neighborhoods.

(f) Council district planning committee means a body of residents of a council district who may choose to be formed from representatives of the neighborhood planning committees to coordinate council district plans. (Code 1965, Sec. 19-1/2-1)

Editorial Note: The provisions of this article are derived from an ordinance of the council, approved August 13, 1974.

Section 6-3012
Neighborhood Planning Units

(a) *Designation.* The department of budget and planning shall designate neighborhood planning units, as defined in section 6-3011(b) of this chapter, which shall include all areas of the city. N.P.U.'s may comprise as many, or as few, neighborhoods as practicable and may cross council district boundaries. The designation of the N.P.U. shall be based on criteria previously established by the department of budget and planning and approved by the council, and shall include the consideration of existing citizens' organizations' boundaries which may exist at the time of designation, as well as provisions for the change of neighborhood boundaries when necessary.

(b) *Presentation of information.* The department of budget and planning shall make available to neighborhood planning committees and other residents of neighborhood planning units basic information, including but not limited to, the areas of land use, transportation, community facilities, programmed capital improvements, housing, human resources, social and recreational programs, environmental quality, open space and parks, citizen involvement in planning activities. This information shall be presented in such a manner as to be readily recognizable to the residents of each N.P.U. This information shall be presented graphically when practicable.

(c) *Neighborhood planning committees.* The neighborhood planning committee may recommend an action, a policy or a comprehensive plan to the city

and to any city agency on any matter affecting the livability of the neighbor- hood, including, but not limited to, land use, zoning, housing, community facilities, human resources, social and recreational programs, traffic and transpor-
tation, environmental quality, open space and parks; assist city agencies in
determining priority needs for the neighborhood; and review items for inclusion in the city budget and make recommendations relating to budget items
for neighborhood improvement.

(d) *Accountability.* Neighborhood planning committees shall be accountable
to the residents of the area they represent. (Code 1965, Sec. 19-1/2-2)

Section 6-3013
Public Hearings

(a) *Manner in which hearings are to be held.* The mayor shall cause public
hearing to be held as prescribed in the charter of the city within each council
district on a schedule and at such public or private places which are accessible
to and of sufficient size to accommodate those members of the public desiring
to attend. Notice of those hearings shall be posted conspicuously within the
district and in the newspapers and other media of general circulation in the
district. Adequate time shall be allowed at these public hearings to present
such basic information as is enumerated in section 6-3012(b) of this article to
the residents of each council district and to solicit public statements of goals,
objectives, policies and other advisory information and proposed 15, five (5)
and one-year comprehensive development plans.

(b) *Conduct of hearings.* Each aforementioned public hearing shall consist
of at least two (2) sessions held on succeeding but not necessarily consecutive
days in each council district, and such other sessions as conditions within the
district may warrant. The first session shall be for the purpose of presenting
the information enumerated in section 6-3012(b) of this article to the residents
of the neighborhood planning units which comprise each district. The department of budget and planning shall receive public comments concerning the
preparation of the comprehensive development plan components which affect
the district. The second session held in each district shall be for the purpose of
presenting the 15, five (5) and one-year comprehensive development plans to
the residents of the district. Special emphasis shall be given during the presentation of those parts of the plans which affect the residents of the neighborhood planning units within the district.

(c) *Planning committtees.* Residents of neighborhood planning units may
form neighborhood planning committees or council district planning committees to advise the department of budget and planning on the preparation of the
15, five (5) and one-year comprehensive development plans. The council member for the district may initiate the organization of these committees, but may
not hold any office in any of the committees. These committees may continue
in existence from year to year. (Code 1965, Sec. 19-1/2-3)

Section 6-3014
Reports on Citizen Involvement to the Council and Coordination
of Citizen Participation

(a) The mayor shall prepare an annual report which shall desribe the manner in which citizen involvement shall be solicited and provided for in the preparation of the 15, five (5), and one-year comprehensive development plans.
This report shall be presented to the development committee at a regularly
scheduled meeting in January of each year.

(b) The mayor shall coordinate citizens participation in planning, under provisions of this article and shall be responsible for advising the council on citizen plans. (Code 1965, Sec. 19-1/2-4)

Reorganization Memorandum, December 30, 1975

Duties of the Neighborhood Planning Division

1. To develop the study design, schedules, work program and format for plans for 24 Neighborhood Planning Units.

2. To determine the scope and content of each planning element to be included in each NPU Plan, e.g., transportation, land use and environment, design, housing and neighborhoods, zoning, community facilities and services.

3. To devise procedures, methods and techniques for achieving uniformity and coordination among the planning elements and among the Plans; to establish communications and coordinate work with other City Departments.

4. To measure the overall progress in the preparation of all NPU Plans periodically toward meeting work objectives and target dates.

5. To coordinate the assembly and production of the One-, Five-, and 15-Year Comprehensive Development Plan.

6. To serve on and provide input into the CDP and Budget Task Force.

7. To evaluate and make recommendations to the Information Coordinator on revision to the Citizen Involvement processes and ordinances.

8. To assist the Special Projects Division in the conduct of special studies.

9. To maintain close liaison with City-Wide Development Division on systems planning components; coordinate input and output between the two divisions.

Duties of the City-Wide Development Division

1. To conduct research on major physical and environmental issues and problems facing the City and to develop suitable strategies for their solution, including appropriate goals and objectives for inclusion in the CDP. Specific functional areas of responsibility are: Transportation & MARTA Liaison, Urban form & TSADS, Housing, Land Use, Service and Environment.

2. To work with the Comprehensive Plan and Budget Task Force to establish communication and coordinate with other departments of the City on their programs and projects for the Comprehensive Development Plan.

3. To represent the Bureau on a City-wide design/engineering team as stipulated in the Master Agreement between the City and MARTA.

4. To strive for and achieve extraordinary coordination, both for the Bureau and as a member of the City-wide team, in the design and construction of the rapid transit system; facilitate technical coordination between MARTA and City.

5. To express adopted City goals and policies and advise MARTA and the City of potential conflicts and possible remedies; to serve as advocate for adopted City plans seeking conformity of MARTA system to those plans.

6. To complete TSADS Work Program and to maintain the studies in a current status after initial work is completed, especially the Core Area Design portions.

7. To provide managerial and technical direction in the development and completion of a new Zoning Ordinance; coordinate all necessary reviews, including citizen and business groups; and seek adoption by Council.

8. To develop the study design for updating the Subdivision Ordinance and

provide managerial and technical direction in the development and completion of a revised Subdivision Ordinance; coordinate all necessary reviews, including citizen and business groups; and seek adoption by Council.

9. To perform technical code reviews to determine adequacy and currency.

10. To serve on and provide input into the CDP and Budget Task Force.

11. To evaluate and make recommendations to the Information Coordinator on revisions to the Citizen Involvement Processes and Ordinances.

12. To assist the Special Projects Division in the conduct of special studies.

13. To maintain close liaison with Local Planning Division on NPU planning; coordinate input and output between two divisions.

Appendix D. Additional Tables

Table D.1. Standardized Regression Coefficients for
Local Organizational Characteristics and Measures
of Effectiveness

Program Element	Increased Influence on Officials	Decreased Resistance to Implementation
Neighborhood definition		
Citizen perceptions	.163	.175
Socioeconomic data	.165	−.109
Preexisting districts	.031	−.128
Physical boundaries	.046	.106
Organizers		
Planning staff	.043	.323
Existing local groups	−.174	.066
Local leaders	.160	.103
Method of selecting representatives		
Elected by community	−.168	.128
Appointed	−.235	.261
Elected by committee	−.153	.067
Voluntary	.237	−.094
No official representatives	−.074	−.072
No set method	−.218	−.012

Table D.2. Standardized Regression Coefficients for
Program Structural Characteristics and Measures
of Effectiveness

Program Element	Increased Influence on Officials	Decreased Resistance to Implementation
Method of sanction		
City charter	.224	−.236
Executive order	.116	.060
Council resolution	.342	.444
Informal agreement	.040	−.006
No sanction	−.093	.230
Administering agency		
Planning department	−.212	−.307
Community development	−.210	−.378
Independent	−.072	−.100
Housing department	.205	.214
Mayor/council	.182	−.101
City manager	−.151	.144
Number of tiers	.210	−.107
Recognition of local groups	.024	.230
Support to local groups		
Financial	.338	.062
Staff	.162	.211
Materials	−.095	.072
Information	−.187	−.366

Table D.3. Standardized Regression Coefficients for Program Operational Variables and Measures of Effectiveness

Program Element	Increased Influence on Officials	Decreased Resistance to Implementation
Funding		
Local funds	−.143	.021
Role of planners		
Advocate	−.267	−.016
Educator	−.341	−.509
Liaison	.027	−.230
Mediator	−.145	.210
Organizer	.119	.301
Role of citizens		
Review plans	.348	.147
Develop plans	.561	.245
Monitor projects	−.041	−.022
Self-help	−.120	−.189
Program scope		
Land use	.197	−.118
Socioeconomic	.018	.048
Service delivery	.189	.089
Planners' training	.087	.058
Number of planners	.428	−.294
Year initiated	.197	.148

Table D.4. Standardized Regression Coefficients for
Interorganizational Variables and Measures
of Effectiveness

Program Element	Increased Influence on Officials	Decreased Resistance to Implementation
Current support		
Mayor	−.049	−.438
Council	.173	.088
City agencies	.205	.241
Residents	−.099	−.194
Tie to comprehensive planning program	−.261	.501
Means of citizen pressure		
Speaking at council	−.116	−.288
Media	.192	.231
Voting as a bloc	.035	−.340
Personal contacts	.135	.266
Protests	.068	−.059

Table D.5. Standardized Regression Coefficients for
City Characteristics and Measures of Effectiveness

Program Element	Increased Influence on Officials	Decreased Resistance to Implementation
City size	−.124	−.194
Type of government (0 = mayor-council, 1 = council-manager)	−.242	−.018
Median income	.157	−.086
Percentage owner occupied	−.051	−.006

Bibliography

Addams, Jane. 1895. *Hull House Maps and Papers.* New York: T. Y. Cro-
well. Excerpt reprinted as "The Settlement as a Factor in the Labor
Movement" in *Readings in the Development of Settlement Work*, edited
by L. M. Pacey. New York: Association Press, 1950.
Ahlbrandt, R. S., Jr., and Cunningham, J. Y. 1979. *A New Public Policy for
Neighborhood Preservation.* New York: Praeger.
Alinsky, S. D. 1946. *Reveille for Radicals.* New York: Random House.
————. 1971. *Rules for Radicals.* New York: Random House.
Altschuler, A. 1965. *The City Planning Process.* Ithaca, N.Y.: Cornell Uni-
versity Press.
————. 1970. *Community Control.* New York: Pegasus.
Arnstein, S. R. 1969. "A Ladder of Citizen Participation." *Journal of the
American Institute of Planners* 35:217–27.
Athanasiou, R., and Yoshioka, G. 1973. "The Spatial Character of Friendship
Formation." *Environment and Behavior* 5:43–65.
Bachrach, P., and Baratz, M. S. 1962. "The Two Faces of Power." *American
Political Science Review* 56:947–52.
————. 1970. *Power and Poverty: Theory and Practice.* New York: Ox-
ford University Press.
Barnett, S. 1909. *Toward Social Reform.* London: T. F. Unwin. Excerpt
reprinted as "The Beginnings of Toynbee Hall" in *Readings in the De-
velopment of Settlement Work*, edited by L. M. Pacey. New York: Asso-
ciation Press, 1950.
Bell, W., and Boat, M. D. 1957. "Urban Neighborhoods and Informal Social
Relations." *American Journal of Sociology* 62:391–98.
Black, A. 1968. *The Comprehensive Plan: Principles and Practice of Urban
Planning.* Washington, D.C.: International City Managers' Association.
Branch, M. C. 1972. *Continuous City Planning.* Planning advisory service
report, no. 20. Chicago: American Planning Association.
Campbell, D. T. 1979. "'Degrees of Freedom' and the Case Study." In *Quali-
tative and Quantitative Methods in Evaluation Research*, edited by
T. D. Cash and C. S. Reichardt. Beverly Hills: Sage Publications.
Caplow, T., and Forman, R. 1950. "Neighborhood Interaction in a Homoge-
neous Community." *American Sociological Review* 15:357–66.
Center for Governmental Studies. 1976. "Neighborhood Planning with Resi-
dents: Approaches of Six Local Planning Departments." *Neighborhood
Decentralization* (March-April).
Chapin, F. S., Jr. 1965. *Urban Land Use Planning.* Urbana, Ill.: University
of Illinois Press.
Cloward, R. A., and Ohlin, L. E. 1963. *Delinquency and Opportunity: A
Theory of Delinquent Gangs.* New York: Free Press.
Coit, A. 1892. *Neighborhood Guilds: An Instrument of Social Reform.* Lon-
don: Swan, Sommerschein and Company. Excerpt reprinted as "The
Neighborhood Guild Defined" in *Readings in the Development of Settle-
ment Work*, edited by L. M. Pacey. New York: Association Press, 1950.
Cole, R. L. 1974. *Citizen Participation and the Urban Policy Process.* Lex-
ington: D. C. Heath and Co.

Community Action Program. Office of Economic Opportunity. 1965. *Community Action Program Guide.* Vol. 1, *Instructions for Applicants.* Washington, D.C.: Government Printing Office.

Cook, T. D., and Reichardt, C. S., eds. 1979. *Qualitative and Quantitative Methods in Evaluation Research.* Beverly Hills, Ca.: Sage.

Dahir, J. 1950. *Communities for Better Living.* New York: Harper and Brothers.

Davidoff, P. 1965. "Advocacy and Pluralism in Planning." *Journal of the American Institute of Planners* 31:331–38.

Duncan, O. D., and Duncan, B. 1955. "Residential Distribution and Occupational Stratification." *American Journal of Sociology* 60:493–503.

Durkheim, E. 1964. *Division of Labor in Society.* Translated by George Simpson. Glencoe, Ill.: Glencoe Press

Eames, E., and Goode, J. G. 1977. *Anthropology of the City.* Englewood Cliffs, N.J.: Prentice-Hall.

Elliot, J. 1915. "After Twenty Years in the Tenement Houses of New York." *Standard* 1:250–54. Reprinted in *Readings in the Development of Settlement Work,* edited by L. M. Pacey. New York: Association Press, 1950.

Fischer, C. S. 1982. *To Dwell among Friends: Personal Networks in Town and City.* Chicago: University of Chicago Press.

Fried, M., and Gleicher, P. 1961. "Some Sources of Residential Satisfaction in an Urban Slum." *Journal of the American Institute of Planners* 27:305–15.

Frieden, B. J., and Kaplan, M. 1975. *The Politics of Neglect.* Cambridge, Mass.: MIT Press.

Friedmann, J. 1971. "The Future of Comprehensive Urban Planning: A Critique." *Public Administration Review* 23:315–26.

—————. 1973. *Retracking America: A Theory of Transactive Planning.* Garden City, N.Y.: Anchor Books.

Gans, H. J. 1961. "Planning and Social Life: Friendship and Neighbor Relations in Suburban Communities." *Journal of the American Institute of Planners* 27:134–40.

—————. 1962. *The Urban Villagers.* New York: Free Press.

—————. 1965. "The Failure of Urban Renewal: A Critique and Some Proposals." *Commentary* 39:29–37.

—————. 1967. *The Levittowners.* New York: Pantheon Books.

Gilbert, N., and Specht, H. 1977. *Dynamics of Community Planning.* Cambridge, Mass.: Ballinger Publishing Co.

Glaser, B., and Strauss, A. L. 1967. *The Discovery of Grounded Theory.* Chicago: Aldine.

Greer, S. 1956. "Urbanism Reconsidered: A Comparative Study of Local Areas in a Metropolis." *American Sociological Review* 21:19–25.

—————. 1972. *The Urbane View: Life and Politics in Metropolitan America.* New York: Oxford University Press.

Hallman, H. 1977. *The Organization and Operation of Neighborhood Councils: A Practical Guide.* New York: Praeger.

Hamburg, B. A., and Killilea, M. 1979. "Relation of Social Support, Stress, Illness and the Use of Health Services." In *Healthy People.* Surgeon General's Report on Health Promotions and Disease Prevention Background Papers. Washington, D.C.: Government Printing Office.

Harvey, D. 1973. *Social Justice and the City.* Baltimore: Johns Hopkins University Press.

Holden, A. C. 1922. *The Settlement Idea: A Vision of Social Justice.* New York: Macmillan Company.

House, J. S. 1980. *Work Stress and Social Support.* Reading, Mass.: Addison-Wesley.

Hunter, A. 1974. *Symbolic Communities.* Chicago: University of Chicago Press.

——————. 1975. "The Loss of Community: An Empirical Test Through Replication." *American Sociological Review* 40:537–52.

Isaacs, R. 1948a. "Are Urban Neighborhoods Possible?" *Journal of Housing* 6 (July): 177–80.

——————. 1948b. "The 'Neighborhood Unit' Is an Instrument for Segregation." *Journal of Housing* 6 (August): 215–19.

Janowitz, M. 1952. *The Community Press in an Urban Setting.* Glencoe, Ill.: Free Press, 1952.

——————. 1975. "Sociological Theory and Social Control." *American Sociological Review* 81:82–108.

——————. 1976. *Social Control of the Welfare State.* New York: Elsevier.

Kaplan, M. 1973. *Urban Planning in the 1960s: A Design for Irrelevancy.* New York: Praeger.

Kasarda, J. D., and Janowitz, M. 1974. "Community Attachment in Mass Society." *American Sociological Review* 39:328–39.

Keller, S. 1968. *The Urban Neighborhood: A Sociological Perspective.* New York: Random House.

Klosterman, R. E. 1980. "A Public Interest Criterion." *Journal of the American Institute of Planners* 46:323–33.

Kornblum, W. 1975. *Blue Collar Community.* Chicago: University of Chicago Press.

Kostka, J. V. 1954. *Planning Residential Subdivisions.* Winnipeg: University of Manitoba.

Kotler, M. 1969. *Neighborhood Government.* New York: Bobbs-Merrill Company.

Kuper, L. 1970. "Neighbour on the Hearth." In *Environmental Psychology: Man and His Physical Setting,* edited by H. M. Proshansky, W. H. Ittleson, and L. G. Rivlin. New York: Holt, Rinehart, and Winston.

Lancourt, J. E. 1979. *Confront or Concede.* Lexington, Mass.: Lexington Books.

Lineberry, R. L. 1977. *Equality and Urban Policy: The Distribution of Municipal Public Services.* Beverly Hills: Sage.

MacMahon, J. 1914. "The Scope of Social Settlements." From the Proceedings of the Third National Conference of Catholic Charities. Reprinted in *Readings in the Development of Settlement Work,* edited by L. M. Pacey. New York: Association Press, 1950.

Marris, P., and Rein, M. 1982. *Dilemmas of Social Reform: Poverty and Community Action in the United States.* Chicago: University of Chicago Press.

Mayer, N. S., and Blake, J. L. 1981. *Keys to the Growth of Neighborhood Development Organizations.* Washington, D.C.: Urban Institute.

Meyerson, M., and Banfield, E. C. 1955. *Politics, Planning and the Public Interest.* Glencoe, Ill.: Free Press.

Michelson, W. 1976. *Man and His Urban Environment.* Reading, Mass.: Addison-Wesley.

Mumford, Lewis. 1954. "The Neighborhood and the Neighborhood Unit." *Town Planning Review* 25:256–69.

National Commission on Neighborhoods. 1979. *People Building Neighbor-hoods*. Washington, D.C.: Government Printing Office.

Nesbit, R. 1966. *The Sociological Tradition*. New York: Basic Books.

Pacey, L. M., ed. 1950. *Readings in the Development of Settlement Work*. New York: Association Press.

Pahl, R. E. 1970. *Patterns of Urban Life*. London: Longmans, Green and Co.

Perin, C. 1967. "The Noiseless Succession of the Comprehensive Plan." *Journal of the American Institute of Planners* 33:336-47.

Perry, A. 1929. *A Plan for New York and Its Environs*. Vol. 7. New York: New York Regional Planning Association.

————. 1939. *Housing for the Machine Age*. New York: Russell Sage.

Peterson, P. E. 1970. "Forms of Representation: Participation of the Poor in the Community Action Program." *American Political Science Review* 64 (June): 491-507.

Rafter, D. O. 1980. "Neighborhood Planning." *Planning* 46:23-25.

Rainwater, L. 1966. "Fear and the House as Haven in the Lower Class." *Journal of the American Institute of Planners* 32:23-31.

Report of the President's Task Force on Model Cities: A Step Toward the New Federalism. 1970. Washington, D.C.: U.S. Government Printing Office.

Rich, R. C. 1980. "The Dynamics of Leadership in Neighborhood Organizations." *Social Science Quarterly* 60:570-87.

Rohe, W. M. 1982. "Models of Residential Density and Their Impact on Planning: A Historical and Contemporary Analysis." *Urbanism Past and Present* 7:15-27.

Ross, B. H. 1979. "Improving the Management of Neighborhood Organizations." *South Atlantic Studies* 4:32-41.

Roszak, T. 1973. *Where the Weekend Ends*. New York: Doubleday/Anchor.

Rubin, I. 1969. "Function and Structure of Community: Conceptual and Theoretical Analysis." *International Review of Community Development* 21-22: 111-19.

Schmandt, H. J. 1973. "Decentralization: A Structural Imperative." In *Neighborhood Control in the 1970s: Politics, Administration and Citizen Participation*, edited by G. Frederickson. New York: Chandler Publishing Co.

Schoenberg, S., and Rosenbaum, P. L. 1980. *Neighborhoods That Work: Sources of Viability in the Inner City*. New Brunswick, N.J.: Rutgers University Press.

Scott, M. 1969. *American City Planning since 1890*. Los Angeles: University of California Press.

Sennett, R. 1970. *The Uses of Disorder: Personal Identity and City Life*. New York: Vintage.

Shevskey, E., and Bell, W. 1955. *Social Area Analysis: Theory, Illustrative Applications and Computation Procedures*. Stanford, Calif.: Stanford University Press.

Simkhovitch, M. K. 1938. "The Settlement and Religion." From the *Churchman*. Reprinted in *Readings in the Development of Settlement Work*, edited by L. M. Pacey. New York: Association Press, 1950.

Solow, A. A.; Ham, C. C.; and Donnelly, E. O. 1969. *The Concept of the Neighborhood Unit*. Pittsburgh: Graduate School of Public and International Affairs, University of Pittsburgh.

Spiegel, Hans. 1968. *Neighborhood Power and Control: Implications for Urban Planning*. New York: Columbia University.

Stone, C. 1982. "Social Stratification, Nondecision-making and the Study of Community Power." *American Politics Quarterly* 10:275–302.

Suttles, G. D. 1968. *The Social Order of the Slum*. Chicago: University of Chicago Press.

U.S. Congress. 1966. The Demonstration Cities and Metropolitan Development Act of 1966. 80 Stat 1255 USC 1966 (PL 89–754).

U.S. Congress. House. Committee on Banking and Currency. Subcommittee on Housing. 1973. *Model Cities Impact on Better Communities*. 93d Congress, 1st Session. Washington, D.C.: Government Printing Office.

Warren, R. B., and Warren, D. I. 1977. *The Neighborhood Organizer's Handbook*. Notre Dame: University of Notre Dame Press.

Warren, R. L. 1963. *The Community in America*. Chicago: Rand McNally.

Weaver, R. C. 1965. *Dilemmas of Urban America*. Cambridge: Harvard University Press.

Weiss, C. H. 1972. *Evaluation Research: Methods for Assessing Program Effectiveness*. Englewood Cliffs, N.J.: Prentice-Hall.

Wellman, B. 1977. "Who Needs Neighborhoods?" In *New Perspectives on the American Community*, edited by R. Warren. Chicago: Rand McNally.

Whyte, W. F. 1955. *Street Corner Society*. 2d ed. Chicago: University of Chicago Press.

Woods, Robert A. 1923. *The Neighborhood in Nation-Building*. Boston: Houghton Mifflin Company.

Wright, C. R., and Hyman, H. 1958. "Voluntary Association Memberships of American Adults: Evidence from National Sample Surveys." *American Sociological Review* 23:284–94.

Yates, D. 1973. *Neighborhood Democracy: The Politics and Impacts of Decentralization*. Lexington, Mass.: D. C. Heath.

Yin, R. K.; Lucas, W. A.; Syranton, P. L.; and Spindler, A. 1973. *Citizen Organizations: Increasing Client Control over Services*. Santa Monica, Ca.: Rand.

Zimmerman, J. 1972. *The Federated City: Community Control in Large Cities*. New York: St. Martin's Press.

Index

www.ingramcontent.com/pod-product-compliance
Lightning Source LLC
Chambersburg PA
CBHW020345270326
41926CB00007B/323